SURVIVE IN IT

L.G. Alexander Timothy and

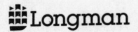
Longman

LONGMAN GROUP LIMITED
London

Associated companies, branches and representatives
throughout the world

© Longman Group Ltd 1980

First published 1980

ISBN 0 582 74710 4
LG 74718 X

Printed in Great Britain

Drawings by Ed McLachlan

Contents

Survive in Italian

A few sounds

PART A: *Study Section*

Survive in Italian

Who is 'Survive in Italian' for?
Anyone going to Italy.
Anyone whose work brings them in touch with Italian speakers.

Why 'Survive'?
To survive in a foreign country, you have to be able to cope with
everyday situations – finding your way around, asking for information,
understanding when you take part in a simple conversation. Survive in
Italian is designed to enable you to do just that.

What is in 'Survive in Italian'?
1 The most commonly used Italian expressions and sentences – printed
   in the book and recorded on the cassette.
2 A 'Mini Dictionary' of about 5000 words to suit your needs, whether
   you are travelling for business or pleasure.
3 A pronunciation key specially designed for English speakers
   beginning to learn Italian.
4 Useful information which you may need when travelling in Italy.

What does this book consist of?
PART A: *Study Section*
This contains sets of key sentence 'patterns' which *you* can adapt to the
situation *you* find yourself in, by inserting in the gaps the words you need
from the Mini Dictionary.

There are eleven small sections of key sentences.

Sections 1–9 cover *general* areas of language useful in more than one
situation eg getting about, expressing wishes, giving information about
yourself, talking about time etc as well as useful basic expressions.

Section 10 contains simple conversations showing you how to use the
key sentences from Sections 1–9 in a variety of *particular* situations.

Section 11 deals with telephoning and emergencies.

The Mini Dictionary is the main feature of this section. It is an alphabetical list of words which will fit into the key sentences in Part A. Each word is followed by the Italian translation and the pronunciation.

The reference section also includes information sections about:

1 Eating out – list of typical items you will find in Italian menus.

2 Signs you may see – on the roads, in shops and public places.

3 Countries – their currencies, nationalities and languages.

4 Motoring – parts of the car and useful expressions.

5 Writing letters – three model letters you may need to write.

6 Equivalents – weights, measures and sizes.

There is also a 'Mini Grammar' – a summary of basic points about Italian which you may want to refer to. This, in addition to the footnotes accompanying the key sentences, gives an idea of how Italian 'works' in comparison with English.

What does the cassette consist of?

All the key sentences and simple conversations in the book (Part A: Study Section) are recorded on the C90 cassette. This gives you the chance to get used to both speaking and listening to real Italian. You can use the cassette with the book or just by itself – at home or in your car cassette recorder, before you travel or while you're travelling.

Key sentences: you will hear first the English expression, then its Italian equivalent, followed by a pause for you to repeat.

Simple conversations: just listen to these a few times to help you to understand what you hear.

How do you find what you want to say?

Suppose that you want a ticket, some coffee, a toothbrush or a room.

1 Turn to 'Wants and needs' (Part A: Study Section 7)

2 You want to say 'I'd like /...../ please'.

3 Find this key sentence pattern and its Italian equivalent – '*Vorrei* /...../ *per favore.*'

4 Look up the word you want in the Mini Dictionary eg ticket.

5 You are now ready to say:
    Vorrei /*un biglietto*/ *per favore* (I'd like a ticket please).

How do you make yourself understood?
'Survive in Italian' uses a simple but effective pronunciation system to help you say correctly all the words you need. The pronunciation system has special symbols for a few sounds in Italian which don't exist in English – you'll find it well worth your while to learn them.

The cassette gives you further help in pronouncing the kind of Italian that will be understood. Copy the key sentences as accurately as you can.

How to get the most out of 'Survive in Italian'
Before you begin to use 'Survive in Italian':
  – look at the contents list to see how the sections are organised.
  – leaf through the whole book to see what is in each section.
  – play through some of the cassette to get the feel of the language.

Any time you spend familiarising yourself with the kit and mastering some of the key sentences will be time well spent.

If you're prepared to spend up to five hours try to master some or all of the introductory section 'Very Basic Survival'. This section, with the help of the cassette and the Mini Dictionary, will take you a long way.

If you're prepared to spend up to twenty hours try to master Part A completely with the aid of the cassette, before setting out on your travels.

This will give you a very good start and will help you survive in a wide variety of situations and begin to communicate with Italian people. Furthermore 'Survive in Italian' provides a sound and accurate basis for further study. The more you put into 'Survive in Italian', the more you'll get out of it.

A FEW HINTS

1 Masculine or feminine?
In Italian all nouns whether they indicate people or things are either masculine or feminine. This is obvious with people:

  un ragazzo (a boy) – masculine
  una ragazza (a girl) – feminine

but not so obvious with things:

  il treno (the train) – masculine
  la macchina (the car) – feminine

Most masculine words end in '*o*' and most feminine words in '*a*.' In the Mini Dictionary any words with different endings will be marked (m) – masculine of (f) – feminine.

Any word which is attached to these masculine or feminine words like 'the/a/some/any' or an adjective like 'big/small/red' must 'agree' with the word:

> *il prossimo treno* (the next train)
> 'train' is masculine, so 'the' (m) is '*il*' and 'next' (m) is '*prossimo*'.

> *una bella macchina* (a beautiful car)
> 'car' is feminine, so 'a' (f) is '*una*' and 'beautiful' (f) is '*bella*'.

But if you confuse the masculine and feminine in Italian, it won't stop you from surviving in Italian!

2 Lei, tu

In Italian there are two ways of saying 'you' when you talk to one person:

> '*Lei*' is the form you will hear most. It is quite formal – always use it in shops, offices, when travelling and with people whom you don't know well.

> '*Tu*' is for people you know very well. Young people use it when talking to each other. The '*tu*' form of some common expressions you may hear or want to use is shown in the Study Section followed by (informal).

(Note that there are also two 'you' forms when you talk to more than one person. '*Loro*' is used in the same way as '*lei*', '*voi*' is used in the same way as '*tu*'.)

3 Signore, Signora, Signorina

Literally, these mean 'Sir', 'Madam', 'Miss'. But they are used all the time in Italian and you should always use them except with very close friends.

4 Buon giorno, buona sera, buona notte

'Good morning', 'good afternoon/evening', 'good night'. These small formalities are used very commonly in Italian. '*Arrivederci*' (Goodbye) can be used when speaking to anybody. '*Ciao*' means both 'hello' and 'goodbye' and is used with someone to whom you would say '*tu*'.

5 C'è, ci sono

You will often hear Italians saying *'C'è'* (there is/is there?) or *'Ci sono'* (there are/are there?) in conversation.

> *C'è del tè?* (Is there any tea?)
> *Ci sono due alberghi in centro* (There are two hotels in the centre)

Learn to recognise them quickly in order to understand spoken Italian. They are quite often used also to mean 'Have you got?'

6 Prego

This is best translated as 'You're welcome'. It is commonly used in Italian after someone has said *'Grazie'* (thank you). It is also used to mean 'Can I help you?' in a shop, restaurant etc.

7 Never mind mistakes

Italians love foreigners trying to speak their language and are always ready to help out. Don't be shy. Jump straight in and never mind your mistakes!

A few sounds

Speaking Italian isn't difficult as long as you remember the following rules.

'c' and 'ch' are usually pronounced 'c' as in '<u>c</u>at':

[k]   <u>c</u>at   <u>c</u>asa (house), <u>c</u>osa (thing), <u>c</u>ucina (kitchen), <u>ch</u>iesa (church)

But before 'e' and 'i', 'c' is pronounced 'ch' as in '<u>ch</u>urch':

[ch]   <u>ch</u>urch   <u>c</u>'è (there is), <u>c</u>ittà (city)

'g' and 'gh' are usually pronounced 'g' as in '<u>g</u>un':

[g]   <u>g</u>un   <u>g</u>atto (cat), <u>g</u>omito (elbow), <u>gh</u>iaccio (ice)

But before 'e' and 'i', 'g' is pronounced 'g' as in '<u>g</u>in':

[j]   <u>j</u>ob, <u>g</u>in   <u>g</u>elato (ice cream), <u>g</u>iovedì (Thursday)

You will find a complete pronunciation key before the Mini Dictionary.

PART A
STUDY SECTION

NB

/   /   means that the word or expression can be replaced by other words or expressions from Part B: The Reference Section, or by other numbers from Part A: Section 1.26.

▭   means that the text recorded on the cassette. * indicates that these words or expressions are recorded within 'Very basic survival' and not repeated on the cassette in later sections.

Stress within a sentence or an individual word is indicated in **bold** type.

1 Very basic survival

1.1 General expressions

Please	Per favore
Thank you	Grazie
Yes	Sì
No	No
Yes please	Sì grazie
No thank you	No grazie
Sorry?	Come?
Sorry!	Scusi!
Excuse me! (to attract someone's attention)	Scusi!
Excuse me! (to pass in front of someone)	Permesso!
I'm sorry	Mi dispiace
That's all right	Va bene!
You're welcome (frequently used)	Prego
OK	Bene
All right	Va bene
Good!	Bene!
Good idea!	Buon'idea!
Great!	Magnifico!

1

Fine!	**Bene!**
Of course!	**Certo**
Look out!	Atten**zion**e!
Nothing	**Nien**te
Everything	**Tut**to
I don't know	Non lo **so**
What's this?	Cos'**è**?
What's the matter	Cosa c'**è**?
I've lost /my passport/	Ho **per**so /il mio passa**por**to/
Now	**O**ra
Soon	**Pres**to
Later	Più **tar**di
And	E
But	Ma
Or	O

1.2 I've got/I haven't got

I've got /a reserved seat/	Ho /un posto preno**ta**to/
I've got /a single room/	Ho /una stanza **sin**gola/
I've got /some tickets/	Ho /dei bi**glie**tti/

I haven't got any /change/	Non ho /**spi**ccioli/
I haven't got any /warm clothes/	Non ho /vestiti da in**ver**no/
I haven't got /enough money/	Non ho /abbastanza de**na**ro/

1.3 Have you got?

Have you got /the ticket/?	Ha /il bi**glie**tto/?
Have you got /the key/?	Ha /la **chia**ve/?
Have you got /a ticket/?	Ha /un bi**glie**tto/?
Have you got /a key/?	Ha /una **chia**ve/?
Have you got /any beer/?	Ha /della **bir**ra/?
Have you got /any tea/?	Ha /del **tè**/?
Have you got /the tickets/?	Ha /i bi**glie**tti/?
Have you got /the keys/?	Ha /le **chia**vi/?
Have you got /any tickets/?	Ha /dei bi**glie**tti/?

1.4 I'd like

I'd like /a ticket/ please	Vorrei /un biglietto/ per favore
I'd like /a room/ please	Vorrei /una stanza/ per favore
I'd like /an envelope/ please	Vorrei /una busta/ per favore
I'd like /some coffee/ please	Vorrei /del caffè/ per favore
I'd like /some tickets/ please	Vorrei /dei biglietti/ per favore
I'd like something to /drink/ please	Vorrei qualcosa da /bere/ per favore
I'd like this please	Vorrei questo per favore
I'd like that please	Vorrei quello per favore
I'd like these please	Vorrei questi per favore
I'd like those please	Vorrei quelli per favore

1.5 Is there?/Are there?

Is there /a train/ to /Milan/ today?	C'è /un treno/ per /Milano/ oggi?
Is there /a letter box/ near here?	C'è /una cassetta delle lettere/ qui vicino?
Is there /a hotel/ near here?	C'è /un albergo/ qui vicino?
Is there /any beer/?	C'è /della birra/?
Is there /any tea/?	C'è /del tè/?
Are there /any seats/?	Ci sono /dei posti/?

1.6 There is /There are

There's /a train/ to /Naples/ today	C'è /un treno/ per /Napoli/ oggi
There's /a letterbox/ near here	C'è /una cassetta delle lettere/ qui vicino
There's /a hotel/ near here	C'è /un albergo/ qui vicino
There's /some beer/ /in the fridge/	C'è /della birra/ /nel frigorifero/
There are /some seats/	Ci sono /dei posti/

3

1.7 There isn't/There aren't

There isn't /a train/ to /Venice/ today	Non c'è /un treno/ per /Ve**ne**zia/ oggi
There isn't /a letterbox/ near here	Non c'è /una cassetta delle **let**tere/ qui vicino
There isn't any /beer/ /in the fridge/	Non c'è /birra/ /nel frigo**ri**fero/
There aren't any /hotels/ near here	Non ci sono /al**ber**ghi/ qui vicino
There aren't any /seats/	Non ci sono /**po**sti/

1.8 Greetings

Hello	Ciao
Hi!	Ciao!
Goodbye	Arrive**der**ci
Bye!	Ciao!
Good morning	Buon **gior**no
Good afternoon	Buon **gior**no
Good evening	Buona **se**ra
Good night	Buona **not**te

1.9 Social

Would you like a drink?	Vuole bere qual**co**sa?
Would you like a drink? (informal)	Vuoi bere qual**co**sa?
Cheers!	Sa**lu**te!
How do you do	Pia**ce**re
How are you?	Come sta?
How are you? (informal)	Come stai?
Very well thank you	Bene **gra**zie
And you?	E **lei**?
And you? (informal)	E **tu**?
Fine thanks	Bene **gra**zie
It was nice to meet you	Piacere di averla cono**sciu**ta
It was nice to meet you (informal)	Piacere di averti cono**sciu**to (conosciuta if addressing a woman)

4

1.10 Indicating

Look!	**Guar**di!
This ... Not this	**Que**sto ... Non **que**sto
That ... Not that	**Quel**lo ... Non **quel**lo
These ... Not these	**Que**sti ... Non **que**sti
Those ... Not those	**Quel**li ... Non **quel**li
For me	Per **me**
For you	Per **lei**
For you (informal)	Per **te**
For him	Per **lui**
For her	Per **lei**
For us	Per **noi**
For you (plural)	Per **loro**
For you (plural informal)	Per **voi**
For them	Per **loro**
Not for me	Non per **me**
(Just add 'non' for 'not')	

1.11 Directions – going places

Which way?	Da quale **parte**?
This way?	Da questa **parte**?
That way?	Da quella **parte**?
Not this way	Non di **qua**
Not that way	Non di **là**
Left	A si**ni**stra
Right	A **de**stra
Straight on	**Drit**to
Here	Qui
There	Là
The station please	Alla sta**zio**ne per favore
The airport please	All'aero**por**to per favore
The air terminal please	Al ter**mi**nale per favore
The airport bus please	L'**au**tobus per l'aero**por**to per favore
A taxi please	Un **ta**xi per favore
I'm in a hurry	Ho **fret**ta
Stop here please	Si fermi **qui** per favore
Where is it please?	Dov'è per favore?

5

Where's /the (nearest) bank/ please?	Dov'è /la **ban**ca (più vicina)/ per favore?
Where's /the (nearest) hotel/ please?	Dov'è /l'al**ber**go (più vicino)/ per favore?
Where can I get /a bus/ to the airport please?	Dove posso prendere /un **au**tobus/ per l'aero**por**to per favore?
Where can I buy /some postcards/ please?	Dove posso comp**rar**e /delle carto**li**ne/ per favore?
Which /platform/ please?	Che /bi**na**rio/ per favore?
A 1st class single to /Florence/ please	Un biglietto di andata prima classe per /**Fi**renze/ per favore
A 2nd class return to /Florence/ please	Un biglietto di andata e ritorno seconda classe per /**Fi**renze/ per favore

---

Now take a part

You meet a friend in a bar one evening.
Buona sera.
Buona sera, Paolo.
Come stai?
Bene grazie. E tu?
Bene grazie.

You want to know which platform your train leaves from.
Che binario per Roma, per favore?
Binario uno.
Da quale parte, per favore?
Dritto.
Grazie.

1.12 Suggestions

Let's go	An**dia**mo
Let's go and /have a drink/	Andiamo a /**be**re qualcosa/
Let's meet /at 9/	Ve**dia**moci /alle **no**ve/

1.13 When?

Today	**O**ggi
This morning	Questa **matt**ina
This afternoon	Oggi pome**rigg**io
This evening	Questa **se**ra
Tonight	Questa **not**te
Tomorrow	Do**ma**ni
Yesterday	**Ie**ri
Not today	Non **o**ggi
(Just add 'non' for 'not')	

When does /the train/ leave?	Quando parte /il **tre**no/?
When does /the bus/ arrive?	Quando arriva /l'**auto**bus/?
When do /the shops/ open?	Quando aprono /i ne**go**zi/?
When do /the banks/ close?	Quando chiudono /le **ban**che/?
When does it begin?	Quando inco**min**cia?
When does it end?	Quando fi**nis**ce?

1.14 Questions

What?	**Co**sa?
When?	**Quan**do?
Where?	**Do**ve?
Who?	**Chi**?
Which?	**Qua**le?
Which one?	**Qua**le?
Whose?	Di **chi**?
How?	**Co**me?
How much? A kilo please	**Quan**to? Un **chi**lo per favore

How many? /Three/ please	**Quan**ti? /**Tre**/ per favore
Why?	Per**chè**?
Because	Per**chè**
Why not?	Per**chè** **no**?
Anything else?	Nient'**al**tro?

7

1.15 Shopping

Can I help you?	Desidera?
I'm just looking	Sto solo guar**dan**do
I'd like to /try this on/	Vorrei /provare **que**sto/
It's in the window	È in ve**tri**na
I'll take it	Lo **pren**do
I'll leave it	Non lo **pren**do

1.16 Money

How much is it please?	Quanto **co**sta per favore?
How much are they please?	Quanto **co**stano per favore?
What's the exchange rate for /the pound/ please?	Qual'è il cambio per /la ster**li**na/ per favore?
Do you take /traveller's cheques/?	Accetta /traveller's cheques/?
In /ten thousands/ please	In /bi**glie**tti da dieci**mi**la/ per favore

The bill please	Il **con**to per favore
Is service included?	È compreso il ser**vi**zio?
Is VAT included?	È compresa l'**IVA**?
(Money see p278)	

1.17 The restaurant

For /4/ please	Per /**qua**ttro/ per favore
What would you like to drink?	Cosa **be**ve?
The menu please	Il me**nu** per favore
What do you recommend?	Cosa mi con**si**glia?
With /chips/	Con /patate **frit**te/
Without /cream/	Senza /**pan**na/
What is it (exactly) please?	Cos'**è** (esattamente) per favore?

1.18 Quantity

Another (masculine)	Un **al**tro
Another (feminine)	Un'**al**tra
A little	Un po'
More	Ancora
Less	Meno
Some more /coffee/ please	Ancora /caffè/ per favore
Enough thank you	**Ba**sta grazie

1.19 Accommodation

Have you got a /double/ room please?	Ha una stanza /**do**ppia/ per favore?
With /bath/	Con /**ba**gno/
Without /bath/	Senza /**ba**gno/
For /2/ nights please	Per /**due**/ **no**tti per favore
Is /breakfast/ included?	È inclusa /la cola**zio**ne/?
Please call me at 7 o'clock	Per favore mi **chia**mi alle **se**tte

---

Now take a part

In a restaurant – you want to order a steak and chips and some beer.

Buona sera.
Buona sera. Vorrei una bistecca, per favore.
Una bistecca. Sì. Con patate fritte?
Sì, per favore.
Con patate fritte. Nient'altro?
Sì. Una birra, per favore.
Una birra. Bene. Grazie.

At a hotel – you want a room.

Buona sera. Desidera?
Ah – sì. Ha una stanza doppia, per favore?
Ah – quante notti?
Per due notti, per favore.
Con bagno o senza bagno?
Con bagno.
Sì, va bene.
Quanto costa per favore?
Una notte ventimila lire.
La prendo, per favore.

1.20 Asking a favour

Could you mind my bag please?	Mi da un'o**cchia**ta alla mia va**li**gia per favore?
Could you keep my seat please?	Mi tiene il **po**sto per favore?

1.21 Information

I'd like some information /about hotels/ please	Vorrei delle informazioni /sugli alberghi/ per favore
I'd like some information /about tours/ please	Vorrei delle informazioni /sulle gite/ per favore

1.22 The petrol station

Fill it up please	Il pieno per favore
/15/ litres please	/Quindici/ litri per favore
/10,000/ lires' worth please	/Diecimila/ lire di benzina per favore

(Equivalents see p280)

1.23 The Post Office

How much is /a letter/ to /England/ please?	Quanto costa spedire /una lettera/ in /Inghilterra/ per favore?
One /200/ lire stamp please	Un francobollo da /duecento/ lire per favore
Two /170/ lire stamps please	Due francobolli da /centosettanta/ lire per favore
Airmail please	Posta aerea per favore
Express please	Espresso per favore

(Money see p278)

1.24 Language

Could you repeat that please	Per favore ripeta
I don't understand	Non capisco
Slower please	Più adagio per favore
I don't speak /Italian/	Non parlo /italiano/
Do you speak /English/?	Parla /inglese/?
Would you write it please	Lo scriva per favore

10

1.25 The telephone

Hello	**Pronto**
Goodbye	**Arrive**der**ci**
May I speak to /Mr Masiero/ please?	Posso par**lare** con /il signor Ma**siero**/ per favore?
I'll call back later	Ri**chiamo** più **tar**di

(See How to cope with the telephone p55)

1.26 Numbers

0	**zero**	76	settanta**sei**
1	**uno**	87	ottanta**sette**
2	**due**	98	novan**tot**to
3	tre	100	**cen**to
4	**quat**tro	101	cento **uno**
5	**cinque**	211	duecento **un**dici
6	sei	322	trecento venti**due**
7	**sette**	433	quattro**cen**to trenta**trè**
8	**otto**	544	cinque**cen**to quaranta**quat**tro
9	**nove**	655	sei**cen**to cinquanta**cin**que
10	**die**ci	766	sette**cen**to sessanta**sei**
11	**un**dici	877	otto**cen**to settanta**sette**
12	**do**dici	988	nove**cen**to ottan**tot**to
13	**tre**dici	1000	**mille**
14	quat**tor**dici	1001	mille **uno**
15	**quin**dici	2112	duemila cento**do**dici
16	**se**dici	3223	tremila duecento venti**trè**
17	dicias**sette**	4334	quattromila trecento trenta**quat**tro
18	di**ciot**to		
19	dician**nove**	10,000	dieci**mila**
20	**ven**ti		
21	ven**tu**no		
32	trenta**due**		
43	quaranta**trè**		
54	cinquanta**quat**tro		
65	sessanta**cin**que		

0.1 = 0,1 **zero** **vir**gola **uno** (literally 'nought comma one')

11

1.27 The days of the week

Monday	Lunedì
Tuesday	Martedì
Wednesday	Mercoledì
Thursday	Giovedì
Friday	Venerdì
Saturday	Sabato
Sunday	Domenica

1.28 The months of the year

January	Gennaio
February	Febbraio
March	Marzo
April	Aprile
May	Maggio
June	Giugno
July	Luglio
August	Agosto
September	Settembre
October	Ottobre
November	Novembre
December	Dicembre

1.29 The alphabet

For the pronunciation, listen to the cassette. See also 3.2

A *a* B *bi* C *ci* D *di* E *e* F *effe* G *gi* H *acca* I *i* J *i-lunga*
K *kappa* L *elle* M *emme* N *enne* O *o* P *pi* Q *cu* R *erre* S *esse*
T *ti* U *u* V *vu* W *vu-doppia* X *ics* Y *ipsilon* Z *zeta*

The Italians very often use names of towns to spell instead of the alphabet:

Ancona; Bari; Catania; Domodossola; Empoli; Firenze; Genova; Hotel; Imola; (J is i-lunga); (K is kappa); Livorno; Milano; Napoli; Otranto; Palermo; Quarto; Roma; Savona; Taranto; Udine; Verona; (W is vu-doppia); (X is ics) (Y is ipsilon); Zara.

Note that J K W X Y are never used with names of towns.

Now take a part

You want to buy some stamps.

Scusi, dove posso comprare dei francobolli, per favore?
Dritto, e a destra.
Grazie.

Buon giorno. Desidera?
Buon giorno. Sì. Quanto costa spedire una lettera in Inghilterra, per favore?
Duecento lire.
Tre francobolli da duecento lire, per favore.
Nient'altro?
No, grazie.
Seicento lire.
Grazie.
Prego.

2 More expressions

*Thanks	**Gra**zie
Thank you very much	Tante **gra**zie
It's very kind of you	È molto gen**ti**le da parte sua
It's very kind of you (informal)	È molto gen**ti**le da parte tua
I'm very sorry	Mi dispiace **mol**to
I'm sorry I'm late	Mi dis**pia**ce di essere in ri**tar**do
I'm sorry I don't know	Mi dis**pia**ce ma non lo **so**
I don't mind	Non im**por**ta
That's right	**Giu**sto
Excellent!	Be**nis**simo!
I don't like it	Non mi **pia**ce
Perhaps	**For**se
It depends	Di**pen**de
If possible	Se pos**si**bile
Give my regards to /Mrs Masiero/	Mi sa**lu**ti /la signora Ma**sie**ro/
See you soon	A **pre**sto
Have a good time!	Si di**ver**ta!
Have a good time! (informal)	Di**ver**titi!

14

Have a good trip!	Buon **viag**gio!
Sleep well!	Dorma **be**ne!
Sleep well! (informal)	Dormi **be**ne!
Is /the plane/ on time?	È in orario /l'aereo/?
Is this seat free please?	È **li**bero questo **po**sto, per favore?

| Do you smoke? | **Fu**ma? |
| What's this called please? | Come si chiama **que**sto per favore? |

| Ready? | **Pron**to? (m) **Pron**ta? (f) **Pron**ti? (mpl) **Pron**te? (fpl) |

Not yet	Non an**co**ra
Just a minute!	Un mo**men**to!
Can I come in?	Posso en**tra**re?
Come in!	A**van**ti!
How does it work?	Come fun**zio**na?
It doesn't work	Non fun**zio**na

| What's the weather like? | Com'è il **tem**po? |
| It's /hot/ | Fa /**cal**do/ |

Now take a part

Saying goodbye to someone you have met.

Arrivederci
Arrivederci e mi saluti Luisa.
Buon viaggio. Piacere di averla conosciuta.
Arrivederci. A presto.

15

3 Personal information

3.1 Name

What's your name please?
My name's /John Harrison/

Come si **chia**ma?
Mi chiamo /John Harrison/

3.2 Name (spelling)

How do you spell it?
J-O-H-N H-A-R-R-I-S-O-N
(Alphabet see 1.29)

Come si **scri**ve?
John J-O-H-N
Harrison H-A-R-R-I-S-O-N

3.3 Telephone number

What's your telephone number please?
(01) 235 1278
(numbers see 1.26)

Qual'è il suo **nu**mero di tele**fo**no per favore?
(Zero uno) due tre **cin**que, uno due sete **ot**to

3.3   See also 3.4, 3.5. *'Il suo numero/il suo indirizzo/la sua data di nascita'* mean literally 'the your number/the your address/the your date of birth'.
'The' in Italian changes according to the noun it precedes (*il numero* – masculine; *la data* – feminine). See other

3.4 Home address

What's your address?	Qual'è il suo indirizzo?
5, Wood Street, London N8 4PS	Wood Street, **cin**que, **Lon**dra N otto quattro PS

3.5 Date of birth

What's your date of birth?	Qual'è la sua data di **na**scita?
9th October 1958 (Dates see 5.5)	Nove ot**to**bre millenove-centocinquan**tot**to

3.6 Home town

Where do you live?	Dove **a**bita?
I live in /London/	**A**bito a /**Lon**dra/

3.7 Country of origin

Where do you come from?	Da dove vi**e**ne?
I come /from England/	Vengo /dall'Inghil**te**rra/

3.3 (cont.)	forms of 'the' p255. 'Your' also changes according to the noun it precedes (*il suo numero* – masculine; *la sua data di nascita* – feminine). See A few hints. Practise saying your phone number in Italian several times. See p55 for more information about the telephone.
3.4	Practise saying your address in Italian several times. When giving the address in Italian you usually give the number of the building after the name of the street eg '*Via Oriani 2*'.
3.5	In Italian the year cannot be shortened as in English eg 1958 'Nineteen fifty-eight'; it has to be '*millenovecentocinquantotto*' (one thousand, nine hundred and fifty-eight). Note that in Italian numbers are sometimes written as one word.
3.6	Other Italianised place names: Dublin – '*Dublino*'; Edinburgh – '*Edimburgo*'; Cornwall – '*Cornovaglia*'. See also list of countries p234.
3.7	'*Dall'Inghilterra*' means literally 'from the England'. 'From' = '*da*'; 'the England' = '*l'Inghilterra*'. '*Da*' (from) + '*l'*' (the) becomes '*dall'*'. Use '*dalla*' (*da + la*) with

17

3.8 Nationality

What nationality are you?	Di che nazionalità è?
I'm /English/	Sono /inglese/

3.9 Place of work

Where do you work?	Dove lavora?
I work in /London/	Lavoro a /Londra/
I work for /Brown & Webster/	Lavoro per /la ditta Brown & Webster/
I haven't got a job	Non ho un impiego

3.10 Occupation

What do you do?	Che lavoro fa?
I'm an /architect/	Sono /architetto/
I'm a /student/ (male)	Sono /studente/
I'm a /student/ (female)	Sono /studentessa/

3.7
(cont.)
feminine nouns beginning with a consonant eg *'dalla Francia'*. Use *'dal' (da + il)* with masculine nouns beginning with a consonant eg *'dal Belgio'*. *'Dagli Stati Uniti'* means 'from the United States'; *'da'* (from) + *'gli'* ('the' masculine plural) becomes *'dagli'*. See p234 for other countries. In Italian, always use 'the' before the name of a country, eg. *'l'Italia'* but not before the name of a town eg *'Vengo da Londra'* 'I come from London'.

3.8
'Sono inglese' means 'I am English' (masculine or feminine). But note *'sono italiano'* 'I am Italian' (masculine); *'sono italiana'* 'I am Italian' (feminine). See p234 for other nationalities.

3.9
'La ditta' means any kind of business or firm.

3.10
'Sono architetto' literally means 'I am architect'. Omit 'a/an' before the name of an occupation. The names of most occupations are the same, whether the holder is masculine or feminine, with some exceptions eg *'commesso'/'commessa'* (male/female shop assistant), *'cameriere'/'cameriera'* (waiter/waitress). See the Mini Dictionary for other occupations.

3.11 Temporary occupation

What are you doing in /Rome/?	Che cosa fa a /**Roma**/?
I'm on holiday	Sono in va**can**za
I'm working	Lavoro

3.12 Temporary address

Where are you staying?	Dove al**loggia**?
I'm staying /at the Hotel Bristol/	Sono /all'albergo Bristol/
I'm staying with /the Berni family/	Sono presso /la famiglia **Ber**ni/
I'm staying with some /friends/	Sono presso /a**mi**ci/

3.13 Health/Mood

*How are you?	Come **sta**?
*How are you (informal)?	Come **stai**?
What's the matter?	Cosa c'**è**?
I'm fine	Sto be**ni**ssimo
I'm not /tired/	Non sono /**stan**co/
I'm /tired/	Sono /**stan**co/
I'm /hot/	Ho /**cal**do/
I'm not feeling very well	Non sto molto **bene**
I've got /a cough/	Ho /la **to**sse/
I've got a stomach upset	Ho lo stomaco distur**ba**to
I've got a pain /in my arm/	Ho male /al **bra**ccio/
I've got a headache	Ho mal di **te**sta

/My leg/ hurts	Mi fa male /la **gam**ba/
I've got a temperature	Ho la **febbre**
(Temperature see p281)	

3.11   *'A Roma'* (in Rome) use *'a'* (in) when talking about towns or cities. Use *'in'* (in) when talking about regions or countries eg *'in Toscana'* (in Tuscany), *'in Italia'* (in Italy).

3.13   Use *'Come stai?'* with people you say *'tu'* to. Use *'Come sta?'* with everyone else.

         'Sono stanco' (I'm tired – masculine). If you are female

3.14 Introductions

This is Mr /Fermi/	Le presento il signor /**Fer**mi/
This is Mrs /Fermi/	Le presento la signora /**Fer**mi/
This is Miss /Fermi/	Le presento la signorina / **Fer**mi/
This is /my mother/	Le presento /mia **ma**dre/
*How do you do	Piacere
This is /Richard/	Questo è /Ric**car**do/
*Hello	Ciao

3.13
(cont.)
you should say *'Sono stanca'*. If the masculine form of adjectives ends in 'o' the feminine ends in 'a'. Adjectives ending in 'e' are the same for both masculine and feminine forms eg *'inglese'* (English). *'Ho caldo'* literally means 'I have heat'. *'Ho freddo/fame/sete'* means 'I am cold/hungry/thirsty'.

'Al braccio' (in the arm) – *'al'* with most masculine words.
'Alla gamba' (in the leg) – *'alla'* with most feminine words.
'The' not 'my' is used with parts of the body.

3.14
'Le presento mia madre' literally means 'to you I introduce my mother'. See p264 for other forms.
Note that *'piacere'* (how do you do) can only be used as a reply to an introduction. See also 1.9.
'Questo' with a man; *'Questa'* with a woman.

Now take a part

At the immigration desk – giving information about yourself.

Da dove viene?
Vengo dall'Inghilterra.
Qual'è il suo indirizzo?
7, Palace Street, Londra N8 4PS.
Come si scrive, per favore?
7, P-A-L-A-C-E S-T-R-E-E-T, L-O-N-D-R-A, N8 4PS.
Grazie. E dove allogia a Roma?
Sono all'albergo Bristol, via Liegi.
Bene. Grazie.

4 Getting about

4.1 General directions (1)

*Which way?	Da quale **par**te?
Can you tell me the way to /the station/ please?	Mi dice dov'è /la sta**zio**ne/ per favore?
Is this the way /to the centre/?	Questa strada porta /al **cen**tro/?
Are you going /to the airport/?	Va /all'aero**por**to/?
*Straight on	**Dri**tto
*On the left	A si**ni**stra
*On the right	A **de**stra
First right	La prima a **de**stra
Second left	La seconda a si**ni**stra
Opposite (. . .)	Di **fron**te (a . . .)
*There	Là
*Here	Qui
Upstairs	Di **so**pra
Downstairs	Di **sot**to

4.1   All nouns in Italian are either masculine or feminine.
        When using 'the' in front of a word, its form changes.
        'The' is *'il'* before most masculine words eg *'il centro'* (the
        centre), *'la'* before most feminine words eg *'la stazione'*
        (the station) and *'l''* before masculine or feminine words
        which begin with a vowel eg *'l'aeroporto'* (airport). See
        p255 for other forms of 'the'. 'To the' is *'al' (a + il)* before

4.2 General directions (2)

Where can I get /a taxi/?	Dove posso **pren**dere /un **ta**xi/?
Where can I buy /a newspaper/?	Dove posso comp**ra**re /un gior**na**le/?
*Where can I buy /some postcards/?	Dove posso comp**ra**re /delle carto**li**ne/?
Where can I get something to /eat/?	Dove posso /man**gia**re/ qualcosa?

4.3 Exact location (1)

*Where's /the (nearest) bank/ please?	Dov'è /la **ban**ca (più vi**ci**na)/ per favore?
*Where's /the (nearest) hotel/ please	Dov'è /l'al**ber**go (più vi**ci**no)/ per favore?
(It's) /opposite/ /the station/	(È) /di fronte/ /alla sta**zio**ne/
(It's) /next to/ /the park/	(È) /vi**ci**no/ /al **par**co/

4.1 (cont.)	most masculine vowels, eg *'al centro'* (to the centre); *'alla'* *(a+la)* before most feminine words eg *'alla stazione'* (to the station); *'all''* *(a+l')* before some masculine or feminine words which take *'l''* eg *'all'aeroporto'* (to the airport). See p256 for other forms.
	'La prima/la seconda'. This is short for *'la prima strada/la seconda strada'* (the first road/the second road). Because *'strada'* is a feminine word, the adjectives *'prima/seconda'* have the feminine form. Compare with *'il primo corridoio'* (the first corridor), which is masculine in form because *'corridoio'* is a masculine word.
	When using *'di fronte'* (opposite) with a building, add the preposition *'a'* eg *'di fronte alla stazione'* (opposite the station). See 4.3.
4.2	The word for 'a' and 'one' is the same in Italian – *'un'* with masculine words eg *'un giornale'* (a newspaper); *'una'* (with feminine words) eg *'una cartolina'* (a postcard).
	With most masculine words, the plural 'some' is *'dei'* eg *'dei giornali'* (some newspapers); with most feminine words 'some' is *'delle'* eg *'delle cartoline'* (some post-cards). See p257 for other forms.
4.3	Words like 'near', 'opposite' are often followed by *'a'* eg

4.4 Exact location (2)

*Which /platform/ please?	Che /binario/ per favore?
Which /station/ please?	Che /stazione/ per favore?
Which /underground station/ please?	Che /stazione della metropolitana/ per favore?
Which /bus/ please?	Che /autobus/ per favore?
Which /bus stop/ please?	Che /fermata/ per favore?
Which /train/ please?	Che /treno/ per favore?
Which /carriage/ please?	Che /carrozza/ per favore?
Which /room/ please?	Che /stanza/ per favore?
Which /office/ please?	Che /ufficio/ per favore?
Which /floor/ please?	Che /piano/ per favore?
Which /number/ please?	Che /numero/ per favore?

4.5 Distance

Is it far?	È lontano?
How far is it to /Venice/?	Quanto è lontana /Venezia/ da qui?
(About) /50/ kilometres	(Circa) /cinquanta/ chilometri
(Distances see p278)	

4.6 Getting there

How do you get there?	Come ci si va?
By /bus/	In /autobus/
Is there /a train/ to /Genoa/ today?	C'è /un treno/ per /Genova/ oggi?
Is this /the bus/ to /the airport/?	È questo /l'autobus/ per /l'aeroporto/?

4.3 (cont.)	'vicino al parco' (near the park), 'di fronte alla stazione' (opposite the station). Remember 'a' + the different forms of 'the', eg 'a' + 'il' becomes 'al', 'a' + 'la' becomes 'alla'. See p256).
4.5	Note that 'lontano' changes to 'lontana' if what you are talking about is feminine eg 'la casa' (the house), 'Venezia' (Venice).
4.6	You can usually use 'in' with methods of transport eg 'in treno' (by train) 'in aereo' (by plane) etc.

Now take a part

You want to find a taxi to take you to the airport.

Scusi.
Sì. Desidera?
Dove posso prendere un taxi, per favore?
Alla stazione. La prima a destra, la seconda a sinistra.
Grazie. È molto gentile.

Sì?
All'aeroporto, per favore.
OK. All'aeroporto.
È lontano?
Non è lontano. Circa cinque chilometri.

5 Time

5.1 General expressions

*Today	**O**ggi
*This morning	Questa mat**ti**na
*This afternoon	Questo pome**ri**ggio
*This evening	Questa **se**ra
*Tonight	Sta**no**tte
*Yesterday	**Ie**ri
Yesterday morning	Ieri mat**ti**na
Yesterday afternoon	Ieri pome**ri**ggio
Yesterday evening	Ieri **se**ra
Last night	Ieri **no**tte
*Tomorrow	Do**ma**ni
Tomorrow morning	Domani mat**ti**na
Tomorrow afternoon	Domani pome**ri**ggio
Tomorrow evening	Domani **se**ra
Tomorrow night	Domani **no**tte

5.1   *'Questa sera', 'ieri sera'. 'Sera'* means evening. But to Italians, the evening lasts until late – 11 pm or even midnight and is commonly used in expressions like *'Che cosa fa questa sera?'* (What are you doing tonight?).

Instead of *'due settimane'* (two weeks) Italians often say *'quindici giorni'* (fifteen days).

This week	Questa settimana
This month	Questo mese
This year	Quest'anno

Last week	La settimana scorsa
Last month	Il mese scorso
Last year	L'anno scorso

/2/ weeks ago	/Due/ settimane fa
/3/ months ago	/Tre/ mesi fa
/4/ years ago	/Quattro/ anni fa

Next week	La settimana prossima
Next month	Il mese prossimo
Next year	L'anno prossimo

| In /2/ weeks | Fra /due/ settimane |
| In /4/ months | Fra /quattro/ mesi |

5.2 The time

What's the time please?   Che ora è per favore?

Sono le sette

Sono le sette e cinque

Sono le sette e dieci

Sono le sette e undici minuti

Sono le sette e un quarto

Sono le sette e venticinque

Sono le sette e mezzo

Sono le otto meno venti

Sono le otto meno un quarto

5.2   You will also hear *'Che ore sono per favore?'* (literally, what hours are they please?) *'Sono'* is used with all hours of the day except 1 and 12 o'clock. This is because you are

5.3 The time (24 hour clock)

When does /the (next) train/ arrive?	Quando arriva /il (prossimo) **tre**no/?
When does /the (last) bus/ leave?	Quando parte /l'(ultimo) **au**tobus/?
When's /the (next) train/ to /Bologna/?	Quando è /il (prossimo) **tre**no/ per /**Bo**logna/?

At 1.03	All'una e **tre**
At 3.12	Alle **tre** e **do**dici
At 4.15	Alle **qua**ttro e **quin**dici
At 15.22	Alle **quin**dici e venti**du**e
At 16.45	Alle **se**dici e quaranta**cin**que
At 17.00	Alle dicias**se**tte
At 17.52	Alle dici as**se**tte e cinquanta**du**e
At 24.00	Alle venti**qua**ttro
(Numbers see 1.26)	

5.4 The date

What's the date today?	Quanti ne ab**bia**mo oggi?

(It's) /January/ 1st	(È) il primo /gen**na**io/
(It's) /February/ 2nd	(E) il due /**feb**braio/
(It's) /March/ 3rd	(È) il tre /**mar**zo/

<table>
<tr><td>5.2
(cont.)</td><td>really saying 'sono le ore sette' (literally 'They are the hours seven'). The exceptions are 'è l'una' (it's one o'clock), 'è mezzogiorno' (it's midday) and 'è mezzanotte' (it's midnight).
'Ora' is feminine so 'la' (the) is shortened to 'l'' before a vowel – 'l'una'. 'The' plural is 'le' eg 'le due' (two o'clock). In Italian the hour is mentioned first, then the minutes. 'Le sette e cinque' (5 past 7) literally means 'the seven and five'. 'Le otto meno venti' (20 to 8) literally means 'the eight less twenty'. Practise telling the time in Italian.</td></tr>
<tr><td>5.3</td><td>'All'una e tre' literally means 'at the one and three' (ie 3 minutes past 1). 'A' + 'l' (before a vowel) becomes 'all''. 'A' + 'le' (feminine plural) becomes 'alle'. See p256.</td></tr>
<tr><td>5.4</td><td>Put 'il' before the date in Italian eg 'il sette agosto' (the 7th</td></tr>
</table>

(It's) /April/ 4th	(È) il quattro/**aprile**/
(It's) /May/ 5th	(È) il cinque /**maggio**/
(It's) /October/ 11th	(È) l'undici /ot**to**bre/

5.5 Specific times (1)

When do you /close/?	Quando si /**chiu**de/?
*When do /the shops/ open?	Quando **a**prono /i ne**go**zi/?
*When do /the banks/ close?	Quando **chiu**dono /le **ban**che/?
When do you serve /breakfast/?	Quando è /la prima cola**zio**ne/?
*When does it /begin/?	Quando /incomin**ci**a/?
*When does it /end/?	Quando /fi**ni**sce/?

At /4/ o'clock	Alle /**quat**tro/
At /2.0/ a.m.	Alle /**due**/ di mattina
At /4.20/ p.m.	Alle /**quat**tro e venti/ del pome**rig**gio
From /8.0/ to /10.0/	Dalle /**ot**to/ alle /**die**ci/

On /Monday/	/Lune**dì**/
On /Mondays/	Di /lune**dì**/
In /June/	In /**giu**gno/
On /July 6th/	Il /sei **lu**glio/
On /Monday August 7th/	/Lune**dì** sette a**go**sto/
In /1995/	Nel /millenove**cen**to novanta**cin**que/
In /summer/	In /es**ta**te/

5.4 (cont.)	August), except when you include the day of the week before the date eg '*Lunedì sette agosto*' (Monday the 7th of August). See 5.5.
	With dates, only '*il primo*' (the first) is an ordinal number in Italian. '*Il due*', '*il tre*' etc literally means 'the two, the three' etc. Practise saying different dates in Italian.
5.5	For the present tense of verbs see p265. Italian has no equivalent for 'on' in phrases like 'on Monday'. You just say the day – '*lunedì*'. But note 'in July' is '*in luglio*'.

29

5.6 Specific times – future (2)

When /will you leave/?	Quando /partirà/?
When /will she arrive/?	Quando /arriverà/?
When will it be /ready/?	Quando sarà /**pron**to/?
When will it be /finished/?	Quando sarà /**fi**nito/?
At /2/ o'clock	Alle /**due**/
Next /Tuesday/	/Marte**dì**/ prossimo
In /3/ hours	Fra /**tre**/ ore
In /2/ days	Fra /**due**/ giorni
I'll be back in /10 minutes/	Torno fra /dieci mi**nu**ti/

5.7 Specific times – past (3)

When /did you (masculine) arrive/?	Quando /è arri**va**to/?
When /did you (feminine) arrive/?	Quando /è arri**va**ta/?
At /3/ o'clock	Alle /**tre**/
Last /Thursday/	/Giove**dì**/ scorso
/2/ days ago	/**Due**/ giorni fa
/5/ minutes ago	/**Cin**que/ minuti fa

5.8 Duration

How long will you be here?	Quanto tempo resterà **qui**?
How long will you be away?	Quanto tempo resterà **via**?
How long will it take?	Quanto ci vor**rà**?

5.6	For the future tense see p268.
	Italians do not use the pronouns 'I/you/he/she' etc much. *'Quando arriverà?'* means literally 'When will arrive?' and could refer to 'you (polite form)/he/she/it'.
	'Pronto', 'finito' – These are masculine forms. If you were talking about a feminine object, you would say *'Quando sarà pronta/finita?'*.
5.7	If you were talking to a woman, you would say *'Quando è arrivata?'* (feminine). See p270 for past tense.
5.8	*'Resterà'* literally means 'will be staying'. *'Ci vorrà'* (it will take) is a useful expression. *'Ci vuole'*

How long will it be /delayed/?	Quanto sarà /in ritardo/?
(About) /an hour and a half/	(Circa) /un'ora e mezza/
/3/ days	/Tre/ giorni
Until /Friday/	Fino a /venerdì/

Now take a part

At the station – you want to find out about train times and then buy a ticket.

Quando è il prossimo treno per Bologna?
Questa sera, alle diciotto e quindici.
Quando arriva il treno?
Arriva alle diciannove e trentasei.
Quanto costa il biglietto?
Andata o andata e ritorno?
Andata, per favore.
Duemila lire.
OK. Un biglietto di andata per Bologna, per favore.
Grazie.

5.8 (cont.)	means 'it takes' eg *'Ci vuole un'ora'* (it takes an hour). But if referring to more than one thing, *'vuole'* becomes *'vogliono'* eg *'Ci vogliono un'ora'*. (they take an hour).

6 Information about things

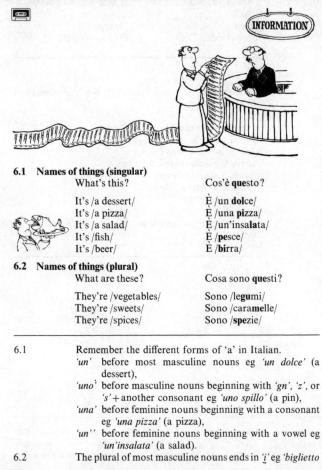

6.1 Names of things (singular)

What's this?	Cos'è **que**sto?
It's /a dessert/	È /un **dol**ce/
It's /a pizza/	È /una **piz**za/
It's /a salad/	È /un'insa**la**ta/
It's /fish/	È /**pe**sce/
It's /beer/	È /**bir**ra/

6.2 Names of things (plural)

What are these?	Cosa sono **que**sti?
They're /vegetables/	Sono /le**gu**mi/
They're /sweets/	Sono /cara**mel**le/
They're /spices/	Sono /**spe**zie/

6.1   Remember the different forms of 'a' in Italian.

'*un*' before most masculine nouns eg '*un dolce*' (a dessert),

'*uno*' before masculine nouns beginning with '*gn*', '*z*', or '*s*'+another consonant eg '*uno spillo*' (a pin),

'*una*' before feminine nouns beginning with a consonant eg '*una pizza*' (a pizza),

'*un'*' before feminine nouns beginning with a vowel eg '*un'insalata*' (a salad).

6.2   The plural of most masculine nouns ends in '*i*' eg '*biglietto*

6.3 Description (singular)

What's it like?	Com'è?
Is it /heavy/?	È /pesante/?

It's like this	È così
It's /big/	È /grande/
It's very /big/	È molto /grande/
It's too /big/	È troppo /grande/
It's not /big/ enough	Non è abbastanza /grande/
It's a little /small/	È un po' /piccolo/
It's got /a key/	Ha /una chiave/

6.4 Description (plural)

What are they like?	Come sono?
Are they /waterproof/?	Sono /impermeabili/?

They're /round/	Sono /rotondi/
They're /sharp/	Sono /affilati/
They're very /long/	Sono molto /lunghi/
They've got /filters/	Hanno /filtri/

6.5 Colour

What colour is it?	Di che colore è?
It's /red/	È /rosso/

6.2 (cont.)	– *biglietti'* (ticket – tickets). The plural of most feminine nouns ends in '*e*' eg *'caramella – caramelle'* (sweet – sweets). Any exceptions to this rule are shown in the Mini Dictionary.
6.3	See also 6.4. Adjectives must 'agree' with the words they describe and most have a feminine and masculine form. Adjectives ending in '*e*' eg *'grande'* are the same in the masculine and feminine singular form. The plural form ends in '*i*' eg *'grandi'*.
	Adjectives which end in '*o*' eg *'piccolo'* in their masculine form, end in '*a*' eg *'piccola'* in their feminine singular form, end in '*i*' eg *'piccoli'* in the masculine plural form, and end in '*e*' eg *'piccole'* in the feminine plural form. See p258.
	All irregular plurals are given in the Mini Dictionary.
6.5	Some adjectives of colours never change their form eg

6.6 What's it made of?

What's it made of?	Di che cosa è **fatto**?
It's made of /metal/ and /plastic/	È fatto di /me**tal**lo/ e /**pla**stica/

6.7 Use

What's it for?	A che cosa **ser**ve?
It's used to /clean shoes/	**Ser**ve per /pulire le **scar**pe/

6.8 Size (clothing) & weight

What size is it?	Che mi**su**ra è?
What size do you want?	Che mi**su**ra **vuo**le?
What shoe size do you take?	Che **nu**mero di **scar**pe porta?
Size /7/ (Size see p278)	**Nu**mero /qua**ran**ta/
How much does it weigh?	Quanto **pe**sa?
(It weighs) /500/ grams (Weight see p280)	(**Pe**sa) /cinque**cen**to/ **gram**mi

6.9 Length & width

How big is it?	Quanto è **gran**de?
It's (about) /15/ cms long	È lungo (circa) /**quin**dici/ centi**me**tri
About /30/ cms wide	Largo circa /**tren**ta/ centi**me**tri
/30/ cms by /15/ cms	/**Tren**ta/ centi**me**tri per /**quin**dici/ centi**me**tri

6.10 Cost

*How much is it please?	Quanto **cos**ta, per favore?
*How much are they please?	Quanto **cos**tano, per favore?

6.5 (cont.)	*'rosa'* (pink), *'porpora'* (crimson) eg *'il vestito rosa'* (the pink dress), *'la cravatta rosa'* (the pink tie). Note that in Italian you usually put the adjective after the word it describes, not before as in English. See p258.
6.7	'What are they for?' is *'A che cosa servono?'*

It's /2,500/ lire	Costa /duemila cinquecento/ lire
They're /2,000/ lire (Money see p278)	Costano /duemila/ lire

6.11 Possession

Whose is it?	Di chi è?
It's /mine/	È /mio/
Is this /yours/?	È /suo/ questo?
*Yes, it is	Sì
*No, it isn't	No

6.12 Likes/Dislikes

Do you like /this colour/?	Le piace /questo colore/?
Do you like /these belts/?	Le piacciono /queste cinture/?
Yes, I do	Sì, mi piace
I like /this style/	Mi piace /questa moda/
No, I don't	No, non mi piace
I don't like /this shape/	Non mi piace /questa forma/
Do you like this?	Le piace questo?

6.11   *'Mio/suo'* – these must change if the thing which they refer to is feminine eg *'Questa è la sua borsetta?'* (Is this your bag?) – *'Sì, è mia'* (Yes, it's mine). (See p263).
'Sì' and *'No'* do not sound brusque when answering in Italian, as they would in English.

6.12   *'Le piace questo colore?'* literally means 'To you pleases this colour?' (Does this colour please you?) Say *'Ti piace . . .?'* (Do you like . . .?) to someone you know well. If you are talking about more than one thing *'piace'* becomes *'piacciono'* eg *'Mi piacciono questi guanti'* (I like these gloves).
Note that *'questo'* (this) changes according to what it is describing *'questo colore'* (this colour – masculine singular), *'questa moda'* (this style – feminine singular), *'questi guanti'* (these gloves – masculine plural), *'queste cinture'* (these belts – feminine plural). See p260.

Yes, I love it	Sì, mi piace **molto**
No, I hate it	**No**, non mi piace af**fatto**
Did you like /the film/?	Le è piaciuto /il **film**/?
No, not very much	No, non **mol**to

Now take a part

You've lost something and you have to describe it.

Buon giorno. Desidera?
Sì. Ho perso la mia valigia.
Com'è?
È piccola è rotonda.
Di che colore è?
È rossa.
Sì. E di che cosa è fatta?
È fatta di plastica.
Va bene. Un momento, per favore. È sua questa?
Sì, è mia. Tante grazie.
Prego.

7 Wants and needs

7.1 Have you got?/I've got/I haven't got (singular)

*Have you got /the ticket/?	Ha /il bi**glie**tto/?
Have you got /a roadmap/?	Ha /una carta stra**da**le/?
Have you got /an appunt**amen**to/?	Ha /un appuntamento/?
*Have you got /any beer/?	Ha /della **bir**ra/?
Have you got /your passport/?	Ha /il passa**por**to/?

7.1   See also 7.2, 7.3. In Italian you do not have to change the
order of words to form questions. You simply change
your tone of voice. *'Ha il biglietto'* can mean 'You've got
the ticket' or 'Have you got the ticket?' depending on the
tone of your voice.

If you are asking a friend informally, *'ha'* becomes *'hai'* eg
'Hai il biglietto?' (Have you got the ticket?)

In Italian, you make less use of 'my/your/his' etc than in
English. *'Ha il passaporto?'* means 'Have you got the
passport?' or 'Have you got your passport?' 'Your' is
understood.

*Yes, I have	Sì
I've got /a reservation/	Ho /una prenotazione/
I've got /some coffee/	Ho /del caffè/

*No, I haven't	No
I haven't got /the ticket/	Non ho /il biglietto/
I haven't got /a ticket/	Non ho /un biglietto/
*I haven't got any /change/	Non ho /spiccioli/

7.2 Have you got?/I've got/I haven't got (plural)

*Have you got /the keys/?	Ha /le chiavi/?
Have you got /any postcards/?	Ha /delle cartoline/?
Have you got /your suitcases/?	Ha /le valige/?

| *Yes, I have | Sì |
| I've got /some stamps/ | Ho /dei francobolli/ |

*No, I haven't	No
I haven't got any /suitcases/	Non ho /valige/
I haven't got any /tickets/	Non ho /biglietti/
I haven't got /the tickets/	Non ho /i biglietti/

7.3 Is there/Are there?

| *Is there /a hotel/ near here? | C'è /un albergo/ qui vicino? |
| Is there /a train/ to /Turin/ this morning? | C'è /un treno/ per /Torino/ questa mattina? |

7.2   'I've got some' – 'some' changes according to whether the thing it refers to is masculine, feminine, singular or plural. It is formed by adding *'di'* to the appropriate form of 'the' eg *'del latte'* (some milk) – *'di'+ 'il'*; *'della birra'* (some beer) – *'di'+ 'la'*; *'dei giornali'* (some newspapers) – *'di'+ 'i'*; *'delle cartoline'* (some postcards) – *'di'+ 'le'*. See p256 for other forms.

'I haven't got any' – in the negative statement there is no equivalent of 'any' or 'some'. You simply say *'Non ho latte'* (literally 'I haven't milk').

38

| *Is there /any tea/? | C'è /del **tè**/? |
| Are there /any restaurants/ near here? | Ci sono /dei risto**ranti**/ qui vicino? |

7.4 There is/There are

*Yes, there is	Sì
There's /a train/ to /Turin/ at /7.50/	C'è /un treno/ per /**Torino**/ alle /**sette** e cin**quan**ta/
*There's /some beer/ /in the fridge/	C'è /della **bi**rra/ /nel frigo**ri**fero/
There are /2/ /hotels/ in the town	Ci sono /due/ /al**ber**ghi/ in città

7.5 There isn't/There aren't

No, there isn't	No, non c'è **ne**
*There isn't any /beer/ /in the fridge/	Non c'è /**bi**rra/ /nel frigo**ri**fero/
*There aren't any /seats/	Non ci sono /**po**sti/

7.6 I'd like

| I'd like /a cut and blow dry/ please | Vorrei /**ta**glio e asciuga**tu**ra al **fon**/ per favore |
| I'd like /a beer and a sandwich/ please | Vorrei /una **bi**rra e un pa**ni**no/ per favore |

7.4   *'Nel frigorifero'* – the preposition 'in' combines with different forms of 'the' like other prepositions; *'in' + 'il'* becomes *'nel'*. See p256 for other forms. Certain fixed phrases do not require 'the' eg *'in città'* (in the town), *'in cucina'* (in the kitchen).

7.5   *'C'è'* (there is) and *'ci sono'* (there are) – don't confuse these with *'è'* (it is) and *'sono'* (they are).

7.6   Remember *'questo'* and *'quello'* become *'questa'* and *'quella'* when referring to feminine things eg *'questa casa'* (this house), *'quella casa'* (that house).

*I'd like /some coffee/ please	Vorrei /del caffè/ per favore
I'd like /some cigars/ please	Vorrei /dei sigari/ per favore
I'd like /breakfast in my room/ please	Vorrei /la colazione in camera/ per favore
*I'd like this please	Vorrei questo per favore
*I'd like that please	Vorrei quello per favore
*I'd like these please	Vorrei questi per favore
*I'd like those please	Vorrei quelli per favore

7.7 Would you like?

What would you like?	Cosa desidera?
What would you like? (informal)	Cosa vuoi?
Would you like /a streetmap/?	Desidera /una pianta della città/?
Would you like /some wine/?	Desidera /del vino/?
Would you like /some biscuits/?	Desidera /dei biscotti/?
*Yes please	Sì grazie
*No thank you	No grazie

7.8 I'd prefer

| I'd prefer /an omelette/ | Preferisco /un'omelette/ |
| I'd prefer /some red wine/ | Preferisco /del vino rosso/ |

7.9 I need

I need /a towel/	Mi occorre /un asciugamano/
I need /some soap/	Mi occorre /del sapone/
I need /some stamps/	Mi occorrono /dei francobolli/
Do I need /a visa/?	Mi occorre /un visto/?
What do I need?	Cosa mi occorre?

7.7   *'Cosa desidera?'* is formal. A slightly less formal, but still polite expression *'Cosa vuole?'* (What do you want?) is also commonly used.

7.9   *'Mi occorre'* literally means 'To me it wants'. It is similar to *'Mi piace'*. See 6.12.

40

7.10 Exact quantities

How many would you like?	Quanti ne desidera?
I'd like /3/	Ne vorrei /**tre**/
How much would you like?	Quanto ne desidera?
I'd like /a slice/ of /ham/ (Numbers see 1.26)	Vorrei /una **fe**tta/ di /pro**sciu**tto/

7.11 Which one?

Which one do you want?	Quale **vuo**le?
Which ones do you want?	Quali **vuo**le?
This one please	**Que**sto per favore
That one please	**Quel**lo per favore
These ones please	**Que**sti per favore
Those ones please	**Quel**li per favore
/The big/ one (masculine)	Quello /**gran**de/
/The big/ one (feminine)	Quella /**gran**de/
The /big/ ones (masculine)	Quelli /**gran**di/
The /big/ ones (feminine)	Quelle /**gran**di/

7.12 Quantities

How many?	**Quan**ti?
How many /apples/ would you like?	Quante /**me**le/ desidera?

7.10   'Ne' – in Italian you can't just say 'I'd like three'; you have to say <u>what</u> you would like. When both the person you are speaking to and you know what you're talking about, you simply add 'ne' before the verb. It means 'of it' or 'of them'. So 'Ne vorrei tre' literally means 'Of them I'd like three'.

7.11   'Quello' is a pronoun meaning 'that one'. 'Quello' (that one) is masculine singular, 'quelli' (those ones) is masculine plural, 'quella' (that one) is féminine singular, 'quelle' (those ones) is feminine plural.
        But it can also be an adjective meaning 'that' followed by a noun with which it must 'agree' eg 'quel formaggio' (that cheese), 'quella mela' (that apple), 'quelli guanti' (those gloves), 'quelle scarpe' (those shoes).

7.12   'Quanto?' (how much?) agrees with the word it refers to

41

Not many - /3/ please	Non **mol**te - /**tre**/ per favore
How much?	**Quan**to?
How much /cream/ would you like?	Quanta /**panna**/ desidera?
Not much	Non **mol**ta
A lot	**Mol**to
*Less	**Me**no
More (...)	Di **più** (...)
Enough	**Ba**sta
A few /tomatoes/	Al**cu**ni /pomo**do**ri/
A little /cream/	Un po' di /**panna**/

7.13 I want/I don't want

I want /some coffee/	Voglio /del caffè/
I want /some stamps/	Voglio /dei franco**bol**li/
I want /some more coffee/	Voglio /ancora caffè/
I don't want many	Non ne voglio **mol**ti
I don't want much	Non ne voglio **mol**to
I don't want so many	Non ne voglio **tan**ti
I don't want so much	Non ne voglio **tan**to

7.14 Comparisons

Have you got anything /bigger/?	Ha qual**co**sa di /più **gran**de/?
I want something /bigger/	Voglio qual**co**sa di /più **gran**de/
I want something more /comfortable/	Voglio qual**co**sa di più /**co**modo/
I want something less /expensive/	Voglio qual**co**sa di meno /cos**to**so/

7.12 (cont.)	like a normal adjective eg *'quanto formaggio?'* (how much cheese?), *'quanta pasta?'* (how much pasta?), *'quanti alberghi?'* (how many hotels?), *'quante mele?'* (how many apples?).
	Use *'Non molto', 'molto/alcuno'* and *'tanto'* in the same way as *'quanto'*. See 7.13 also.
7.14	Use *'più'* for 'more', *'meno'* for 'less'.

7.15 Anything else?/Anything for?

Do you want anything else?	Vuole qualcos'**al**tro?
Do you need anything else?	Le occorre qualcos'**al**tro?
Would you like anything else?	Vorrebbe qualcos'**al**tro?
Have you got anything for /a cough/?	Ha qualcosa per /la **to**sse/?
Have you got anything for /children/?	Ha qualcosa per /bam**bi**ni/?

7.16 Food (style, variety, flavour)

How would you like it?	Come lo **vuo**le?
I'd like it /well done/ please	Lo vorrei /cotto **be**ne/ per favore
What kind of /sandwich/ would you like?	Che tipo di /pa**ni**no/ vuole?
I'd like a /ham/ sandwich please	Vorrei un panino col /pro**sciu**tto/ per favore
I'd like /an ice cream/ please	Vorrei /un ge**la**to/ per favore
What flavour would you like?	Che gusto **vuo**le?
/Vanilla/ please	/**Cre**ma/ per favore

7.14 (cont.)	There is no difference between 'bigger' and 'biggest' or 'more comfortable' and 'most comfortable' in Italian eg *'la borsa più grande'* means both 'the bigger bag' and 'the biggest bag'.
7.15	*'Qualcos'altro'* – *'qualcosa'* and *'altro'* are joined together because of the two adjoining vowels. *'Qualcosa per la tosse'* literally means 'something for the cough'. In Italian you say *'Ho la tosse'* (I've got the cough) rather like in English you say 'I've got the flu'. See also 3.13.

Now take a part

Buying some groceries.

Buon giorno. Desidera?
Buon giorno. Ha del caffè?
Sì, quanto ne desidera?
Ne vorrei un mezzo chilo, per favore.
Bene. Nient'altro?
Sì. Vorrei delle mele, per favore.
Quante?
Non molte – basta.
OK. È duemila cinquecento lire, per favore.
Grazie.

8 Getting help – getting things done

8.1 General expressions

How does it work?	Come funziona?
Like this	Così
It works with /batteries/	Funziona a /pile/
It doesn't work	Non funziona
It's broken	È rotto
It's out of order	È guasto
It makes a /funny/ noise	Fa uno /strano/ rumore
I can't open it	Non riesco ad aprirlo
I can't do it	Non riesco a farlo

8.2 (Could you) please?

Could you /call/ /a taxi/ for me	Mi /chiami/ /un taxi/ per favore
Could you tell me when we get there	Mi dice quando siamo arrivati per favore
*Please /call/ me at /7/ o'clock	Per favore mi /chiami/ alle /sette/
Please leave me alone	Mi lasci in pace per favore

8.1   'Non riesco' means 'I don't succeed in' (doing something).
The verb 'fare' (do) loses its final 'e' to become 'far' when
it is followed by something – 'far' + 'lo' (it) becomes
'farlo' (the pronoun 'it' is joined onto the verb).

8.3 Getting things done

I'd like to have /this shirt/ /washed/ please

Vorrei far /lavare/ /questa camicia/ per favore

I'd like to have /this film/ /developed/ please

Vorrei far /sviluppare/ /questo rullino/ per favore

I'd like to have /this camera/ /repaired/ please

Vorrei far /aggiustare/ /questa **ma**cchina foto**gra**fica/ per favore

I'd like to have /this skirt/ /cleaned/ please

Vorrei far /pulire a secco/ / questa **gonna**/ per favore

I'd like to have /this/ /delivered/ please

Vorrei far /recapitare a casa/ /**que**sto/ per favore

Now take a part

You take your camera to a camera shop to be repaired.

Buon giorno. Desidera?

Buon giorno. Sì. Vorrei far aggiustare questa macchina fotografica, per favore.

Cose c'è?

Non lo so. Non funziona. Non riesco ad aprirla.

Sì. Va bene. Un momento, per favore. Come si chiama, per favore?

Mi chiamo Anderson. John Anderson.

Grazie.

Quando sarà pronta?

Venerdì prossimo.

Grazie. Buon giorno.

Buon giorno.

8.3   *'Vorrei far lavare'* literally means 'I'd like to make to wash'. *'Fare'* loses its final *'e'* as it is followed by something (the infinitive *'lavare'* – to wash). See 8.1.

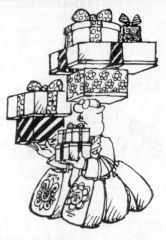

9.1 Wishes

Do you want to /hire/ /a car/?	Vuole /noleggiare//una macchina/?
I want to /hire/ /a car/	Voglio /noleggiare/ /una macchina/
I don't want to /go/ by /bus/	Non **vo**glio /andare/ in /**au**tobus/
What would you like to do?	Cosa vorrebbe **fa**re?
Would you like to /go/ to /Leghorn/?	Vorrebbe /andare/ a /**Livo**rno/?
Would you like to /do some shopping/?	Vorrebbe /**fa**re delle **spe**se/?

9.1   *'Vorrei', 'vorrebbe'* (I would like, you would like). See p267 for other parts of the verb.

I'd love to /go/ to /Leghorn/	Mi piacerebbe **mol**to /andare/ a /Livorno/
I'd like to /do some shopping/	Vorrei /**fa**re delle **spe**se/
I'd like to see you again	Vorrei rive**der**la/
I'd prefer to /go to the cinema/	Prefe**ri**sco /andare al **ci**nema/

9.2 Possibility

| Can I /hire/ /a car/? | Posso /noleg**gia**re/ /una ma**cchi**na/? |
| Where can I /hire/ /a bicycle/? | Dove posso /noleg**gia**re/ /una bici**clet**ta/? |

| I can /meet you/ /tomorrow/ | Posso /ve**der**la/ /do**ma**ni/ |
| I can't /meet you/ /tomorrow/ | Non posso /ve**der**la/ /do**ma**ni/ |

9.3 Permission

| May I /borrow/ /your pen/? | Posso /**pren**dere in pre**sti**to/ / la sua **pen**na/? |
| Yes, of course | Sì, **cer**to |

9.4 Necessity

Must I /pay/ now?	Devo /pa**ga**re/ **o**ra?
Where must I /go/?	Dove devo /an**da**re/?
I must /leave early/	Devo /partire **pre**sto/
I must /catch/ /the next train/	Devo /**pren**dere/ /il prossimo **tre**no/
I needn't /catch/ /the next train/	Non debbo /**pren**dere/ /il prossimo **tre**no/

9.3   *'La sua penna'* literally means 'the your pen'. Both 'the' and 'your' agree with *'penna'* (pen – feminine singular). *'Sua'* is the polite form of 'your'.

9.5 Intention

Are you going to /hire/ /a car/?	Ha intenzione di /noleggiare/ /una macchina/?
I'm going to /buy/ /a map/	Ho intenzione di /comprare/ /una mappa/
I'm going to /see him/ tomorrow	Ho intenzione di /vederlo/ domani

9.6 Suggestions

*Let's go	Andiamo
Let's go and /eat/	Andiamo a /mangiare/
Let's go /to the cinema/	Andiamo /al cinema/
Let's go /shopping/	Andiamo a /fare le spese/
Let's go /swimming/	Andiamo a /fare il bagno/
Let's meet /tomorrow/	Vediamoci /domani/
Let's meet /next Tuesday/	Vediamoci /martedì prossimo/
*Let's meet at /9/	Vediamoci alle /nove/

Now take a part

Arranging to meet someone again.

Vorrei rivederla. Possiamo vederci domani?
Sì. Magnifico. Quando?
Alle sei – va bene?
Sì. Dove?
Al suo albergo. Cosa vorrebbe fare?
Andiamo al cinema.
Bene. A domani sera.
Ciao.

9.5   *'Ha intenzione di'* literally means 'I have intention of' and must be followed by the infinitive form of the verb eg *'vedere'* (to see).

'Vederlo' (to see him) – *'vedere' + 'lo'*. If there is a pronoun eg *'lo'* (him) *'la'* (you/her) *'ti'* (you informal) etc after the verb, the *'e'* is omitted and the verb and pronoun are joined together. See also 9.1 and 9.2.

10 A variety of situations

The language you have learned in all the previous Study Sections can of course be used in many different situations. This section contains a number of examples of the sorts of conversations you should be able to take part in or understand. Even if you don't understand every word, you will often be able to get the gist of what people are saying depending on the situation you are in. The figures on the right refer, where applicable, to sections you have already studied.

10.1 Meeting someone – Someone you don't know is meeting you at the airport.

– Scusi! Lei è Arthur Smith?	1.1
– Sì, sono io.	1.1
– Buon giorno. Io sono Bruno Negrente.	1.8
Lavoro per la ditta Bonetti.	3.9
Sono architetto.	3.10
– Piacere. Smith.	1.9
– Mi da la valigia.	—
– Grazie.	1.1
– Andiamo.	1.12/9.6
– Sì. Grazie.	1.1

10.2 Introductions – Someone introduces you to a 3rd person.

– Le presento la signorina Andreoli il
  signor Smith.   3.14
– Piacere. Andreoli.   1.9
– Piacere. Smith.   1.9
– Quando è arrivato, signor Smith?   5.7
– Ieri sera.   5.1
– Quanto tempo resterà qui?   5.8
– Tre giorni.   5.8

10.3 The hotel – Mr and Mrs Smith and their two children have just
arrived at a hotel. They previously booked two rooms.

– Buon giorno, signore.   1.8
– Buon giorno.   1.8
  Mi chiamo Smith. Ho una
  prenotazione.   3.1/7.1
– Smith – come si scrive per favore?   3.2
– S-M-I-T-H   1.29

– Ah, sì! I signori Smith con due
  bambini.   1.1
  Due stanze doppie con bagno.   1.19
– *Esatto*.   —
– Mi dia i passaporti per favore.   —
– *Eccoli*.   —
– Grazie. Numeri 401 e 402.   1.26
  Ecco le chiavi.   1.1
– Grazie. Che piano per favore?   4.4
– *Quarto* piano.   —

Esatto (That's right). *Eccoli* (Here they are). *Ecco* (Here
are). *Quarto* (fourth).

10.4 Making reservations . . .

10.4.1 . . . at the theatre

– Vorrei due posti in *platea* per favore.   7.6
– Per quando?   1.13
– Sabato sera, per favore.   5.4
– Sì. Ci sono ancora posti.   —
– Quanto costano per favore?   6.10
– 11,000 lire.   1.26

	– Vorrei spendere meno per favore.	—
	– Ci sono due *balconate*, prima fila a 7,000 lire.	1.6
	– Prendo quelli.	7.11

Platea (stalls), *balconata* (dress circle).

10.4.2 ... at a restaurant

	– Vorrei un tavolo per questa sera per favore.	1.4/1.13
	– Per quanti?	7.12
	– Per quattro.	1.17/1.26
	– Per che ora scusi?	—
	– Per le otto e mezzo.	5.2
	– Ho un tavolo libero per le nove. Va bene?	7.1
	– Benissimo grazie.	2/1.1
	– Come si chiama?	3.1
	– Wrapson. W-R-A-P-S-O-N.	—
	– Grazie signore.	1.1

10.5 The restaurant – You are ordering food.

	– Il menu per favore.	1.17
	– Certo signore.	1.1
	– Desidera anche *la lista dei vini*?	7.7
	– Sì per favore.	1.1
	– Posso ordinare ora?	9.2/1.1
	– Certo. Cosa desidera?	1.1/7.7
	– Vorrei *spaghetti alla carbonara*. *Poi* una bistecca.	7.16
	– Come la vuole?	7.16
	– La vorrei cotta bene, per favore.	7.16
	Vorrei anche patate fritte e *insalata mista*.	7.6
	– Cosa beve?	1.17
	– *Una bottiglia di Bardolino*, per favore.	—

La lista dei vini (wine list). *Spaghetti alla carbonara* (spaghetti with bacon and egg sauce). *Poi* (then). *Insalata mista* (mixed salad). *Una bottiglia di Bardolino* (a bottle of Bardolino).

10.6 Travel – at a Tourist Information Office – You want to know how to get to Venice.

–	Buon giorno.	1.8
–	Voglio andare a Venezia.	9.1
	Vorrei delle informazioni sui treni, per favore.	1.21/7.6
	Quando parte il prossimo treno?	5.3
–	Alle quattordici e venti.	5.3/1.26
–	Quanto costa un biglietto di andata e ritorno?	6.10/1.11
–	9,700 lire.	1.26
–	Grazie.	1.1

10.7 Shopping

10.7.1 . . . buying a pair of shoes

–	Desidera?	1.15
–	C'è un paio di scarpe in vetrina.	1.15
	Vorrei provarle per favore.	1.15
–	Certo.	1.1
	Che numero di scarpe porta?	6.8
–	Numero 40.	6.8/1.26
–	*Provi queste.*	—
–	Grazie.	1.1
–	*Le vanno bene?*	—
–	Sì, sono molto comode.	6.4
	Quanto costano, per favore?	6.10
–	25,000 lire.	1.26
–	Le prendo. Grazie.	1.15

Provi queste (try these). *Le vanno bene?* (Are they all right?/Do they fit?).

10.7.2 . . . deciding not to buy

–	Vorrei una macchina fotografica, per favore.	1.4
	Quanto costa questa?	6.10
–	83,000 lire.	1.26
–	*Vuole vederla?*	7.15
–	Sì, per favore.	1.1

È bella, ma voglio qualcosa di meno
   costoso.   6.3/7.14
– Le piace questa?   6.12
– No, grazie, non la prendo.   1.15

Vuole vederla? (Would you like to see it?)

PLACE THIS TICKET INSIDE THE
WINDSCREEN VISIBLE FROM THE OUTSIDE

CITY OF BIRMINGHAM

DATE   MONTH   HOUR   MINUTE   FEE PAID
ENTRY TIME

30C 13 OCT 10:43

DATE   MONTH   HOUR   MINUTE   FEE PAID
DEPARTURE TIME

13 OCT 14:51

DATE   MONTH   HOUR   MINUTE   FEE PAID
13 OCT 10:47

DETACH FOR RECEIPT OR REMINDER

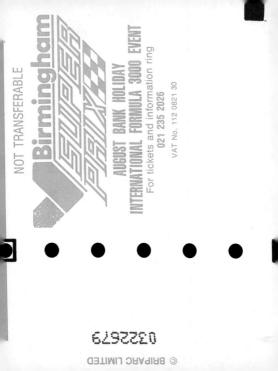

NOT TRANSFERABLE

Birmingham
SUPER PRIX

AUGUST BANK HOLIDAY
INTERNATIONAL FORMULA 3000 EVENT
For tickets and information ring
021 235 2026

VAT No. 112 0821 30

0322679

© BRIPARC LIMITED

11 How to cope with

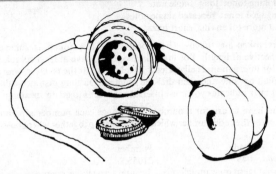

11.1 The telephone

Where to find a phone: In bars, indicated by a yellow telephone dial sign hanging outside. There are also call boxes in the street, and always at stations.

Money: 'Gettoni' (tokens) are used for public telephones; buy them in bars, or from machines in or near the call box.

Inland calls: You can dial direct throughout Italy. See list of codes ('teleselezione') which is usually found in the call box or near the bar phone.

International calls: See list of international code numbers in telephone directory – most international calls can be dialled direct. To call Britain from Italy, dial 0044 then the code for the British town and then the number.

NB If the British code starts with 0, omit it eg to dial London (code 01) dial 0044 1, followed by the number.

General expressions

Where's the (nearest) phone please?	Dov'è il telefono (più vicino) per favore?
May I use your phone please?	Posso usare il suo telefono per favore?
Have you got a telephone directory?	Ha un elenco telefonico?
Have you got a code book?	Ha il libretto dei prefissi telefonici?

How to make a telephone call from a public telephone in Italy

Dialling tone: repeated pairs of short notes
Ringing tone: long, single note
Engaged tone: repeated single notes
Put more tokens in: short buzz

Insert token or tokens. (For local calls, one token is sufficient, irrespective of length. For long distance calls, have at least six tokens, and for international calls at least 20 tokens.) Lift the receiver, wait for the dialling tone and then dial the number. On long distance calls, a short buzz indicates you must insert more tokens to go on speaking.

If you have to ask for a number, pronounce each number separately, except for the code number which Italians group together where possible eg

	Code	Number
Verona	045	21055
	zero quarantacinque	due uno zero cinque cinque

Directory enquiries

See the local telephone directory for Directory Enquiries number, which varies from town to town. For calls to the United States or other non-European countries, dial Italcable (170).

Directory Enquiries	Informazioni
Which town please?	Che città per favore? /Roma/
I'd like a telephone number in /Urbino in the Marches/	Vorrei un numero telefonico di /Urbino nelle Marche/
Name?	Cognome? /Fratta/
First name?	Nome? /Luisa/
Address?	Indirizzo? /Via Palladio 85/
What is the code for /Vicenza/ please?	Qual'è il prefisso di /Vicenza/ per favore?

Operator

There is no general purpose 'operator' in Italy. Look in the opening pages of the telephone directory for the specific service you require.

Number please?	Mi dia il numero per favore? /Perugia 35261/
What's your number please?	Che numero ha per favore? /Roma 7439022/

56

I'd like a personal call to /Mr Cook/, /Oxford 56762/

Vorrei una chiamata personale con /il signor Cook/, /Oxford 56762/

I'd like a transferred charge call to /York 33582/

Vorrei chiamare /York 33582/ con pagamento a destinazione

Can I have a line please?

Mi dà una linea per favore?

Could you call me at /7 o'clock/ please?

Mi può chiamare alle /7/ per favore?

Hold the line please

Resti in linea prego

The line's engaged

La linea è occupata

There's no reply

Non risponde

Difficulties

I want /London 327 5389/. I can't get through

Voglio /Londra 327 5389/. Non riesco ad ottenere il numero

I was speaking to /Turin 384529/. I was cut off

Stavo parlando con /Torino 384529/. Siamo stati interrotti

PHONE CALLS

1 Informal

Hello

Pronto

Hello. Is that /Mr Strabbioli/?

Pronto. Parlo con /il signor Strabbioli/?

Speaking

Sì, sono io

This is /Jane Butcher/ here. May I speak to /Mrs Strabbioli/?

Qui parla /Jane Butcher/. Posso parlare con /la Signora Strabbioli/?

She's out at the moment

È fuori in questo momento

I'll ring back later

Richiamo più tardi

2 Wrong number

Hello. May I speak to /John/ please?

Pronto. Posso parlare con /Giovanni/ per favore?

I'm sorry. There's no one of that name here. This is /413624/

Mi dispiace. Qui non abita nessuno di quel nome. Questo è il /413624/

Sorry. Wrong number

Scusi. Ho sbagliato numero

3 Business

Hello. /Marini's/. Can I help you?	Pronto. /Ditta Marini/. Desidera?
/Mr Frasson/, extension 56 please	Vorrei /il signor Frasson/, interno 56 per favore
Hold the line please	Resti in linea prego
I'm putting you through	Le passo il numero
Hello. /Mr Frasson's/ office	Pronto. Ufficio del /signor Frasson/
Hello. Could I speak to /Mr Frasson/ please?	Pronto. Posso parlare con /il signor Frasson/ per favore?
I'm sorry, he's /in a meeting/	Mi dispiace. Ha /una riunione/
Can I leave a message?	Posso lasciar detto qualcosa?
Yes, of course	Sì, certo
Could you tell him /Mr Cook/ called?	Vuole dirgli che ha chiamato /il signor Cook/?
Yes, certainly	Non dubiti
Thank you. Goodbye	Grazie. Buon giorno
Goodbye	Buon giorno

11.2 Emergencies

The emergency number is the same throughout Italy – 113 – and can be dialled from any type of phone (you have to pay one token when calling from public phone boxes). Having dialled 113 you are put through to the service you require.

NB You have to pay for the ambulance service according to the distance travelled; the sum also varies from place to place.

Emergency calls

113. Which service do you want?	Cento tredici. Desidera?
Police	Polizia
Fire brigade	Pompieri
Ambulance	Ambulanza
There's been an accident on /Via Roma/	C'è stato un incidente in /Via Roma/

Where exactly?	Dove esattamente?
Near the supermarket	Vicino al supermercato
There's a fire on /Via Ortigara/	C'è un incendio in /Via Ortigara/
Send an ambulance to /9, Via Fratta/ please	Mandi un'ambulanza in /Via Fratta nove/ per favore
What's your number please?	Che numero ha per favore?

General expressions

Where's the /British/ Embassy?	Dov'è l'ambasciata /britannica/?
Help!	Aiuto!
Help me please!	Mi aiuti per favore!
Quick!	Presto!
Look out!	Attenzione!
Careful!	Adagio!
Call /the police/!	Chiami /la polizia/!
Call /the fire brigade/!	Chiami /i pompieri/!
Call /an ambulance/!	Chiami /un'ambulanza/!
Call /a doctor/!	Chiami /un dottore/!
Are you insured?	È assicurato?
Please give me your name and address	Mi dia il suo nome e indirizzo per favore

At the hospital

The casualty department (Pronto Soccorso) of a hospital deals with emergencies.

Where's /the (nearest) hospital/ please?	Dov'è /l'ospedale (più vicino)/ per favore?
I'm /diabetic/	Ho /il diabete/
I'm /pregnant/	Sono /incinta/
(I think) it's /my heart/	(Credo) sia /il cuore/
Is it /broken/?	È /rotto/?
I'd like /a painkiller/	Vorrei /un analgesico/
I'm allergic /to penicillin/ (male)	Sono allergico /alla penicillina/
I'm allergic /to penicillin/ (female)	Sono allergica /alla penicillina/
Please notify /Mr Davis/ at /the Hotel Bristol/	Per favore avvisi /il signor Davis/ all'/Hotel Bristol/

At the police station

If you've lost something or somebody go to the nearest police or carabinieri headquarters (the carabinieri are part of the Italian armed forces and deal with all types of police work).

Where's /the (nearest) police station/ please?	Dov'è /la stazione di polizia (più vicina)/ per favore?
Where's /the carabinieri/ please?	Dove sono /i carabinieri/ per favore?
I've lost /my passport/	Ho perso /il passaporto/
I've lost /my wallet/	Ho perso /il portafoglio/
/My handbag/ has been stolen	Mi hanno rubato /la borsetta/
/My luggage/ has been stolen	Mi hanno rubato /i bagagli/
I've run out of money	Sono rimasto senza soldi
I want /a lawyer/	Voglio /un avvocato/

PART B
REFERENCE SECTION

Pronunciation key

Sounds you don't have to worry about – they're very close to English sounds:

		Italian words
[b]	bath	bagno (bath)
[d]	date	data (date)
[f]	fire	fuoco (fire)
[ks]	taxi	taxi (taxi)
[l]	lemon	limone (lemon)
[m]	me	mi (me)
[n]	nose	naso (nose)
[p]	place	posto (place)
[R]	red	rosso (red) – the 'r' is always rolled
[s]	sausage	salsiccia (sausage)
[t]	tea	tè (tea)
[v]	veal	vitello (veal)
[z]	zoo	rosa (rose), zoo (zoo)

There are five basic vowels sounds in Italian which are all very clearly pronounced:

[a]	between hat and hut	gatto (cat)
[e]	between hate and egg	bello (beautiful)
[ēē]	he	italiano (Italian)
[o]	between home and knot	troppo (too)
[ōō]	zoo	brutto (ugly)

Sounds which are also close to English sounds but which may look different when written in Italian:

[ch]	church	città (city)
[dz]	loads	mezzo (middle, half)
[g]	gun	gatto (cat), ghiaccio (ice)
[j]	job, gin	gelato (ice cream)
[k]	cat	casa (house), chiesa (church), quando (when)
[ly]	million	aglio (garlic)
[ny]	onion	gnocchi (type of dumplings)
[sh]	shoe	pesce (fish)
[ts]	cats	ragazza (girl)
[w]	worry	quasi (almost), uomo (man)
[y]	yes	italiano (Italian)

62

'c' before 'i' or 'e' is pronounced 'ch' as in 'church'; otherwise 'c' as in 'cat'.

'g' before 'i' or 'e' is pronounced soft as 'gin'; otherwise hard as in 'gun'.

To help you, the Italian vowel sounds 'e' and 'o' have been simplified. In Italian an 'e' can be long as the 'a' in 'hate' or short as in 'egg'. The Italian 'o' can also be long as in 'home' or short as in 'knot'. The short vowels for both 'e' and 'o' have been used as the difference between the long and the short vowels is much less marked in Italian.

In Italian the accent usually falls on the next to last syllable. To help you, the stressed syllable is always marked in bold type eg limone (lemon).

Mini Dictionary

The words in this Mini Dictionary have been selected to fit into the key sentence 'patterns' in the Study Section. The more familiar you are with the Study Section the more you will get out of the Mini Dictionary. Here are a few notes which will help you..

1 How to get the most out of the Mini Dictionary

1.1 *Abbreviations*

(adj)	adjective
(adv)	adverb
(n)	noun
(prep)	preposition
(vb)	verb
(m)	Most masculine words end in 'o'. All masculine words which do not end in 'o' are followed by (m) eg '*incidente* (m)' (accident).
(f)	Most feminine words end in 'a'. All feminine words which do not end in 'a' are followed by (f) eg '*nave* (f)' (boat).
(m & f)	Words which are both masculine and feminine eg '*artista* (m & f)' (artist).
(pl)	Words which have no singular or which are mainly used in the plural eg '*spiccioli* (mpl)' (small change).
(s)	Words which are singular in Italian eg '*roba* (s)' (belongings).
(infml)	Colloquial words or expressions used in everyday or informal speech eg '*bici* (infml)' (bike).
(tdmk)	Trademark names of products which are commonly used as ordinary words eg '*pullman* (tdmk)' (coach).
*	Verbs which follow the '*finire*' pattern. See p266.

1.2 *Plurals*

With masculine words ending in 'o' the plural is formed by taking off the 'o' and adding 'i'. With feminine words ending in 'a' the plural is formed by taking off the 'a' and adding 'e'. With all nouns ending in 'e' the plural is formed by taking off the 'e' and adding 'i'. All other plurals are given eg '*formica –che*' (ant), together with their pronunciation. Some words do not change in the plural and are followed by – eg '*aerosol* (m) – ' (aerosol).

64

1.3 *Feminine and plural forms of adjectives*

Adjectives are given in the masculine singular form. Use the following table if you want to use the feminine or plural forms.

	masculine	feminine	masculine plural	feminine plural
blue	azzur**ro**	azzur**ra**	azzur**ri**	azzur**re**
sad	trist**e**	trist**e**	trist**i**	trist**i**

All adjectives which have an irregular feminine or plural form are given eg '*cieco –chi* (mpl) *–che* (fpl)' together with their pronunciation.

1.4 *Substitutions*

/ / Two oblique lines show that a word or an expression between the lines can be replaced by another in the key sentence eg '*Vorrei /dei sigari/*' (I'd like /some cigars/), '*Vorrei /dei biscotti/*' (I'd like /some biscuits/). In this case, if the word you want to use is feminine, '*dei*' must be changed to '*delle*' egg '*Vorrei /delle mele/*' (I'd like /some apples/). The table at the bottom of some pages in the Mini Dictionary will help you to choose the appropriate translation of 'the/a/some' etc.

1.5 *Verbs*

Verbs are given in the 'infinitive' form eg '*chiudere*' (to close). See the Mini Grammar p265 for how to form the present tense of verbs.

The past tense is only touched on in the Survival kit but should you want to use it, you will find more details in the Mini Grammar p270. Only the past participles of irregular verbs are given eg '*chiudere*' (close) '*chiuso*' (closed). To form the past participles of regular verbs, verbs ending in :

–are	change to	*–ato*	eg *lavare* (wash)	*lavato* (washed)
–ere	change to	*–uto*	eg *avere* (have)	*avuto* (had)
–ire	change to	*–ito*	eg *spedire* (send)	*spedito* (sent)

Certain verbs ending in '*mi*' are given in the Mini Dictionary eg '*lavarmi*' (have a wash). This is the first person infinitive form of 'reflexive' verbs, the form you will be most likely to need :

    Vorrei lavarmi   I'd like to have a wash

If you are talking to someone else and using the polite '*lei*' form of the verb, then you must change '*mi*' to '*si*' :

    Vorrebbe lavarsi?   Would you like to have a wash?

For more information about reflexive pronouns see the Mini Grammar p263.

2 A note on quantity

How to indicate quantity using *'del'*, *'dell''*, *'della'*, *'dei'*, *'delle'* etc is fully
covered in Section 7 of the Study Section. Words like *'del'* and *'dei'* are
used to indicate a quantity in a general way:

Vorrei /del caffè/ per favore   I'd like /some coffee/ please
Ha /dei francobolli/?   Have you got /any stamps/?

With the help of the Mini Dictionary you can also ask for precise
amounts. For example, if you look up 'match' (*fiammifero*) you will find
'a box of matches' (*una scatola di fiammiferi*).

Quantity can also be indicated precisely in terms of volume or weight eg
20 litres of petrol, a kilo of tomatoes, etc. See Equivalents p280.

Remember these five 'quantity words' and you will be able to ask for
almost anything:

una bottiglia di /birra/	a bottle of /beer/
un bicchiere di /latte/	a glass of /milk/
un pacchetto di /sigarette/	a packet of /cigarettes/
una fetta di /prosciutto/	a slice of /ham/
un barattolo di /pomodori/	a tin of /tomatoes/

3 Precise information

The Mini Dictionary also gives more precise information in other areas.
If you look up 'ticket' (*biglietto*) you will find a list of different types of
ticket so that you can choose the kind of ticket you want.

A

about (=approximately)	circa	cheeRka
about (=concerning)	circa	cheeRka
above	sopra	sopRa
a. /my head/	s. /la testa/	sopRa /la testa/
abroad	all'estero	alesteRo
he's a.	è all'e.	e alesteRo
accept	accettare	achetaRe
accident	incidente (m)	eencheedente
accommodation	alloggio	alojo
accountant	ragioniere (m)	Rajonyere
ache	male (m)	male
I've got backache	ho mal di schiena	o mal dee skyena
I've got earache	ho mal d'orecchio	o mal doRekyo
I've got stomachache	ho mal di stomaco	o mal dee stomako
across	attraverso	atRaveRso
walk a. /the street/	attraversare /la strada/	atRaveRsaRe /la stRada/
actor	attore (m)	atoRe
actress	attrice (f)	atReeche
adaptor plug	spina	speena
add	aggiungere – aggiunto	ajoonjere – ajoonto
address	indirizzo	eendeeReetso
temporary a.	i. provvisorio	eendeeReetso proveesoRyo
adjust	aggiustare	ajoostaRe
admission (=cost)	entrata	entRata
adult	adulto	adoolto
adults only	solo per adulti	solo peR adooltee
advance (a. of money)	anticipo	anteecheepo
in a.	in a.	een anteecheepo
a. booking	prenotazione (f)	pRenotatsyone
advantage	vantaggio	vantajo
advertise	fare pubblicità	faRe poobleecheeta
advertisement	avviso pubblicitorio	aveeso poobleecheetaRyo
advice	consiglio	konseelyo
I'd like some a.	vorrei un c.	voRey oon konseelyo
advise a rest	consigliare riposo	konseelyaRe Reepozo
aerial	antenna	antena
aeroplane	aeroplano	aeRoplano
by air	per via aerea	peR veea aeRea

aerosol	aerosol (m) –	aerosol
afraid		
be a. (of / /)	aver paura (di / /) – avuto paura (di / /)	aver paoora (dee / /) – avooto paoora (dee / /)
I'm a. of / /	ho p. di / /	o paoora dee / /
after	dopo	dopo
afternoon	pomeriggio	pomereejo
this a.	oggi p.	ojee pomereejo
tomorrow a.	domani p.	domanee pomereejo
yesterday a.	ieri p.	yeree pomereejo
aftershave lotion	dopo barba (m) –	dopo barba
afterwards	dopo	dopo
again	ancora	ankora
against	contro	kontro
age	età –	eta
agency	agenzia	ajentseea
agenda	ordine (m) del giorno	ordeene del jyorno
agree	essere d'accordo – stato d'accordo	esere dakordo – stato dakordo
I a.	sono d'a.	sono dakordo
ahead	avanti	avantee
air	aria	arya
a. pressure	pressione (f) atmosferica	presyone atmosfereeka
by a.	per via aerea	per veea aerea
some fresh a.	a. fresca	arya freska
air conditioning	aria condizionata	arya kondeetsyonata
air letter	lettera aerea	letera aerea
airline	linea aerea	leenea aerea
airmail	posta aerea	posta aerea
by a.	per via aerea	per veea aerea
airport	aeroporto	aeroporto
a. bus	autobus (m) dell'a.	aootoboos del aeroporto
air terminal	terminale aereo	termeenale aereo
a. t. bus	autobus (m) del t. a.	aootoboos del termeenale aereo
alarm clock	sveglia	zvelya
alcohol	alcool (m)	alko-ol
alcoholic (adj)	alcoolico	alkooleeko
alive	vivo	veevo
he's a.	vive	veeve
all	tutto	tooto
a. /the time/	t. /il tempo/	tooto /eel tempo/

allergic	allergico	aleRjeeko
I'm a. to /penicillin/	sono a. /alla penecillina/	sono aleRjeeko /ala penetheleena/
allow	permettere – permesso	peRmetere – peRmeso
a. /smoking/	p. di /fumare/	peRmetere dee /foomaRe/
allowed	permesso	peRmeso
almost	quasi	kwazee
alone	solo	solo
alphabet	alfabeto	alfabeto
already	già	ja
also	anche	anke
alter (change)	cambiare	kambyaRe
alter (=clothes)	cambiare	kambyaRe
alternative (n)	alternativa	alteRnateeva
always	sempre	sempRe
a.m	di mattina	dee mateena
/4/ a.m.	/le quattro/ di m.	/le kwatRo/ dee mateena
ambassador	ambasciatore (m)	ambashatoRe
ambulance	ambulanza	amboolantsa
amenities	comodità (fpl)	komodeeta
among	tra	tRa
amusement arcade	sala giochi	sala jyokee
amusing	divertente	deeveRtente
anaemic	anemico	anemeeko
anaesthetic (n)	anestetico	anesteteeko
anchor	ancora	ankoRa
angry	arrabbiato	aRabyato
I'm a. with /him/	sono a. con /lui/	sono aRabyato kon /looee/
animal	animale (m)	aneemale
ankle	caviglia	kaveelya
a. socks	calzini (mpl)	kaltseenee
anniversary	anniversario	aneeveRsaryo
wedding a.	a. del matrimonio	aneeveRsaryo del matReemonyo
announcement	dichiarazione (f)	deekyaRatsyone
make an a.	fare una d.	faRe oona deekyaRatsyone
annoying	fastidioso	fasteedyozo
annual	annuale	anooale

	words ending in –o or marked (m)	words ending in –a or marked (f)
the	il/l'/lo	la/l'
the (plural)	i/gl'/gli	le/l'

69

anorak	giacca –che a vento	jaka a vento jake a vento
another (= additional)	un altro (m) un'altra (f)	ōōn altro ōōn altra
a. /glass of wine/	un altro /bicchiere di vino/	ōōn altro /beekyere dee veeno/
another (different)	un altro (m) un'altra (f)	ōōn altro ōōn altra
answer (n)	risposta	reesposta
answer (vb)	rispondere – risposto	reespondere – reesposto
ant	formica –che	formeeka formeeke
antibiotic	antibiotico	anteebyoteeko
antique (n)	oggetto di antiquariato	ojeto dee anteekwaryato
antique shop	negozio di antiquariato	negotsyo dee anteekwaryato
antiseptic	antisettico	anteeseteeko
a. cream	crema antisettica	krema anteeseteeka
tube of a. (cream)	tubetto di crema antisettica	toobeto dee krema anteeseteeka
aperitif	aperitivo	apereeteevo
apologise	domandare scusa	domandare skooza
I a.	domando scusa	domando skooza
apology	scusa	skooza
appendicitis	appendicite (f)	apendeecheete
apple	mela	mela
a. juice	succo di m.	sooko dee mela
application form	modulo di domanda	modoolo dee domanda
apply for /a licence/	fare domanda per /un permesso/	fare domanda per /ōōn permeso/
a. to /someone/	rivolgermi a /qualcuno/	reevoljermee a /kwalkoono/
appointment	appuntamento	apōōntamento
make an a.	fissare un a.	feesare ōōn apōōntamento
apricot	albicocca –che	albeekoka albeekoke
April	aprile (m)	apreele
aqualung	autorespiratore (m)	aōōtorespeeratore
architect	architetto	arkeetetto
area (of country)	regione (f)	rejyone
area (of town)	area	area
argue	discutere – discusso	deeskootere – deeskooso
argument	discussione (f)	deeskoosyone

arm	braccio (m) braccia (fpl)	bRacho bRacha
army	esercito	ezeRcheeto
around	intorno	eentorno
arrange	organizzare	oRganeetsare
a. /a meeting/	o. /un incontro/	oRganeetsare /oon eenkontRo/
arrangement	accordo	akoRdo
arrival	arrivo	areevo
time of a.	ora di a.	ora dee areevo
arrive on /Monday/	arrivare /lunedì/	areevare /loonedee/
arrive /at 4.30/	a. /alle quattro e mezzo/	areevare /ale kwatro e medzo/
a. in /July/	a. in /luglio/	areevare een /loolyo/
arrow	freccia –ce	fRecha fReche
art gallery	galleria d'arte	galereea daRte
artichoke	carciofo	kaRchofo
artificial	artificiale	aRteefeechale
artificial respiration	respirazione (f) artificiale	Respeeratsyone aRteefeechale
artist	artista (m & f)	aRteesta
ashamed		
be a. (of / /)	vergognarmi (di / /)	veRgonyaRmee (dee / /)
I'm a. of /him/	mi vergogno di /lui/	mee veRgonyo dee /looee/
ashtray	portacenere (m)	poRtachenere
ask	domandare	domandare
please a. how much it is	domandi quanto è, per favore	domandee kwanto e peR favore
ask (a favour)	chiedere	kyedere
asleep	addormentato	adoRmentato
he's a.	è a.	e adoRmentato
asparagus	asparagi	aspaRajee
aspirin	aspirina	aspeereena
a bottle of aspirins	una bottiglia di aspirinas	oona boteelya dee aspeereenas
a packet of aspirins	un pachetto di aspirinas	oon paketo dee aspeereenas
assistant	assistente (m & f)	aseestente
shop a.	commesso (m) commessa (f)	komeso komesa
asthma	asma	azma
at	a	a
a. 7.30	alle sette e mezzo	ale sete e medzo
a. the hotel	all'albergo	alalbeRgo
atlas	atlante (m)	atlante

71

attack (n)	attacco	atako
an a. of / /	un a. di / /	o͞on atako dēē / /
attend	assistere – assistito	asēēstere – asēēstēēto
a. a /Catholic/ service	a. ad una funzione /cattolica/	asēēstere ado͞ona fo͞ontsyone /katolēēka/
attendant	guardiano	gwaRdyano
attractive	attraente (m & f)	atraente
aubergine	melanzana	melantsana
auction (n)	asta	asta
auction (vb)	vendere all'asta	vendere alasta
audience	pubblico	po͞oblēēko
August	agosto	agosto
aunt	zia	dsēēa
au pair	ragazza alla pari	Ragatsa ala paRēē
author	autore (m)	ao͞otore
authorities	autorità (fpl)	ao͞otorēēta
automatic	automatico	ao͞otomatēēko
autumn	autunno	ao͞oto͞ono
in a.	in a.	ēēn ao͞oto͞ono
available	disponibile (m & f)	dēēsponēēbēēle
avalanche	valanga	valanga
average (n)	media	medya
avocado	avocado	avokado
avoid	evitare	evēētare
awake	sveglio	zvelyo
he's a.	è s.	e zvelyo
away	via	vēēa
he's a.	è v.	e vēēa
away (absent)	assente (m & f)	asente
awful (of people)	antipatico	antēēpatēēko
awful (of things)	orribile (m & f)	orēēbēēle

B

baby	bambino (m) bambina (f)	bambēēno bambēēna
baby-sit	fare la baby-sitter	faRe la bebēē-sēēteR
baby-sitter	baby-sitter (m & f)	bebēē-sēēteR
back	schiena	skyena
backache	mal di s.	mal dēē skyena

	words ending in –o or marked (m)	words ending in –a or marked (f)
a	un/uno	una/un'
some	del/dell'/dello	della/dell'
some (plural)	dei/degl'/degli	delle

back door	porta di dietro	porta dēē dyetro
backwards	in dietro	ēēn dyetro
bacon	pancetta	pancheta
bad	cattivo	katēēvo
badly	male	male
b. hurt	ferito m.	ferēēto male
badminton	volano	volano
a game of b.	una partita a v.	ōōna partēēta a volano
bag	borsa	borsa
carrier b.	sacchetto	saketo
paper b.	sacchetto di carta	saketo dēē karta
plastic b.	sacchetto di plastica	saketo dēē plastēēka
string b.	b. di rete	borsa dēē rete
bake	cuocere al forno – cotto al forno	kwochere al forno koto al forno
baker's	panetteria	paneterēēa
balcony	balcone (m)	balkone
bald	calvo	kalvo
ball	palla	pala
b. of /string/	gomitolo di /filo/	gomēētolo dēē /fēēlo/
beach b.	p. da spiaggia	pala da spyaja
footb.	pallone (m)	palone
golf b.	pallina da golf	palēēna da golf
squash b.	pallina da squash	palēēna da skwosh
table tennis b.	pallina da ping-pong	palēēna da pēēng pong
tennis b.	p. da tennis	pala da tenēēs
ball (=dance)	ballo	balo
ballet	balletto	baleto
b. dancer	ballerino (m) ballerina (f)	balerēēno balerēēna
balloon	palloncino	palonchēēno
ballpoint pen	penna a sfera	pena a sfera
ballroom	sala da ballo	sala da balo
banana	banana	banana
band (=orchestra)	banda	banda
bandage (n)	benda	benda
bandage (vb)	bendare	bendare
bank	banca	banka
bank account	conto	konto
current account	c. corrente	konto korente
bar (=for drinks)	bar (m)	bar
barbecue	festa campestre	festa kampestre
bare (=naked)	nudo	nōōdo
bare (of room etc)	nudo	nōōdo

73

bargain (n)	affare (m)	afaʀe
bargain (vb)	contrattare	kontʀatare
b. with /someone/	c. con /qualcuno/	kontʀatare kon /kwalkōōno/
barrel	barile (m)	baʀēēle
b. of / /	b. di / /	baʀēēle dēē / /
barrier	barriera	baʀyeʀa
basement	seminterrato	semēēnteʀato
basket	cesto	chesto
a b. of / /	un c. di / /	ōōn chesto dēē / /
shopping b.	cestino per la spesa	chestēēno peʀ la speza
waste paper b.	cestino per la carta straccia	chestēēno peʀ la kaʀta stracha
basketball (=game)	pallacanestro	palakanestro
a game of b.	una partita a p.	ōōna paʀtēēta a palakanestro
bat (cricket)	mazza	matsa
bath	bagno	banyo
have a b.	fare un b.	faʀe ōōn banyo
Turkish b.	b. turco	banyo tōōrko
bathe (eyes etc)	bagnare	banyaʀe
bathe (in the sea etc)	fare il bagno	faʀe ēēl banyo
bathing cap	cuffia da bagno	kōōfya da banyo
bathing costume (one piece)	costume (m) da bagno	kostōōme da banyo
bathing trunks	pantaloncini (mpl) da bagno	pantalonchēēnēē da banyo
bath mat	tappeto di bagno	tapeto dēē banyo
bathroom	(stanza da) bagno	(stantsa da) banyo
bath salts	sali (mpl) da bagno	salēē da banyo
battery (car)	batteria	bateʀēēa
battery (radio)	pila	pēēla
bay (=part of sea)	baia	baya
be	essere – stato	eseʀe – stato
beach	spiaggia –gge	spyaja – spyaje
b. hut	cabina per bagnanti	kabēēna peʀ banyantēē
b. umbrella	ombrellone (m)	ombʀelone
beads	perline (fpl)	peʀlēēne
string of b.	filo di p.	fēēlo dēē peʀlēēne
beans	fagioli (mpl)	fajolēē
broad b.	fave (fpl)	fave
french b.	fagiolini (mpl)	fajolēēnēē
beautiful	bello	belo
beauty salon	salone (m) di bellezza	salone dēē beletsa

because	perchè	peRke
b. /of the weather/	a causa /del tempo/	a kaooza /del tempo/
bed	letto	leto
b. and beakfast	l. e colazione	leto e kolatsyone
double b.	l. matrimoniale	leto matreemonyale
go to b.	andare a l.	andaRe a leto
in b.	a l.	a leto
make the b.	fare il l.	faRe eel leto
single b.	l. singolo	leto seengolo
bed clothes	coperte (fpl)	kopeRte
bedpan	padella da letto	padela da leto
bedroom	camera da letto	kameRa da leto
bee	ape (f)	ape
b. sting	puntura d'a.	pootooRa dape
beef	manzo	mandso
b. sandwich	panino di m.	paneeno dee mandso
beer	birra	beeRa
a b.	una b.	oona beeRa
a bottle of b.	una bottiglia di b.	oona boteelya dee beeRa
a can of b.	un barattolo di b.	oon baRatolo dee beeRa
a pint of b.	un mezzo litro di b.	oon medzo leetRo dee beeRa
beetroot	barbabietola	baRbabyetola
before	prima	pReema
behalf		
on b. of / /	da parte di / /	da paRte dee / /
behaviour	comportamento	kompoRtamento
behind (prep)	dietro	dyetRo
b. /the house/	d. /alla casa/	dyetRo /ala kaza/
beige	beige	bej
believe	credere	kRedeRe
b. /me/	creder/mi/	kRedeR/mee/
I don't b. it	non ci credo	non chee kRedo
bell	campanello	kampanelo
belongings	roba (s)	Roba
below	sotto	soto
belt	cintura	cheentooRa
bend (in a road)	curva	kooRva
bend (vb)	piegare	pyegaRe

	words ending in –o or marked (m)	words ending in –a or marked (f)
the	il/l'/lo	la/l'
the (plural)	i/gl'/gli	le/l'

BENT

bent (adj)	piegato	pyegato
beret	berretto	beReto
berth	cuccetta	kōōcheta
/four/-b. cabin	cabina da /quattro/ cuccette	kabēēna da /kwatRo/ kōōchete
lower b.	c. di sotto	kōōcheta dēē soto
upper b.	c. di sopra	kōōcheta dēē sopRa
beside	accanto	akanto
b. /her/	a. a /lei/	akanto a /ley/
best	migliore	mēēlyoRe
the b. /hotel/	il m. /albergo/	ēēl mēēlyoRe /albeRgo/
bet (n)	scommessa	skomesa
bet (vb)	scommettere – scommesso	skometeRe – skomeso
better	meglio	melyo
he's b. (health)	sta m.	sta melyo
it's b. (things)	va m.	va melyo
betting shop	allibratore (m)	alēēbRatoRe
between /London/ and /Rome/	tra /Londra/ e /Roma/	tRa /londRa/ e /Roma/
beyond	oltre	oltRe
b. /the station/	o. /alla stazione/	oltRe /ala statsyone/
bib	bavaglino	bavalyēēno
Bible	Bible	bēēbya
bicycle/bike	bicicleta/bici (f) – (infml)	bēēchēēkleta/bēēchēē
big	grande	gRande
bikini	bikini (m)	bēēkēēnēē
bill (for food, hotel, etc)	conto	konto
billiards	biliardo (s)	bēēlyaRdo
a game of b.	una partita a b.	ōōna paRtēēta a bēēlyaRdo
bingo	tombola	tombola
binoculars	binocolo (s)	bēēnokolo
a pair of b.	uno b.	ōōno bēēnokolo
bird	uccello	ōōchelo
biro (tdmk)	biro (f) –	bēēRo
birth certificate	certificato di nascita	cheRtēēfēēkato dēē nashēēta
date of b.	data di n.	data dēē nashēēta
place of b.	luogo di n.	lwogo dēē nashēēta
birthday	compleanno	kompleano
biscuit	biscotto	bēēskoto
bite (=insect b.)	puntura	pōōntōōRa

bitter (adj)	amaro	amaro
black	nero	nero
b. coffee	caffè	kafe
blackberry	mora	mora
blackcurrant	ribes nero (m) –	reebes nero
blanket	coperta	koperta
bleach (n) (laundry)	candeggina	kandejeena
bleach (vb) (laundry)	imbiancare	eembyankare
bleed	sanguinare	sangweenare
my nose is bleeding	mi sanguina il naso	mee sangweena eel nazo
stop the bleeding	fermi il sangue	fermee eel sangwe
blind (adj)	cieco –chi	chyeko chyekee
blinds (=Venetian-type)	persiane (fpl)	persyane
blister	vescica –che	vesheeka vesheeke
blocked (eg drain)	bloccato	blokato
block of flats	condominio	kondomeenyo
blonde	biondo	byondo
blood	sangue (m)	sangwe
b. group	gruppo sanguigno	groopo sangweenyo
b. pressure	pressione (f) del sangue	presyone del sangwe
blotting paper	carta assorbente	karta asorbente
blouse	camicetta	kameecheta
blue	azzurro	adsooro
blunt (eg knife)	spuntato	spoontato
board (n) (=cost of meals)	pensione (f)	pensyone
full b.	p. completa	pensyone kompleta
half b.	mezza p.	medsa pensyone
board (vb) (eg a plane)	salire	saleere
boarding card	foglio di imbarcazione	folyo dee eembarkatsyone
boat	nave (f)	nave
by b.	in n.	een nave
lifeb.	scialuppa di salvataggio	shaloopa di salvatajo
motor-b.	motoscafo	motoskafo
body	corpo	korpo
boil (vb)	bollire	boleere
hardboiled egg	uovo sodo	wovo sodo
softboiled egg	uovo alla coque	wovo ala kok
bomb	bomba	bomba
bone	osso –a	oso osa

book	libro	lēēbro
guide b.	guida	gwēēda
paperback	edizione (f) economica	edēētsyone ekonomēēka
booking	prenotazione (f)	prenotatsyone
advance b.	p.	prenotatsyone
booking office	biglietteria	bilyeterēēa
bookmaker	allibratore (m)	alēēbratore
bookshop	libreria	lēēbrerēēa
boots	stivali (mpl)	stēēvalēē
a pair of b.	un paio di s.	ōōn payo dēē stēēvalēē
rubber b.	s. di gomma	stēēvalēē dēē goma
ski-b.	s. da sci	stēēvalēē da shēē
border (=frontier)	frontiera	frontyera
bored	annoiato	anoyato
I'm b.	sono a.	sono anoyato
borrow /a pen/	prendere in prestito /una penna/	prendere ēēn prestēēto /ōōna pena/
both	ambedue/tutti e due (m) tutte e due (f)	ambedōōe/tōōtēē e dōōe tōōte e dōōe da ambo ēē latēē
b. /sides/	da ambo /i lati/	da ambo /ēē latēē/
bother (vb)	disturbare	dēēstōōrbare
don't b.	non si disturbi	non sēē dēēstōōrbēē
I'm sorry to b. you	mi dispiace disturbarla	mēē dēēspyache dēēstōōrbarla
bottle	bottiglia	botēēlya
a b. of / /	una b. di / /	ōōna botēēlya dēē / /
b.-opener	cava-tappi (m) –	kava-tapēē
feeding b.	biberon (m) –	bēēberon
bottom (part of body)	sedere (m)	sedere
the b. of / /	il fondo di / /	ēēl fondo dēē / /
bowl	zuppierina	dzōōpyerēēna
bowling (=ten pin bowling)	bocce (fpl)	boche
b. alley	corsia per b.	korsēēa per boche
bows (of ship)	prua (s)	prōōa
bow tie	cravatta a farfalla	kravata a farfala

	words ending in –o or marked (m)	words ending in –a or marked (f)
a	un/uno	una/un'
some	del/dell'/dello	della/dell'
some (plural)	dei/degl'/degli	delle

box	scatola	skatola
a b. of / /	una s. di / /	ōōna skatola dee / /
boxer	pugilatore (m)	pōōjeelatore
boxing	pugilato	pōōjeelato
b. match	incontro di p.	ēenkontro dee pōōjeelato
box office	biglietteria	beelyetereea
boy	ragazzo	ragatso
boyfriend	ragazzo	ragatso
bra	reggipetto	rejeepeto
bracelet	braccialetto	brachaleto
silver b.	b. d'argento	brachaleto darjento
braces	bretelle (fpl)	bretele
a pair of b.	un paio di b.	ōōn payo dee bretele
branch (of company)	filiale (m)	feelyale
brand (= of make)	marca	marka
b. name	m.	marka
brandy	cognac (m) –	konyak
a bottle of b.	una bottiglia di c.	ōōna boteelya dee konyak
a b.	un c.	ōōn konyak
bread	pane (m)	pane
a loaf of b.	pagnotta	panyota
a slice of b.	una fetta di p.	ōōna feta dee pane
b. and butter	p. e burro	pane e bōōro
brown b.	p. nero	pane nero
b. roll	panino	paneeno
sliced b.	p. carrè	pan kare
break (vb)	rompere – rotto	rompere – roto
breakfast	colazione (f)	kolatsyone
bed and b.	letto e c.	leto e kolatsyone
b. for /2/	c. per /due/	kolatsyone per /dōōe/
b. in my room	c. in camera	kolatsyone ēen kamera
continental b.	c. continentale	kolatsyone konteenentale
English b.	c. inglese	kolatsyone ēengleze
have b.	fare c.	fare kolatsyone
serve b.	servire la c.	serveere la kolatsyone
breast	petto	peto
breast-feed	allattare	alatare

breath	respiro	RESPEERO
out of b.	senza fiato	sentsa fyato
breathe	respirare	RESPEERARE
bride	sposa	spoza
bridegroom	sposo	spozo
bridge	ponte (m)	ponte
toll b.	p. a pedaggio	ponte a pedajo
bridge (= card game)	bridge (m)	brēēj
a game of b.	una partita a b.	ōōna partēēta a brēēj
bridle	briglia	brēēlya
briefcase	cartella	kartela
bring	portare	portare
broadcast (n)	trasmessione (f)	trasmesyone
broadcast (vb)	trasmettere – trasmesso	trasmetere – trasmeso
broccoli	broccoli (mpl)	brokolēē
brochure	opuscolo	opōōskolo
broken	rotto	roto
brooch	spilla	spēēla
cameo b.	cammeo	kameo
brother	fratello	fratelo
brother-in-law	cognato	konyato
brown	marrone	marone
bruise (n)	livido	lēēvēēdo
bruised	contuso	kontōōzo
brush	scopa	skopa
clothes b.	spazzola per i vestiti	spatsola per ēē vestēētēē
hair-b.	spazzola per i cappelli	spatsola per ēē kapelēē
nail-b.	spazzolino per le unghie	spatsolēēno per le ōōngye
paint-b.	pennello	penelo
shaving b.	pennello da barba	penelo da barba
shoe-b.	spazzola per le scarpe	spatsola per le skarpe
tooth-b.	spazzolino da denti	spatsolēēno da dentēē
bucket	secchiello	sekyelo
b. and spade	s. e paletta	sekyelo e paleta
buckle	fibbia	fēēbya
Buddhist	Buddista (m)	budēēsta
buffet car	vagone (m) ristorante	vagone rēēstorante
builder	costruttore (m)	kostrōōtore

building	edificio –ci	edēēfēēcho
		edēēfēēchēē
public b.	e. pubblico	edēēfēēcho pōōblēēko
bulb (=light b.)	lampadina	lampadēēna
40/60/100/200 watt	40/60/100/200 candele	kwaranta/sesanta/ chento/dōōechento kandele
bun (bread)	focaccia –ce	fokacha fokache
bun (hair)	crocchia	krokya
in a b. (hair)	in c.	ēēn krokya
bunch	mazzo	matso
a b. of /flowers/	un m. di /fiori/	ōōn matso dēē /fyorēē/
bungalow	bungalow (m) –	bōōngalo
bunk bed	letto a castello	leto a kastelo
buoy	boa	boa
burglary	furto con scasso	fōōrto kon skaso
burn (n)	scottatura	skotatōōra
burn (vb)	bruciare	brōōchare
burnt	bruciato	brōōchato
burst (adj)	scoppiato	skopyato
a b. pipe	un tubo s.	ōōn tōōbo skopyato
bury	seppellire	sepelire
bus	autobus (m) –	aōōtobōōs
b. station	stazione (f) di a.	statsyone dēē aōōtobōōs
b. stop	fermata di a.	fermata dēē aōōtobōōs
by b.	in a.	ēēn aōōtobōōs
the b. for / /	l'a. per / /	laōōtobōōs per / /
bus driver	conducente (m)	kon dōōchente
businessman	uomo d'affari –mini d'affari	womo dafarēē womēēnēē dafarēē
busy	occupato	okōōpato
butane	butano	bōōtano
butcher's	macelleria	machelerēēa
butter	burro	bōōro
butterfly	farfalla	farfala
button	bottone (m)	botone
buy /an umbrella/	comprare /un ombrello/	komprare /ōōn ombrelo/
bypass (n)	circonvallazione (f)	chēērkonvalatsyone
	words ending in –o or marked (m)	words ending in –a or marked (f)
the	il/l'/lo	la/l'
the (plural)	i/gl'/gli	le/l'

81

cabbage	cavolo	**ka**volo
cabin	cabina	ka**bee**na
c. cruiser	panfilo	**pan**fee̅lo
/four/ berth c.	c. a /quattro/ cucette	ka**bee**na a /**kwa**tʀo/ ko̅o̅chete
cable (n)	cavo	**ka**vo
cable car	teleferica –che	telefeʀe̅e̅ka telefeʀe̅e̅ke
café	caffè (m)/bar (m)	kafe/baʀ
caffeine	caffeina	kafe̅e̅na
cake	torta	**toʀ**ta
a piece of c.	una fetta di t.	o̅o̅na feta de̅e̅ **toʀ**ta
cake shop	pasticceria	paste̅e̅cheʀe̅e̅a
calculate /the cost/	calcolare /il prezzo/	kalkola**ʀe** /e̅e̅l **pʀe**tso/
calculator	calcolatrice (f)	kalkolatʀe̅e̅che
calendar	calendario –ri	kalen**da**ryo kalen**da**ʀe̅e̅
call (n) (telephone c.)	chiamata	kya**ma**ta
alarm c.	c. d'allarme	kya**ma**ta da**laʀ**me
c. box	cabina telefonica	ka**bee**na telefon**ee**ka
early morning c.	sveglia	**zve**lya
international c.	c. internazionale	kya**ma**ta e̅e̅nteʀnatsyo**na**le
local c.	c. urbana	kya**ma**ta o̅o̅ʀ**ba**na
long distance c.	c. interurbana	kya**ma**ta e̅e̅nteʀo̅o̅ʀ**ba**na
make a c.	fare una telefonata	**fa**ʀe o̅o̅na telefo**na**ta
personal c.	c. personale	kya**ma**ta peʀso**na**le
transferred charge c.	conversazione (f) con pagamento a destinazione	konveʀsa**tsyo**ne kon paga**men**to a deste̅e̅na**tsyo**ne
call (vb) (=telephone)	chiamare	kya**ma**ʀe
c. again later	c. più tardi	kya**ma**ʀe pyo̅o̅ **taʀ**de̅e̅
c. /the police/	c. /la polizia/	kya**ma**ʀe /la pole̅e̅**tse̅e̅**a/
call on / / (=visit)	andare a trovare / /	an**da**ʀe a tʀo**va**ʀe / /
calm (of sea)	calmo	**kal**mo
calor gas	calor gas (m)	**ka**loʀ gaz
calories	calorie (fpl)	kaloʀe̅e̅e̅
cameo	cammeo	ka**me**o

camera	macchina (fotografica)	makéena (fotoqrafeéka)
cine c.	cinepresa	chéenepreza
35 mm c.	m. a 35 millimetri	makéena a tRentachéenkwe méeléemetRée
camera shop	negozio fotografico	negotsyo fotoqrafeéko
camp (n)	campeggio –ggi	kampejo kampejée
holiday c.	c. di vacanze	kampejo dée vakantse
camp bed	branda	bRanda
campfire	fuoco all'aperto – fuochi all'aperto	fwoko alapeRto fwokée alapeRto
camping	campeggio	kampejo
go c.	fare il c.	faRe éel kampejo
campsite	campeggio –ggi	kampejo kampejée
can (n)	barattolo	baRatolo
a c. of /beer/	un b. di /birra/	óon baRatolo dée /béeRa/
can (vb)	potere	poteRe
canal	canale (m)	kanale
cancel /my flight/	cancellare /il mio volo/	kanchelaRe /éel méeo volo/
cancellation	annullamento	anóolamento
cancelled	annullato	anóolato
candle	candela	kandela
canoe (n)	canoa	kanoa
canoeing	fare il c.	faRe éel kanotajo
go c.	fare il c. – fatto il c.	faRe éel kanotajo fato éel kanotajo
canvals (=material)	tela	tela
c. bag	borsa di t.	boRsa dée tela
cap (= hat)	berretto	beReto
shower c.	cuffia	kóofya
swimming c.	cuffia	kóofya
cap (n) (for tooth)	capsula	kapsóola
cap (vb) (tooth)	incapsulare	éenkapsóolaRe
cape (=cloak)	cappa	kapa
cape (eg Cape of Good Hope)	capo	kapo
captain	capitano	kapéetano
car	macchina	makéena
by c.	in m.	éen makéena
buffet c.	vagone (m) ristorante	vagone RéestoRante
c. ferry	traghetto per macchine	tRageto peR makéene

c. hire	auto noleggio	aōōto nolejo
c. park	parcheggio –ggi	paʀkejo paʀkejēē
c. wash	lavaggio macchine	lavajo makēēne
sleeping c.	vagone (m) letto	vagone leto
carafe	caraffa	kaʀafa
a c. of /wine/	una c. di /vino/	ōōna kaʀafa dēē /vēēno/
carat	carato	kaʀato
/9/ c. gold	oro a /nove/ carati	oʀo a /nove/ kaʀatēē
caravan	roulotte (f)	rōōlot
c. site	campeggio per r.	kampejo peʀ rōōlot
/four/ berth c.	r. a /quattro/ cuccette	rōōlot a /kwatʀo/ kōōchete
card (business c.)	biglietto	beelyeto
birthday c.	cartolina di buon compleanno	kaʀtolēēna dēē bwon kompleano
cardigan	golf	golf
cards	carte (fpl)	kaʀte
a game of c.	una partita a c.	ōōna paʀtēēta a kaʀte
a pack of c.	un mazzo de c.	ōōn matso dēē kaʀte
careful	prudente	prōōdente
careless	imprudente	imprōōdente
caretaker	custode (m)	kōōstode
carnation	garofano	gaʀofano
carnival	carnevale (m)	kaʀnevale
car park	parcheggio	paʀkejo paʀkejēē
carpet	tappeto	tapeto
fitted c.	moquette (f)	moket
carriage (in a train)	carrozza	kaʀotsa
carrier bag	sacchetto	saketo
carrot	carota	kaʀota
carry	portare	poʀtaʀe
carrycot	culla portatile	kōōla poʀtatēēle
carton of /cigarettes/ (=200)	stecca di /sigarette/	steka dēē /sēēgaʀete/
a c. of /milk/	un cartone di /latte/	ōōn kaʀtone dēē /late/
cartridge (=film c.)	rotolo	ʀotolo
cartridge (for gun)	cartuccia –ce	kaʀtōōcha kaʀtōōche
	words ending in –o or marked (m)	words ending in –a or marked (f)
a	un/uno	una/un'
some	del/dell'/dello	della/dell'
some (plural)	dei/degl'/degli	delle

case (=suitcase)	valigia	valeeja
cigarette c.	porta sigarette (m)	porta seegarete
cash (n)	contanti (mpl)	kontantee
c. payment	pagamento in c.	pagamento een kontantee
c. price	prezzo all'ingrosso	pretso al eengroso
pay by c.	pagare in c.	pagare een kontantee
cash (vb)	incassare	eenkasare
c. /a traveller's cheque/	incassare /un traveller's cheque/	eenkasare /oon travelers chek/
cash desk	cassa	kasa
cashier	cassiere (m) cassiera (f)	kasyere kasyera
cashmere	cachemire (m)	kashmeer
c. sweater	golf (m) di c.	golf dee kashmeer
casino	casinò	kazeeno
casserole (container)	casseruola	kaseroola
casserole (meal)	stufato	stoofato
cassette	cassetta	kaseta
c. player	mangianastri (m)	manjanastree
c. recorder	registratore (m)	rejeestratore
pre-recorded c.	c. preregistrata	kaseta prererejeestrata
c60/90/120	C60/90/120	chee sesanta/chee novanta /chee chentoventee
castle	castello	kastelo
cat	gatto	gato
catalogue	catalogo –ghi	katalogo katalogee
catch /an illness/	prendere /una malattia/ – preso /una malattia/	prendere /oona malateea/ – prezo /oona malateea/
catch /the train/	prendere /il treno/– preso /il treno/	prendere /eel treno/ – prezo /eel treno/
cathedral	cattedrale (m)	katedrale
Catholic (adj)	cattolico	katoleeko
cattle	bestiame (ms)	bestyame
cauliflower	cavolfiore (m)	kavolfyore
cause (n)	causa	kaooza
cave	caverna	kaverna
ceiling	soffitto	sofeeto
celery	sedano	sedano
cellar	cantina	kanteena
cement (n)	cemento	chemento
cemetery	cimitero	cheemeeetero

centimetre	centimetro	chentēēmetro
central heating	riscaldamento centrale	rēēskaldamento chentrale
centre	centro	chentro
in the c.	in c.	ēēn chentro
shopping c.	shopping (m)	shopēēng
town c.	c. città	chentro chēēta
century	secolo	sekolo
ceramic	ceramica –che	cheramēēka cheramēēke
cereal (=breakfast c.)	cereale	chereale
a bowl of c.	una ciatola di c.	ōōna chatola dēē chereale
ceremony	cerimonia	cherēēmonya
certain	sicuro	sēēkōōro
I'm c.	sono s.	sono sēēkōōro
certainly	certamente	chertamente
certificate	certificato	chertēēfēēkato
chain	catena	katena
chain store	negozio a catena	negotsyo a katena
chair	sedia	sedya
high c.	seggiolone (m)	sejolone
wheel c.	s. a rotelle	sedya a rotele
c. lift	s. ascensore	sedya ashensore
chairman	presidente (m)	prezēēdente
chalet	chalet (m) –	shale
chambermaid	cameriera	kameryera
champagne	sciampagna	shampanya
a bottle of c.	una bottiglia di s.	ōōna botēēlya dēē shampanya
change (n) (= alteration)	cambiamento	kambyamento
change (n) (=money)	resto	resto
small c.	spiccioli (mpl)	spēēcholēē
change (vb)	cambiare	kambyare
I'd like to c. /some traveller's cheques/	vorrei c. /dei traveller's cheques/	vorey kambyare /dey travelers cheks/
change at / / (of train)	cambiare a / /	kambyare a / /
do I have to change?	devo c.?	devo kambyare
changing room	spogliatoio	spolyatoyo
charcoal	carbone (m) di legna	karbone dēē lenya
charge (n) (=payment)	prezzo	pretso
charge (vb) (=payment)	far pagare – fatto pagare	far pagare – fato pagare

charming	incantevole	eenkantevole
chart (= sea map)	carta marina	karta mareena
charter flight	volo (m) charter	volo charter
chauffeur	autista (m) –i	aooteesta aooteestee
cheap	economico	ekonomeeko
cheat (vb)	imbrogliare	eembrolyare
check (vb)	controllare	kontrolare
check in (vb) (=of hotel/plane)	registrarmi	rejeestrarmee
check out (vb) (=of hotel)	pagare il conto	pagare eel konto
check up (n) (=of health)	controllo generale	kontrolo jenerale
cheek (of face)	guancia –ce	gwancha gwanche
cheese	formaggio	formajo
c. /omelette/	/omelette/ al f.	/omelet/ al formajo
chemist's	farmacia	farmacheea
cheque	assegno	asenyo
c. book	libretto di assegni	leebreto dee asenyee
c. card	carta di credito	karta dee kredeeto
traveller's c.	traveller's cheque (m)	travelers chek
pay by c.	pagare con a.	pagare kon asenyo
cherry	ciliegia –ge	cheelyeja cheelyeje
chess	scacchi (mpl)	skakee
a game of c.	una partita a s.	oona parteeta a skakee
chest (part of body)	torace (m)	torache
chestnuts	castagne (fpl)	kastanye
chest of drawers	cassettone (m)	kasetone
chewing gum	ciunga	choonga
chicken	pollo	polo
chicken pox	varicella	vareechela
chilblain	gelone (m)	jelone
child	bambino (m)	bambeeno bambeena
	bambina (f) figli (mpl)	feelyee
chill	raffreddare	rafredare
chimney	camino	kameeno
chin	mento	mento
china	porcellana	porchelana
	words ending in –o or marked (m)	words ending in –a or marked (f)
the	il/l'/lo	la/l'
the (plural)	i/gl'/gli	le/l'

chips	patate frite (fpl)	patate frēēte
chiropodist	pedicure (m)	pedeekōōre
chocolate	cioccolata	chokolata
a bar of c.	una stecca di c.	ōōna steka dee chokolata
a box of chocolates	una scatola di cioccolatini	ōōna skatola dee chokolatēēnēē
choice	scelta	shelta
c. between / / and / /	s. tra / / e / /	shelta tra / / e / /
choir	coro	koro
choose	scegliere – scelto	shelyere – shelto
c. between / / and / /	s. tra / / e / /	shelyere tra / / e / /
chop (n)	braciola	brachola
lamb c.	b. di agnello	brachola dee anyelo
pork c.	b. di maiale	brachola dee mayale
chop (vb)	tagliare	talyare
chopsticks	bacchette (fpl) per mangiare alla cinese	bakete per manjare ala chēēneze
Christ	Cristo	krēēsto
Christian	cristiano	krēēstyano
Christmas	Natale	natale
C. card	cartolina di N.	kartolēēna dee natale
C. Day	il giorno di N.	eel jorno dee natale
church	chiesa	kyeza
a /Protestant/ C.	una c. /protestante/	ōōna kyeza /protestante/
cider	sidro	sēēdro
a bottle of c.	una bottiglia di s.	ōōna botēēlya dee sēēdro
a c.	un s.	ōōn sēēdro
cigar	sigaro	sēēgaro
a box of cigars	une scatola di sigari	ōōna skatola dee sēēgarēē
a Havana c.	un s. avana	ōōn sēēgaro avana
cigarette (American type)	sigaretta americana	sēēgareta amerēēkana
c. (French type)	s. francese	sēēgareta francheze
smoke a c.	fumare una s.	fōōmare ōōna sēēgareta
cigarette case	porta sigarette (m)	porta sēēgarete

cigarette lighter	accendino	achendēēno
gas lighter	accendigas (m) –	achendēēgaz
cigarette paper	carta da sigarette	karta da sēēgarete
cigarettes	sigarette (fpl)	sēēgarete
a carton of c. (=200)	una stecca di s.	ōōna steka dēē sēēgarete
a packet of c.	un pacchetto di s.	ōōn paketo dēē sēēgarete
filter-tipped c.	s. col filtro	sēēgarete kol feeltro
cinema	cinema –	chēēnema
circus	circo –chi	cheerko cheerkēē
citizen	cittadino	cheetadēēno
city	città –	cheeta
the new part of the c.	la parte nuova della c.	la parte nōōova dela cheeta
the old part of the c.	la parte vecchia della c.	la parte vekya dela cheeta
civilisation	civiltà –	cheeveelta
civil servant	impiegato statale (m)	ēēmpyegato statale
	impiegata statale (f)	ēēmpyegata statale
claim /damages/	reclamare /danni/	reklamare /danēē/
claim on the insurance	reclamare dall'assicurazione	reklamare dal aseekōōratsyone
clarify	chiarificare	kyareefēē kare
class	classe (f)	klase
cabin c.	c. cabina	klase kabēēna
/first/ c.	/prima/ c.	/prēēma/klase
tourist c.	c. turistica	klase tōōreestēēka
class (in a school)	classe (f)	klase
classical (eg music)	classico	klasēēko
clean (adj)	pulito	pōōlēēto
clean (vb)	pulire	pōōleere
cleaner's	lavasecco	lavaseko
cleansing cream	crema detergente	krema deterjente
clear (=obvious)	evidente	eveedente
clear (=transparent)	chiaro	kyaro
clear goods through Customs	passare per la dogana	pasare per la dogana
clever (of people)	bravo	bravo
client	cliente (m & f)	klyente
cliff	scogliera	skolyera
climate	clima	klēēma
climb (vb) (=c. mountains)	scalare	skalare
climbing	scalata	skalata
go c.	fare s.	fare skalata

89

clinic	clinica	klēēnēēka
private c.	c. privata	klēēnēēka prēēvata
cloakroom	guardaroba –	gwardaroba
clock	orologio –gi	orolojo orolojēē
alarm c.	sveglia	zvelya
clogs	zoccoli (mpl)	tsokolēē
a pair of c.	un paio di z.	ōōn payo dēē tsokolēē
close (vb)	chiudere – chiuso	kyōōdere – kyōōzo
closed (adj)	chiuso	kyōōzo
cloth (=dishcloth)	strofinaccio –ci	strofēēnacho strofēēnachēē
clothes	vestiti (mpl)	vestēētēē
c. brush	spazzola per i v.	spatsola per ēē vestēētēē
c. line	corda per stendere	korda per stendere
c. peg	molletta	moleta
cloud	nuvola	nōōvola
cloudy	nuvoloso	nōōvoloso
club	circolo	chēērkolo
gambling c.	c. per il gioco d'azzardo	chēērkolo per ēēl joko dadzardo
golf c. (institution)	c. di golf	chēērkolo dēē golf
golf c. (object)	mazza da golf	matsa da golf
coach	pullman (f) – (infml)	pōōlman
by c.	in p.	ēēn pōōlman
c. (on a train)	carrozza	karotsa
coal	carbone (m)	karbone
coarse (of person)	ruvido	rōōvēēdo
coast (n)	costa	kosta
coastguard	polizia costiera	polēētsēēa kostyera
coastline	linea costiera	lēēnea kostyera
coat	cappotto	kapoto
coat hanger	attaccapanni (m) –	atakapanēē
cockroach	scarafaggio –gi	skarafajo skarafajēē
cocktail	cocktail (m)	kokteyl
cocoa	cacao	kakao
a cup of c.	una tazza di c.	ōōna tatsa dēē kakao
coconut	noce (f) di cocco	noche dēē koko
cod	merluzzo	merlōōtso

	words ending in –o or marked (m)	words ending in –a or marked (f)
a	un/uno	una/un'
some	del/dell'/dello	della/dell'
some (plural)	dei/degl'/degli	delle

code	codice (m)	kodeeche
dialling c.	prefisso	prefeeeeso
postal c.	c. postale	kodeeche postale
codeine	codeina	kodeeena
coffee	caffè	kafe
a cup of c.	una tazza di c.	oona tatsa dee kafe
a percolated c.	c. filtrato	kafe feeltrato
a pot of c.	un bricco di c.	oon breeko dee kafe
black c.	c. expresso	kafe espreso
decaffeinated c.	c. decaffeinizzato	kafe dekafeyneedzato
ground c.	c. macinato	kafe macheenato
instant c.	c. solubile	kafe soloobeele
white c.	caffellatte	kafelate
white c. (smaller cup-frothy and with less milk)	cappuccino	kapoocheeno
coffeepot	caffettiera	kafetyera
coffin	bara	bara
coin	moneta	moneta
cold (adj)	freddo	fredo
I'm c.	ho f.	o fredo
it's c. (of things)	è f.	e fredo
it's c. (of weather)	fa f.	fa fredo
cold (n)	raffreddore (m)	rafredore
I've got a c.	sono raffreddato	sono rafredato
collar	colletto	koleto
c. bone	clavicola	klaveekola
dog c.	collare (m)	kolare
colleague	collega (m & f) –ghi (mpl) –ghe (fpl)	kolega kolegee kolege
collect /from/	ritirare /di/	reeteerare /dee/
c. /my luggage/	r. /le mie valigie/	reeteerare /le meee valeeje/
collection (in a church)	colletta	koleta
collection (of objects)	raccolta	rakolta
last c. (of post)	ultima r.	oolteema rakolta
college	collegio –gi	kolejo kolejee
cologne	colonia	kolonya
colour	colore (m)	kolore
comb (n)	pettine (m)	peteene
come /from/	venire /da/ – venuto /da/	veneere /da/ – venooto /da/
comfortable	comodo	komodo
comic (=funny paper)	fumetti (mpl)	foometee

commerce	commercio	komercho
commission (=payment)	commissione (f)	komeesyone
common (=usual)	normale	normale
company (=firm)	ditta	deeta
compartment (in train)	scompartimento	skomparteemento
non-smoking c.	s. per non fumatori	skomparteemento per non foomatoree
smoking c.	s. per fumatori	skomparteemento per foomatoree
compass	bussola	boosola
compensation	compenso	kompenso
competition	gara	gara
complain /to the manager/	protestare /col direttore/	protestare /kol deeretore/
c. about /the noise/	p. per /il rumore/	protestare per /eel roomore/
complaint	protesta	protesta
complete (adj)	completo	kompleto
compulsory	obbligatorio –ri	obleegatoryo obleegatoree
computer	computer (m)	kompooter
concert	concerto	koncherto
concert hall	sala concerti	sala konchertee
condition	condizione (f)	kondeetsyone
in bad c.	in cattive condizioni (fpl)	een kateeve kondeetsyonee
in good c.	in buone condizioni (fpl)	een buone kondeetsyonee
conditioner (for hair)	lozione (f) rinforzante	lotsyone reenfortsante
a bottle of hair c.	una bottiglia di l. r. per i capelli	oona boteelya dee lotsyone reenfortsante peree kapelee
conducted tour	visita guidata	veezeeta gweedata
go on a c. t.	fare una v. g.	fare oona veezeeta gweedata
conference	congresso	kongreso
confirm /my flight/	confermare /il mio volo/	konfermare /eel meeo volo/
confused	confuso	konfoozo
I'm c.	sono c.	sono konfoozo
congratulate /you/ on / /	congratularmi con /lei/ per / /	kongratoolarmee kon /ley/ per / /
congratulations	complimenti (mpl)	kompleementee

92

connect	collegare	kolegaʀe
connecting flight	volo in coincidenza	volo ēen koēencheēdentsa
constipated	soffrire di stitichezza – sofferto di s.	sofʀēēʀe dēē steēteēketsa – sofeʀto dēē steēteēketsa
consul	console (m)	konsole
consulate	consolato	konsolato
the /British/ C.	il c. /britannico/	ēel konsolato /bʀeētaneēko/
contact lenses	lenti (fpl) a contatto	lentēē a kontato
contagious	contagioso	kontajoso
contents (eg of a parcel)	contenuto (s)	kontenōōto
continental	continentale	konteēnentale
c. breakfast	colazione c.	kolatsyone konteēnentale
continual	continuo	konteēnwo
continue /a journey/	proseguire /un viaggio/	pʀozegweēʀe /ōōn vyajo/
contraceptives	anticoncezionali (mpl)	anteēkonchetsyonalēē
the Pill	la pillola	la peēlola
a packet of sheaths (=Durex)	un pacchetto di Durex	ōōn paketo dēē dōōʀeks
contract (n)	contratto	kontʀato
convenient (of time and distance)	comodo	komodo
cook (vb)	cuocere – cotto	kwocheʀe – koto
cooked	cotto	koto
cooker	cucina	kōōcheēna
electric c.	c. elettrica	kōōcheēna eletʀeēka
gas c.	c. a gas	kōōcheēna a gaz
cooking	cucinare	kōōcheēnaʀe
do the c.	far da mangiare – fatto da m.	faʀ da manjaʀe – fato da manjaʀe
cool (adj)	fresco –chi	fʀesko fʀeskeē
cool (vb)	raffreddare	ʀafʀedaʀe
copper	rame (m)	ʀame
copy (n)	copia	kopya
copy (vb)	copiare	kopyaʀe
coral	corallo	koʀalo

	words ending in –o or marked (m)	words ending in –a or marked (f)
the	il/l'/lo	la/l'
the (plural)	i/gl'/gli	le/l'

cord	corda	koRda
corduroy	velluto	velōōto
cork	tappo	tapo
corkscrew	cavatappi (m) –	kavatapēē
corn	grano	gRano
sweet c.	granoturco dolce	granotōōRko dolche
corn (eg on a toe)	callo	kalo
c. pads	callifughi (mpl)	kaleēfōōgee
corner	angolo	angolo
cornflakes	cornflakes (mpl)	koRnfleks
correct (adj)	corretto	koReto
correct (vb)	correggere – corretto	koRejere – koReto
correction	correzione (f)	koRetsyone
corridor	corridoio	koRēēdoyo
corset	busto	bōōsto
cost (n)	prezzo	pRetso
cost (vb)	costare	kostaRe
cot	lettino	letēēno
cottage	villino	vēēlēēno
cotton	cotone	kotone
a reel of c.	un rocchetto di c.	ōōn Roketo dēē kotone
cotton wool	cotone (m) idrofilo	kotone ēēdRofeēlo
couchette	cuccetta	kōōcheta
cough (n)	tosse (f)	tose
cough (vb)	tossire	tosēēre
cough mixture	sciroppo per la tosse	sheēRopo peR la tose
a bottle of c. m.	una bottiglia di s. per la t.	ōōna botēēlya dēēsheēRopo peR la tose
cough pastilles	pastiglie (fpl) per la tosse	pasteēlye peR la tose
count (vb)	contare	kontaRe
country (=countryside)	campagna	kampanya
country (=nation)	paese (m)	paeze
countryside	campagna	kampanya
couple (married c.)	coppia	kopya
coupon	buono	bwono
/petrol/ c.	b. per /la benzina/	bwono peR /la bentsēēna/
courrier	corriere (m)	koRyere
course (of food)	piatto	pyato
first c.	primo p.	pRēēmo pyato
main c.	p. principale	pyato pRēēncheēpale
last c.	ultimo p.	ōōltēēmo pyato

court (law)	corte (f)	koʀte
tennis c.	campo da tennis	kampo da tenées
cousin	cugino (m) cugina (f)	kooȷééno koojééna
cow	mucca	mooka
crab	granchio	gʀankyo
crack (n)	fessura	fesoora
cracked	rotto	ʀoto
cramp (n)	crampo	kʀampo
crash (car c.)	incidente (m)	eencheedente
crash helmet	casco da guidatore	kasko da gwéédatoʀe
crayon	pastello	pastelo
cream (from milk)	panna	pana
cream (=lotion)	crema	kʀema
crease (vb)	sgualcire	sgwalchééʀe
does it c.?	si sgualcisce?	sée sgwalchééshe
credit	credito	kʀedééto
on c.	a c.	a kʀedééto
c. terms	condizioni (fpl) di c.	kondéétsyonée dée kʀedééto
credit card	carta di credito	kaʀta di kʀedééto
crew	equipaggio –ggi	ekwéépajo ekwéépajée
air c.	e. dell'aereo	ekwéépajo delaeʀeo
ground c.	personale (m) di servizio a terra	peʀsonale dée seʀvéétsyo a teʀa
ship's c.	e. della nave	ekwéépajo dela nave
cricket	cricket (m)	kʀéékeet
a game of c.	una partita a c.	oona paʀtééta a kʀéékeet
crime	delinquenza	deleenkwentsa
criminal	criminale	kʀééméénale
crisps	patatine (fpl)	patatééne
crocodile (leather)	di coccodrillo	dée kokodʀéélo
c. bag	borsa di c.	boʀsa dée kokodʀéélo
cross /the road/	attraversare /la strada/	atʀaveʀsaʀe /la stʀada/
crossed (eg a cheque)	sbarrato	sbaʀato
crossroads	incrocio –ci	eenkʀocho eenkʀochée
crossword puzzle	parole incrociate (fpl)	paʀole eenkʀochate
crowd	folla	fola
crowded	affollato	afolato
crown (vb) (tooth)	mettere una corona – messo una c.	meteʀe oona koʀona – meso oona koʀona

cruise	crociera	кrochera
go on a c.	fare una c.	fare ōōna кrochera
cry (vb)	piangere – pianto	pyanjere – pyanto
the baby's crying	il bambino piange	eel bambeeno pyanje
cucumber	cetriolo	chetryolo
cuff links	gemelli (mpl)	jemelee
a pair of c. l.	un paio di g.	ōōn payo dee jemelee
cup	tazza	tatsa
a c. of / /	una t. di / /	ōōna tatsa dee / /
/plastic/ c.	t. /di plastica/	tatsa dee /plasteeka/
cupboard	armadio	armadyo
cure (n) (health)	guarigione (f)	gwareejone
cure (vb) (health)	*guarire	gwareere
curl (vb)	arricciare	areechare
curlers	bigodini (mpl)	beegodeenee
currants	uva passa (fs)	ōōva pasa
currency	valuta	valōōta
current (=electric c.)	corrente (f)	korente
A.C.	c. alternata	korente alternata
D.C.	c. continua	korente konteenwa
120/240 volt	cento venti/due centi venti volt	chento ventee/dōōechento ventee volt
current (of water)	corrente (f)	korente
strong c.	c. forte	korente forte
curry	curry (m)	kuree
c. powder	polvere (f) di radice di curcuma	polvere dee radeeche dee kōōrkōōma
curtain	tenda	tenda
cushion	cuscino	kōōsheeno
custom	abitudine (f)	abeetōōdeene
Customs	dogana	dogana
c. declaration form	dichiarazione (f) per la d.	deekyaratsyone per la dogana
cut (n)	taglio	talyo
c. and blow dry	t. e asciugare al fon	talyo e ashōōgare al fon
cut (vb)	tagliare	talyare

	words ending in –o or marked (m)	words ending in –a or marked (f)
a	un/uno	una/un'
some	del/dell'/dello	della/dell'
some (plural)	dei/degl'/degli	delle

cutlery	posateria	pozater**ēē**a
cutlet	costoletta	kostoleta
lamb c.	c. di agnello	kostoleta d**ēē** anyelo
veal c.	c. di vitello	kostoleta d**ēē** v**ēē**telo
cut off (eg of telephone)	interrottare	**ēē**nteRotare
i've been c. o.	sono stato interrotto (m) sono stata interrotta (f)	**sono stato** **ēē**nteRoto – **sono stata** **ēē**nteRota
cycling	ciclismo	ch**ēē**kl**ēē**zmo
go c.	andare in bicicletta	and**a**Re **ēē**n b**ēē**ch**ēē**kleta

D

daily	giornaliero	jyoRnalyeRo
damage (n)	danno	**da**no
damaged	danneggiato	danejato
damages (=compensation)	danni (mpl)	dan**ēē**
damnl	accidenti!	ach**ēē**dent**ēē**
damp (adj)	umido	**ōō**m**ēē**do
dance (n)	ballo	b**a**lo
dance (vb)	ballare	bal**a**Re
dance hall	sala da ballo	s**a**la da b**a**lo
dancer	ballerino (m) ballerina (f)	baleR**ēē**no baleR**ēē**na
dancing	ballare	bal**a**Re
go d.	andare a b.	and**a**Re a bal**a**Re
dandruff	forfora (s)	foRfora
danger	pericolo	peR**ēē**kolo
dangerous	pericoloso	peR**ēē**koloso
dark (=d. haired)	scuro	sk**ōō**Ro
dark (=d. skinned)	scuro	sk**ōō**Ro
dark (of colour)	scuro	sk**ōō**Ro
dark (=time of day)	buio	b**ōō**yo
it's d.	è b.	e b**ōō**yo
darn (vb)	rammendare	Ramend**a**Re
dartboard	bersaglio	beRs**a**lyo
darts	tirassegno (s)	t**ēē**Rasenyo
a game of d.	una partita a t.	**ōō**na paRt**ēē**ta a t**ēē**Rasenyo
date (calendar)	data	d**a**ta
d. of birth	d. di nascita	d**a**ta d**ēē** nash**ēē**ta

97

DATES

English	Italian	Pronunciation
dates (=fruit)	datteri (mpl)	dat̄erēe
daughter	figlia	fēelya
daughter-in-law	nuora	nwoʀa
dawn (n)	alba	alba
day	giorno	jyoʀno
every d.	ogni g.	ony jyoʀno
dead	morto	moʀto
deaf	sordo	soʀdo
decaffeinated	decaffeinizzato	dekafeynēedzato
December	dicembre (m)	dēechembʀe
decide	decidere – deciso	dechēedere – dechēezo
d. to / /	d. di / /	dechēedere dēe / /
d. on /a plan/	d. ad /un piano/	dechēedere ad /ōon pyano/
deck	ponte (m)	ponte
lower d.	p. inferiore	ponte ēenfeʀyoʀe
upper d.	p. superiore	ponte sōopeʀyoʀe
deckchair	sedia a sdraio	sedya a sdʀayo
declare /this watch/	dichiarare /quest'orologio/	dēekyaʀaʀe /kwestoʀolojo/
deduct	togliere – tolto	tolyeʀe – tolto
d. /2000 lire/ from the bill	t. /duemila lire/ dal conto	tolyeʀe /dōomēela lēeʀe/ dal konto
deep	profondo	pʀofondo
deep freeze (=machine)	freezer (m)	frēedzer
definite	definitivo	defēenēetēevo
definitely	definitivamente	defēenēetēevamente
degree (=university d.)	laurea	laōoʀea
degrees	gradi	gʀadēe
Centigrade	centigrado	chentēegʀado
Fahrenheit	fahrenheit	faʀenayt
delay (n)	ritardo	ʀēetaʀdo
delayed (of people)	ritardato	ʀēetaʀdato
delayed (of things)	ritardato	ʀēetaʀdato
delicate (health)	delicato	delēekato
delicatessen (=food shop)	rosticceria	ʀostēecheʀēea
deliver to	consegnare a	konsenyaʀe a
denim (=material)	stoffa da blue jeans	stofa da blōo jēenz
a pair of d. jeans	jeans (mpl)	jēenz
dentist	dentista (m & f) –i	dentēesta dentēestēe
I must go to the dentist's	devo andare dal d.	devo andaʀe dal dentēesta
dentures	dentiera (s)	dentyeʀa

98

deodorant	deodorante (m)	deodoʀante
depart on /Monday/	partire /lunedì/	paʀteeʀe /loonedee/
d. at 4.30 a.m.	p. alle quattro e mezzo	paʀteeʀe ale kwatʀo e medzo
d. in /July/	p. in /luglio/	paʀteeʀe een /loolyo/
department	reparto	ʀepaʀto
children's d.	r. bambini	ʀepaʀto bambeenee
men's d.	r. uomini	ʀepaʀto womeenee
women's d.	r. donne	ʀepaʀto done
department store	grande magazzino	gʀande magadzeeno
departure lounge	sala di partenza	sala dee paʀtentsa
departure time	ora di partenza	oʀa dee paʀtentsa
depend /on the weather/	fidarmi /del tempo/	feedaʀmee /del tempo/
deposit (n)	deposito	depozeeto
deposit /some money/	depositare /del denaro/	depozeetaʀe /del denaʀo/
d. /these valuables/	d. /questi oggetti di valore/	depozeetaʀe /kwestee ojetee dee valoʀe/
depth	profondità –	pʀofondeeta
describe	descrivere – descritto	deskʀeeveʀe – deskʀeeto
description	descrizione (f)	deskʀeetsyone
design (n)	disegno	deezenyo
design (vb)	disegnare	deezenyaʀe
desk	scrivania	skʀeevaneea
dessert	dessert (m)	deseʀt
dessertspoonful of / /	cucchiaio di / /	kookyayo dee / /
destination	destinazione (f)	desteenatsyone
detail	particolare (m)	paʀteekolaʀe
detergent	detergente (m)	deteʀjente
detour	deviazione (f)	devyatsyone
make a d.	fare una d.	faʀe oona devyatsyone
develop	sviluppare	zveeloopaʀe
d. and print (a film)	s. e stampare	zveeloopaʀe e stampaʀe
diabetes	diabete (m)	dyabete
diabetic	diabetico	dyabeteeko

	words ending in –o or marked (m)	words ending in –a or marked (f)
the	il/l'/lo	la/l'
the (plural)	i/gl'/gli	le/l'

99

DIAL

dial	comporre un numero	kompoRe ōōn nōōmero –
	– composto un n.	komposto ōōn nōōmero
diamond	diamante (m)	dyamante
diarrhoea	diarrea	dyaRea
diary	diario	dyaRyo
dice	dado	dado
dictionary	vocabulario	vokabōōlaRyo
English/Italian d.	v. inglese/italiano	vokabōōlaRyo ēēngleze/ēētalyano
Italian/English d.	v. italiano/inglese	vokabōōlaRyo ēētalyano/ēēngleze
pocket d.	v. tascabile	vokabōōlaRyo taskabēēle
die (vb)	morire – morto	moRēēRe – moRto
diet (=slimming d.)	dieta	dyeta
be on a d.	essere a d. – stato a d.	eseRe a dyeta – stato a dyeta
difference	differenza	dēēfeRentsa
different	diverso	dēēveRso
d. from / /	d. di / /	dēēveRso dēē / /
difficult	difficile	dēēfēēchēēle
difficulty	difficoltà –	dēēfēēkolta
dig	vangare	vangaRe
dinghy	dinghy (m) –	dēēngēē
rubber d.	d. di gomma	dēēngēē dēē goma
sailing d.	d. a vela	dēēngēē a vela
dining room	sala da pranzo	sala da pRantso
dinner (=evening meal)	cena	chena
d. jacket	smoking (m)	zmokēēng
have d.	cenare	chenaRe
diplomat	diplomatico	dēēplomatēēko
direct (adj)	diretto	dēēReto
d. line	linea diretta	lēēnea dēēReta
d. route	percorso d.	peRkoRso dēēReto
direction	direzione (f)	dēēRetsyone
director	direttore (m)	dēēRetoRe
directory	elenco	elenko
telephone d.	e. telefonico	elenko telefonēēko
D. Enquiries	Informazioni (fpl)	ēēnfoRmatsyonēē
dirty	sporco	spoRko
disagree with	non essere d'accordo	non eseRe dakoRdo
it disagrees with /me/ (food)	/mi/ fa male	/mēē/ fa male
I d. with /you/	non sono d'accordo con /lei/	non sono dakoRdo kon /ley/

100

disappointed	deluso	delo_oso
disc	disco	deesko
a slipped d.	un d. fuori posto	oon deesko fworee posto
disco	discoteca	deeskoteka
disconnect	distaccare	deestakare
discount (n)	sconto	skonto
disease	malattia	malateea
disembark	sbarcare	zbarkare
disgusting	schifoso	skeefoso
dish (container for food)	piatto	pyato
dish (food)	piatto	pyato
dishcloth	strofinaccio –ci	strofeenacho strofeenachee
dishonest	disonesto	deesonesto
dishwasher	lavastoviglie (m) –gli	lavastoveelye lavastoveelyee
disinfectant	disinfettante (m)	deeseenfetante
a bottle of d.	una bottiglia di d.	oona boteelya dee deeseenfektante
disposable	da buttar via	da bootar veea
d. nappies	pannolini da buttare	panoleenee da bootare
distance	distanza	deestantsa
dive into / /	tuffarmi dentro / /	toofarmee dentro / /
diversion	deviazione (f)	devyatsyone
divide (vb)	dividere – diviso	deeveedere – deeveezo
diving	tuffare	toofare
go d.	andare a tuffarmi	andare a toofarmee
skin-d.	t. in apnea	toofare een apnea
divorced	divorziato	deevortsyato
dizzy	stordito	stordeeto
I feel d.	ho le vertigini	o le verteejeenee
do	fare – fatto	fare – fato
d. /some shopping/	fare /delle spese/	fare /dele speze/
d. /me/ a favour	far/mi/ un favore	far/mee/ oon favore
docks	bacini (mpl) portuali	bacheenee portwalee
doctor	medico –ci	medeeko medeechee
I must go to the doctor's	devo andare dal m.	devo andare dal medeeko

documents	documenti (mpl)	dokōōmentēē
travel d.	d. di viaggio	dokōōmentēē dee vyajo
car d.	d. della macchina	dokōōmentēē dela makēēna
dog	cane (m)	kane
d. collar	collare (m) di c.	kolaRe dēē kane
doll	bambola	bambola
dollar	dollaro	dolaRo
domestic help	colf (m)	kolf
dominoes	domino (s)	domēēno
a game of d.	una partita a d.	ōōna paRtēēta a domēēno
donkey	asino	azēēno
door	porta	poRta
back d.	p. di dietro	poRta dēē dyetRo
front d.	p. davanti	poRta dēē davantēē
doorbell	campanello	kampanelo
doorman	portiere (m)	poRtyeRe
dose of /medecine/	dose (f) di /medicina/	doze dēē /medēēchēēna/
double	doppio	dopyo
a d. room	una stanza doppia	ōōna stantsa dopya
a d. whisky	un whisky d.	ōōn wēēskēē dopyo
pay d.	pagare d. prezzo	pagaRe dopyo pretso
doubt (vb)	dubitare	dōōbēētare
I d. it	dubito	dōōbēēto
down	giù	jōō
downstairs	giù dalle scale	jōō dale skale
dozen	dozzina	dodzēēna
a d. /eggs/	una d. di /uova/	ōōna dodzēēna dēē /wova/
half a d.	una mezza d.	ōōna medza dodzēēna
drains (=sanitary system)	fogne (fpl)	fonye
the drain's blocked	lo scarico è bloccato	lo skaRēēko e blokato
draught (of air)	corrente (f)	koRente
draughts (game)	dama (f)	dama
a game of d.	una partita a d.	ōōna paRtēēta a dama

	words ending in —o or marked (m)	words ending in —a or marked (f)
a	un/uno	una/un'
some	del/dell'/dello	della/dell'
some (plural)	dei/degl'/degli	delle

102

draughty		
it's very d.	c'è molta corrente	che molta korente
draw (a picture)	disegnare	deezenyare
drawer	cassetto	kaseto
dreadful	orribile	oreebeele
dress (n)	vestito	vesteeto
dress (vb) (a wound)	fasciare	fashare
dressing (medical)	fasciatura	fashatoora
dressing (=salad d.)	condimento	kondeemento
dressing gown	vestaglia	vestalya
dressmaker	sarta	sarta
dress /oneself/	vestir/mi/	vesteer/mee/
d. /the baby/	vestire /il bambino/	vesteere /eel bambeeno/
dress shop	negozio di abbigliamento	negotsyo dee abeelyamento
drink (n) (usually alcoholic)	bibita	beebeeta
soft d.	b. analcolica	beebeeta analkoleeka
drink (vb)	bere – bevuto	bere – bevooto
drip-dry	lavare e asciugare	lavare e ashyoogare
a d.-d. shirt	camicia che non si stira	kameecha ke non see steera
drive (n) (=entrance)	viale (m)	vyale
drive (vb)	guidare	gweedare
go for a d.	fare un giro in macchina	fare oon jeero een makeena
driver	autista (m & f) –i	aooteesta aooteeestee
driving licence	patente (m)	patente
international d. l.	p. internazionale	patente eenternatsyonale
drop /of water/	goccia /d'acqua/	gochya /dakwa/
drug	droga	droga
drunk (adj) (=not sober)	ubriaco –chi	oobryako oobryakee
dry (adj) (of drinks)	secco –chi	seko sekee
dry (adj) (of the weather)	secco –chi	seko sekee
dry (adj) (of things)	asciutto	ashyooto
dry (vb)	asciugare – asciutto	ashyoogare – ashyooto
dry cleaner's	lavasecco	lavaseko
dryer		
hair d.	fon (m)	fon
dual carriageway	strada a doppia corsia	strada a dopya korseea
duck/duckling	anitra/anatrocolo	aneetra/anatrokolo

English	Italian	Pronunciation
due (to arrive)	atteso	atezo
/the train/'s d. /at 2 p.m./	/il treno/ deve arrivare /alle due/	/eel tʀeno/ deve aʀeevare /ale dooe/
dull (of people and entertainments)	noioso	noyozo
dull (of the weather)	uggioso	oojozo
dummy (baby's d.)	tettarella	tetaʀela
during /the night/	durante /la notte/	dooʀante /la note/
dusk	crepuscolo	kʀepooskolo
dust	polvere (f)	polveʀe
dustbin	bidone (m) per i rifiuti	beedone peʀ ee ʀeefyootee
dustman	netturbino	netooʀbeeno
duty (= obligation)	dovere (m)	doveʀe
duty (=tax)	dazio –zi	datsyo datsee
duty-free goods	merce (fs) esente dal dazio	meʀche ezente dal datsyo
duty-free shop	negozio esente da dogana	negotsyo ezente da dogana
duvet	piumone (m)	pyoomone
d. cover	copertina per p.	kopeʀteena peʀ pyoomone
dye (vb)	tingere – tinto	teenjeʀe – teento
d. /this sweater/ /black/	t. di /nero/ /questo golf/	teenjeʀe dee /neʀo/ /kwesto golf/
dysentery	dissenteria	deesenteʀeea

E

English	Italian	Pronunciation
each	ciascuno	chyaskoono
e. /of the children/	c. /dei bambini/	chyaskoono /dey bambeenee/
ear	orecchio –chi	oʀekyo oʀekee
earache	mal d'o.	mal doʀekyo
early	presto	pʀesto
e. train	treno di mattina p.	tʀeno dee mateena pʀesto
leave e.	partire p.	paʀteeʀe pʀesto
earn	guadagnare	gwadanyaʀe
earplugs	tappi (mpl) per gli orecchi	tapee peʀ ly oʀekee
earrings	orecchini (mpl)	oʀekeenee
clip-on e.	o. con la clip	oʀekeenee kon la kleep

e. for pierced ears	o. per orrecchi con foro	oꞧekēēnēē peꞧ oꞧekēē kon foꞧo
earth (= the e.)	terra	teꞧa
easily	facilmente	fachēēlmente
east	est (m)	est
Easter	Pasqua	paskwa
easy	facile	fachēēle
eat	mangiare	manjaꞧe
eau-de-Cologne	acqua di cologna	akwa dēē kolonya
a bottle of e.-d.-C.	una bottiglia di a. d. c.	ōōna botēēlya dēē akwa dēē kolonya
education	istruzione (f)	ēēstꞧōōtsyone
educational	istruttivo	ēēstꞧōōtēēvo
efficient	efficiente (m & f)	efēēchente
egg	uovo –a	wovo wova
boiled e.	u. alla coque	wovo ala kok
fried e.	u. fritto	wovo fꞧēēto
poached e.	u. in camicia	wovo ēēn kamēēcha
scrambled eggs	u. strapazzato	wovo stꞧapatsato
elaborate (adj)	elaborato	elaboꞧato
elastic (n)	elastico	elastēēko
elastic band	elastico	elastēēko
Elastoplast (tdmk)	cerotto	cheꞧoto
elbow	gomito	gomēēto
election	elezione (f)	eletsyone
electric	elettrico	eletꞧēēko
e. shock	scossa elettrica	skosa eletꞧēēka
electrical appliance shop	negozio di elettricità	negotsyo dēē eletꞧēēchēēta
electrician	elettricista (m) –sti	eletꞧēēchēēsta eletꞧēēchēēstēē
electricity	elettricità	eletꞧēēchēēta
elsewhere	altrove	altꞧove
embarcation	imbarcazione (f)	ēēmbaꞧkatsyone
embark	imbarcarmi	ēēmbaꞧkaꞧmēē
embassy	ambasciata	ambashata
the /British/ E.	l'a. /britannica/	lambashata /bꞧēētanēēka/
embroidery	ricamo	ꞧēēkamo
emergency	emergenza	emeꞧjentsa
emergency exit	uscita di sicurezza	ōōshēēta dēē sēēkōōꞧetsa

	words ending in –o or marked (m)	words ending in –a or marked (f)
the	il/l'/lo	la/l'
the (plural)	i/gl'/gli	le/l'

emotional	emotivo	emot__ee__vo
she's very e.	è molto nervosa	e **molto** neʀvosa
employed by / /	impiegato da / /	__ee__mpyegato da / /
empty (adj)	vuoto	**vw**oto
empty (vb)	vuotare	**vw**otaʀe
enclose	accludere – accluso	akl__oo__deʀe – akl__oo__zo
please find enclosed	qui troverete unito	kw__ee__ tʀoveʀete __oo__n__ee__to
end (n)	fine (f)	f__ee__ne
end (vb)	*finire	f__ee__n__ee__ʀe
endorse	vistare	v__ee__staʀe
e. my ticket to / /	v. mio biglietto per / /	v__ee__staʀe m__ee__o b__ee__lyeto peʀ / /
engaged (telephone)	occupato	ok__oo__pato
engaged (to be married)	fidanzato	f__ee__dantsato
engaged (toilet)	occupato	ok__oo__pato
engagement ring	anello di fidanzamento	anelo d__ee__ f__ee__dantsamento
engine (eg for a car)	motore (m)	motoʀe
engineer	ingegnere (m)	__ee__njenyeʀe
engrave	intagliare	__ee__ntalyaʀe
enjoyable	piacevole (m & f)	pyachevole
enjoy oneself	divertirmi	d__ee__veʀt__ee__ʀm__ee__
enlarge	ingrandire	__ee__ngʀand__ee__ʀe
enough	abbastanza	abastantsa
e. money	a. denaro	abastantsa denaʀo
fast e.	a. veloce	abastantsa veloche
enroll	iscrivere – iscritto	__ee__skʀ__ee__veʀe – __ee__skʀ__ee__to
enter	entrare	entʀaʀe
e. /a country/	e. in /un paese/	entʀaʀe __ee__n /__oo__n paeze/
entertaining	divertente (m & f)	d__ee__veʀtente
entitled		
be e. to /petrol coupons/	aver diritto ad avere /i buoni per la benzina/	aveʀ d__ee__ʀ__ee__to ad aveʀe /__ee__ bwon__ee__ peʀ la bendz__ee__na/
entrance	entrata	entʀata
e. fee	biglietto di e.	b__ee__lyeto d__ee__ entʀata
main e.	e. principale	entʀata pʀ__ee__nch__ee__pale
side e.	e. di fianco	entʀata d__ee__ **fy**anko

106

envelope	busta	bōosta
a packet of envelopes	un pacchetto di buste	ōōn paketo dēē bōoste
airmail e.	b. aerea	bōosta aerea
epidemic (n)	epidemia	epēedemēea
epileptic (adj)	epilettico	epēeletēeko
equal	uguale (m & f)	ōōgwale
equip	equipaggiare	ekwēepajare
equipment	equipaggiamento	ekēēpajamento
photographic e.	e. fotografico	ekwēēpajamento fotografēēko
eraser	gomma per cancellare	goma per kanchelare
escape from / /	scappare da / /	skapare da / /
escort (n)	scorta	skorta
escort (vb)	scortare	skortare
espresso coffee	espresso	espreso
estate agent	agente (m) per case e terrene	ajente per kaze e terene
estimate (n)	stima	stēema
even (surface)	perfino	perfēēno
evening	sera	sera
this e.	questa s.	kwesta sera
tomorrow e.	domani s.	domanēē sera
yesterday e.	ieri s.	yerēē sera
evening dress (for men)	smoking (m)	zmokēēng
evening dress (for women)	vestito lungo	vestēēto lōōngo
every	ogni	ony
every day	ogni giorno	ony jorno
everyone	ognuno	onyōōno
everything	tutto	tōōto
everywhere	dappertutto	dapertōōto
exact	preciso	prechēēzo
exactly	precisamente	prechēēzamente
examination	visita	vēēzeeta
medical e.	v. medica	vēēzeeta medēeka
examine (medically)	visitare	vēēzeetare
example	esempio	ezempyo
for e.	per e.	per ezempyo
excellent	eccellente (m & f)	echelente
except	eccetto	echeto
excess	eccesso	echeso
e. baggage	bagaglio in eccedenza	bagalyo een echedentsa
e. fare	supplemento	sōōplemento

exchange	scambiare	skambyaRe
e. /this sweater/	s. /questo golf/	skambyaRe /kwesto golf/
exchange rate	tasso di cambio	taso dee kambyo
excited	eccitato	echeetato
exciting	emozionante (m & f)	emotsyonante
excursion	gita	jeeta
go on an e.	fare una g.	faRe oona jeeta
excuse (n)	scusa	skooza
make an e.	fare una s.	faRe oona skooza
excuse (vb)	scusare	skoozaRe
exhibition	mostra	mostRa
exit	uscita	oosheeta
emergency e.	u. di sicurezza	oosheeta dee seekooRetsa
expedition	spedizione (f)	spedeetsyone
expensive	costoso	kostozo
experienced	di esperienza	dee espeRyentsa
expert (adj)	esperto	espeRto
expert (n)	esperto	espeRto
expire (= run out)	scadere	skadeRe
/my visa/ has expired	/il mio visto/ è scaduto	/eel meeo veesto/ e skadooto/
explain	spiegare	spyegaRe
explanation	spiegazione (f)	spyegatsyone
export (vb)	esportare	espoRtaRe
exposure meter	esposimetro	espozeemetRo
express	espresso	espReso
e. letter	lettera espressa	leteRa espResa
e. mail	posta espressa	posta espResa
e. service	servizio e.	seRveetsyo espReso
e. train	treno rapido	tReno Rapeedo
extension (telephone)	estensione (f)	estensyone
extra	extra	ekstRa
extras	extra (mpl)	ekstRa
eye	occhio –chi	okyo okee
eyebrow	sopracciglio –gli	sopRacheelyo sopRacheely
eyelid	palpebra	palpebRa
eye make-up	trucco per gli occhi	tRooko peR ly okee

	words ending in –o or marked (m)	words ending in –a or marked (f)
a	un/uno	una/un'
some	del/dell'/dello	della/dell'
some (plural)	dei/degl'/degli	delle

F

English	Italian	Pronunciation
face	faccia –cce	fachya – fache
facecloth	panno per il viso	pano per eel veeso
facial (=face massage) ****17120	massaggio –ggi	masajo – masajee
fact	fatto	fato
factory	fabbrica –che	fabreeka fabreeke
factory worker	operaio (m) operaia (f)	operayo operaya
faded	sbiadito	sbyadeeto
faint (vb)	svenire	zveneere
I fell f.	mi sento s.	mee sento zveneere
fair (adj) (hair)	biondo	byondo
fair (adj) (=just)	giusto	joosto
that's not f.	non è g.	non e joosto
fair (adj) (skin)	chiaro	kyaro
fair (=entertainment)	luna park (m)	loona park
fall (n)	caduta	kadoota
fall (vb)	cadere	kadere
I fell downstairs	sono caduto giù per le scale	sono kadooto joo per le skale
false	falso	falso
f. teeth	dentiera (s)	dentyera
family	famiglia	fameelya
famous	famoso	famozo
fan (n) (electric)	ventilatore (m)	venteelatore
fan (n) (sports)	tifoso	teefoso
fancy dress	costume (m)	kostoome
far	lontano	lontano
fare	tariffa	tareefa
air f.	t. aerea	tareefa aerea
bus f.	t. dell'autobus	tareefa delaootoboos
full f.	t. intera	tareefa eentera
half f.	t. ridotta	tareefa reedota
return f.	t. di andata e ritorno	tareefa dee andata e reetorno
single f.	t. singola	tareefa seengola
train f.	t. ferroviaria	tareefa ferovyarya
farm	fattoria	fatoreea
farmer	fattore (m)	fatore
farmhouse	casa della fattoria	kaza dela fatoreea
fashionable	di moda	dee moda
fast	veloce	veloche
f. train	rapido	rapeedo

fasten	chiudere – chiuso	kyōoderе – kyōozo
fat (adj)	grasso	grаsо
father	padre (m)	padrе
father-in-law	suocero	swосhеrо
fattening	ingrassante (m & f)	ēengrаsante
fatty (of food)	grasso	grаsо
fault	colpa	kolpa
it's my f.	è c. mia	e kolpa mēea
faulty	difettoso	dēefetozo
favour	favore (m)	favorе
do me a f.	farmi un f.	farmēe ōon favorе
favourite (adj)	preferito	preferēeto
feather	piuma	pyōoma
February	febbraio	febrayo
fed up		
be f. u.	essere stufo	eserе stōofo
I'm f. u.	sono s.	sono stōofo
feeding bottle	biberon (m) –	bēeberоn
feel	sembrare	sembrarе
it feels /rough/	sembra /ruvido/	sembra /rōovēedo/
feel	sentire	sentēerе
I f. ill	mi sento male	mēe sento male
I f. sick	sento nausea	sento naōosea
felt (material)	feltro	feltrо
felt-tip pen	pennarello	penarelo
female (adj)	femmina	femēena
feminine	femminile	femēenēele
ferry	traghetto	trageto
by f.	in t.	ēen trageto
car f.	t. per le macchine	trageto per le makēene
festival	festa	festa
fetch	andare a prendere	andarе a prenderе
fever	febbre (f)	febrе
feverish	febbrile (m & f)	febrēele
few	pochi (mpl)	pokēe
a f.	qualche	kwalkе
f. /people/	poca /gente/	poka /jente/
fewer	meno	meno
fiancé	fidanzato	fēedantsato
fiancée	fidanzata	fēedantsata
field (n)	campo	kampo
fig	fico –chi	fēeko fēekēe
fight (n)	lotta	lota
fight (vb)	lottare	lotarе
figure (=body)	figura	fēegōora
fill in(form)	riempire	ryempēerе

fill (tooth)	otturare	otooᴚaᴚe
fill (vessel)	riempire	ᴚyempeeᴚe
fillet (n)	filetto	feeleto
fillet (vb)	tagliare	talyaᴚe
filling (tooth)	otturazione (f)	otooᴚatsyone
filling station	distributore (m)	deestᴚeebootoᴚe
film	pellicola	peleekola
ASA (tdmk)	ASA	asa
black and white f.	rulino bianco e nero	ᴚooleeno byanko e neᴚo
cartridge f.	rotolo	ᴚotolo
colour f.	rulino a colori	ᴚooleeno a koloᴚi
DIN (tdmk)	DIN	deen
Polaroid f. (tdmk)	p. polaroid	peleekola polaᴚoeed
Super 8	Super 8	sooᴘeᴚ oto
16mm	16mm	peleekola sedeechee meeleemetᴚee
35mm 20/36 exposures	35mm con 20/36 pose	tᴚentacheenkwe meeleemetᴚee kon ventee/tᴚentasey poze
120, 127, 620	120, 127, 620	chento/chento venteesete/ seychenteeventee
film (=entertainment)	film (m)	feelm
horror f.	f. di orrore	feelm dee oᴚoᴚe
pornographic f.	f. pornografico	feelm poᴚnogᴚafico
thriller	f. giallo	feelm jalo
Western	Western	westeᴚn
filter-tipped cigarettes	sigarette (fpl) con filtro	seegaᴚete kon feeltᴚo
find	trovare	tᴚovaᴚe
f. /this address/	t. /quest'indirizzo/	tᴚovaᴚe /kwest eendeeᴚeetso/
fine (adj) (of weather)	bello	belo
it's f.	fa b.	fa belo
fine (adj) (=sum of money)	multa	moolta
pay a f.	pagare una m.	pagaᴚe oona moolta
finger	dito –a	deeto deeta

	words ending in –o or marked (m)	words ending in –a or marked (f)
the	il/l'/lo	la/l'
the (plural)	i/gl'/gli	le/l'

finish	*finire	feenee̅e̅re
f. /my breakfast/	f. /mia colazione/	feenee̅e̅re /mee̅a kolatsyone/
fire (n)	incendio –di	ee̅nchendyo ee̅chendee̅
on f.	incendiato	ee̅nchendyato
fire alarm	allarme (m) d'incendio	alarme dee̅nchendyo
fire brigade	pompieri (mpl)	pompyere̅e̅
fire engine	camion (m) dei pompieri	kamyon dey pompyere̅e̅
fire escape	uscita di sicurezza	oo̅she̅e̅ta dee̅ se̅e̅koo̅retsa
fire extinguisher	pompa antiincendio	pompa antee̅e̅e̅nchendyo
fireman	pompiere (m)	pompyere
fireworks (pl)	fuochi (mpl) d'artificio	fwoke̅e̅ dartee̅fee̅cho
firework display	spettacolo di f. d'a.	spetakolo dee̅ fwoke̅e̅ dartee̅fee̅cho
firm (n) (=company)	ditta	de̅e̅ta
first	primo	pre̅e̅mo
at f.	innanzitutto	ee̅nantse̅e̅too̅to
f. of all	prima di tutto	pre̅e̅ma dee̅ too̅to
first aid	pronto soccorso	pronto sokorso
f. a. kit	equipaggiamento di p. s.	ekwe̅e̅pajamento dee̅ pronto sokorso
first class (adj)	di prima classe	de̅e̅ pre̅e̅ma klase
first class (n)	prima classe	pre̅e̅ma klase
first name	nome (m)	nome
fish	pesce (m)	peshe
f. and chips	p. con patate fritte	peshe kon patate fre̅e̅te
fishing	pescare	peskare
go f.	andare a p.	andare a peskare
fishing line	lenza	lentsa
fishing rod	canna da pesca	kana da peska
fishmonger's	pescivendolo	peshe̅e̅vendolo
fit	adattare	adatare
it doesn't f. me	non mi sta bene	non me̅e̅ sta bene
it's a good f.	mi sta bene	me̅e̅ sta bene
fit (adj)	adatto	adato
he's f.	è in forma	e ee̅n forma
fit (n) (=attack)	convulsione (f)	konvoo̅lsyone
fitting room (in shop)	stanza per le prove	stantsa per le prove
fix (vb) (=mend)	fissare	fe̅e̅sare

fizzy	frizzante (m & f)	frɛētsante
flag	bandiera	bandyeɾa
flame (n)	fiamma	fyama
flannel (=cloth)	flanella	flanela
flash	lampo	lampo
f. bulb	l. di magnesio	lampo dēē manyezyo
f. cube	cubo al magnesio	kōōbo al manyezyo
flask (vacuum f.)	fiasco –chi	fyasko fyaskēē
flat (adj)	piatto	pyato
flat (n)	appartamento	apaɾtamento
furnished f.	a. ammobiliato	apaɾtamento amobēēlyato
unfurnished f.	a. non ammobiliato	apaɾtamento non amobēēlyato
flavour	gusto	gōōsto
banana f.	g. di banana	gōōsto dēē banana
blackcurrant f.	g. di ribes	gōōsto dēē ɾēēbes
chocolate f.	g. di cioccolata	gōōsto dēē chokolata
strawberry f.	g. di fragola	gōōsto dēē fɾagola
vanilla f.	g. di vaniglia	gōōsto dēē vanēēlya
flea	pulce (f)	pōōlche
fleabite	morso di pulce	moɾso dēē pōōlche
flea market	mercato delle pulci	meɾkato dele pōōlchēē
flea powder	polvere (f) contro le pulci	polveɾe kontɾo le pōōlchēē
flight	volo	volo
charter f.	v. charter	volo chaɾtɛɾ
connecting f.	v. in coincidenza	volo ēēn koēēnchēēdentsa
scheduled f.	v. di linea	volo dēē lēēnea
student f.	v. per studenti	volo peɾ stōōdentēē
flippers	pinne (fpl)	pēēne
a pair of f.	un paio di p.	ōōn payo dēē pēēne
float (vb)	galleggiare	galejaɾe
flood (n)	diluvio –vi	dēēlōōvyo dēēlōōvēē
flooded	inondato	ēēnondato
floor (of building)	piano	pyano
basement (B)	seminterrato	semēēnteɾato
ground f. (g)	pianterreno	pyanteɾeno
/first/ f.	/primo/ p.	/pɾēēmo/ pyano
top f.	ultimo p.	ōōltēēmo pyano
floor (of room)	pavimento	pavēēmento

floor (=the ground)	pavimento	paveemento
florist's	fioraio –ai	fyoRAyo fyoRAyee
flour	farina	faReena
flower	fiore (m)	fyoRe
a bunch of flowers	un mazzo di fiori	oon matso dee fyoRee
flower pot	vaso da fiori	vazo da fyoRee
flu	influenza	eenflwentsa
fly to / /	volare verso / /	volaRe veRso / /
fly (=insect)	mosca –che	moska moske
fly spray	sprai (m) contro le mosche	spRay kontRo le moske
flying	volo	volo
go f.	andare a volare	andaRe a volaRe
fog	nebbia	nebya
foggy	nebbioso	nebyozo
it's f.	è n.	e nebyozo
fold	piegare	pyegaRe
folding /bed/	/letto/ pieghevole	/leto/ pyegevole
folk (adj)	folk	folk
f. art	arte (f) f.	aRte folk
f. dancing	ballo f.	balo folk
f. music	musica f.	moozeeka folk
folklore	folklore (m)	folkloRe
follow	seguire	segweeRe
fond		
(be) fond of	aver simpatia per – avuto simpatia per	aveR seempateea peR – avooto seempateea peR
I'm fond of /him/	ho simpatia per /lui/	o seempateea peR /looee/
food	cibo	cheebo
where can I get some f.?	dove posso trovare del c.?	dove poso tRovaRe del cheebo
f. poisoning	avvelenamento da c.	avelenamento da cheebo
health f.	c. dietetico	cheebo dyeteteeko
fool (n)	stupido	stoopeedo
foolish	sciocco –chi	shyoko shyokee
foot (distance)	piede (m)	pyede
foot (=part of body)	piede (m)	pyede
on f.	a piedi	a pyedee
football (=ball)	pallone (m)	palone

	words ending in –o or marked (m)	words ending in –a or marked (f)
a	un/uno	una/un'
some	del/dell'/dello	della/dell'
some (plural)	dei/degl'/degli	delle

English	Italian	Pronunciation
football (=game)	calcio	kalchyo
a game of f.	una partita di c.	ōōna partēēta dēē kalchyo
footpath	sentiero	sentyero
for (prep)	per	peR
forehead	fronte (f)	fronte
foreign	straniero	stranyero
foreigner	straniero (m) straniera (f)	stranyero stranyera
forest	foresta	foresta
forget	dimenticare	dēēmentēēkare
forgive	perdonare	perdonare
fork (cutlery)	forchetta	forketa
form (=document)	modulo	modōōlo
fortunately	fortunatamente	fortōōnatamente
forward to	inoltrare a	ēēnoltrare a
please forward	pregasi inoltrare	pregasēē ēēnoltrare
fountain	fontana	fontana
fountain pen	penna stilografica	pena stēēlografēēka
foyer (in hotels and theatres)	entrata	entrata
fragile	fragile	frajēēle
f. with care (=on labels)	f.	frajēēle
frame (n) (=picture f.)	cornice (f)	kornēēche
frame (vb)	incorniciare	ēēnkornēēchare
free (=unconstrained)	libero	lēēbero
free (=without payment)	gratis	gratēēs
freeze	congelare	konjelare
freezing	ghiacciato	gyachato
it's f.	si gela	sēē jela
frequent (adj)	frequente	frekwente
fresh	fresco (m) freschi (mpl) fresca (f) fresche (fpl)	fresko freskēē freska freske
f. food (not stale, not tinned)	cibo f.	chēēbo fresko
f. water (ie not salt)	acqua dolce	akwa dolche
Friday	venerdì (m)	venerdēē
on Friday	v.	venerdee
on Fridays	di v.	dēē venerdee
fridge	frigorifero	frēēgorēēfero
friend	amico (m) –ci (pl) amica (f) –che (pl)	amēēko amēēchēē amēēka amēēke

115

FRIENDLY

friendly	amichevole (m & f)	ameekevole
fringe (hair)	frangia –ge	franja franje
from	da	da
front	fronte (m)	fronte
in f. of / /	di f. a / /	dee fronte a / /
frontier	frontiera	frontyera
frost	gelo	jelo
frosty	gelato	jelato
frozen (=deep f.)	congelato	konjelato
f. /food/	/cibo/ c.	/cheebo/ konjelato
fruit	frutta –	froota
fresh f.	f. fresca	froota freska
tinned f.	f. in scatola	froota een skatola
fruit juice (see also under juice)	succo di frutta	sooko dee froota
a bottle of f. j.	una bottiglia di s. di f.	oona boteelya dee sooko dee froota
a glass of f. j.	un bicchiere di s. di f.	oon beekyere dee sooko dee froota
fry	friggere – fritto	freejere – freeto
frying pan	padella	padela
full	pieno	pyeno
f. board	pensione completa	pensyone kompleta
fun	divertimento	deeverteemento
have f.	divertirmi	deeverteermee
funeral	funerale (m)	foonerale
funicular	funicolare (f)	fooneekolare
funny (=amusing)	ridicolo	reedeekolo
fur	pelo	pelo
f. coat	pelliccia	peleechya
lined with f.	foderato di pelliccia	foderato dee peleechya
furnish	ammobiliare	amobeelyare
furnished /flat/	/appartamento/ ammobiliato	/apartamento/ amobeelyato
furniture	mobili (mpl)	mobeelee
furniture shop	negozio di mobili	negotsyo dee mobeelee
further	più lontano	pyoo lontano
fuse (n)	valvola fusibile	valvola foozeebeele
/3 / amp f.	valvola da /tre/ amp	valvola da /tre/ amp
f. wire	filo della valvola	feelo dela valvola
fuse (vb)	saltare	saltare
the lights have fused	le luci sono saltate	le loochee sono saltate
future (adj)	futuro	footooro
future (n)	futuro	footooro

116

G

gabardine coat	gabardina	gabaʀdeena
gadget	aggeggio –ggi	ajejo ajejee
gale	burrasca	booʀaska
gallery	galleria	galeʀeea
art g.	g. d'arte	galeʀeea daʀte
gallon	gallone (m)	galone
gallop	galoppare	galopaʀe
gamble (vb)	giocare d'azzardo	jokaʀe dadzaʀdo
gambling	gioco d'azzardo	joko dadzaʀdo
gambling club	circolo di gioco	cheeʀkolo dee joko
game	partita	paʀteeta
a g. of /tennis/	una p. a /tennis/	oona paʀteeta a /tenees/
game (animals)	selvaggina	selvajeena
hare	lepre (f)	lepʀe
quail	quaglia	kwalya
wild boar	cinghiale (m)	cheengyale
gaol	prigione (f)	pʀeejone
in g.	in p.	een pʀeejone
garage	garage (m)	gaʀaje
garden	giardino	jyaʀdeeno
garlic	.aglio	alyo
gas	gas (m)	gaz
gate (=airport exit)	uscita	oosheeta
gate (=door)	cancello	kanchelo
gear	equipaggiamento	ekweepajamento
climbing g.	e. per scalare	ekweepajamento peʀ skalaʀe
diving g.	e. subacqueo	ekweepajamento soobakweo
general (adj)	generale	jeneʀale
generator	generatore (m)	jeneʀatoʀe
generous	generoso	jeneʀoso
Gent's (lavatory)	gabinetto per gli uomini	gabeeneto peʀ ly womeenee
genuine	genuino	jenweeno
germ	germe (m)	jeʀme
German measles	rosolia	ʀozoleea
get /a taxi/	prendere /un taxi/ – preso /un taxi/	pʀendeʀe /oon taksee/ – pʀezo /oon taksee/
get off at / /	salire a / /	saleeʀe a / /

	words ending in –o or marked (m)	words ending in –a or marked (f)
the	il/l'/lo	la/l'
the (plural)	i/gl'/gli	le/l'

get on at / /	scendere a / / – sceso a / /	shendere a / / – shezo a / /
gift	regalo	regalo
gift shop	negozio di regali	negotsyo dee regalee
gin	gin (m)	jeen
a bottle of g.	una bottiglia di g.	oona boteelya dee jeen
a g.	un g.	oon jeen
a g. and tonic	un gin e tonico	oon jeen e toneeko
ginger (flavour)	zenzero	dzendzero
girl	ragazza	ragatsa
girlfriend	ragazza	ragatsa
give	dare – dato	dare – dato
g. it to /me please	/me/ lo dia, per favore	/me/ lo deea per favore
glacier	ghiacciaio –ai	gyachyayo gyachyay
glad	contento	kontento
he's g.	è c.	e kontento
glass	bicchiere (m)	beekyere
a g. /of water/	un b. /d'acqua/	oon beekyere /dakwa/
a wine g.	un b. da vino	oon beekyere da veeno
set of glasses	servizio di bicchieri	serveetsyo dee beekyeree
glass (=substance)	vetro	vetro
glasses	occhiali (mpl)	okyalee
a pair of g.	un paio di o.	oon payo dee okyalee
glassware shop	negozio di vetrerie	negotsyo dee vetrereee
gliding	vola a vela	volo a vela
go g.	fare v. a v. – fatto v. a v.	fare volo a vela – fato volo a vela
gloves	guanti (mpl)	gwantee
a pair of g.	un paio di g.	oon payo dee gwantee
glue	colla	kola
go	andare	andare
g. /home/	a. a /casa/	andare a /kaza/
g. /on a picnic/	a. a /fare un picnic/	andare a /fare oon peeknek/
g. out with / /	uscire insieme con / /	oosheere eensyeme kon / /
g. /shopping/	a. a /fare la spesa/	andare a /fare la speza/
let's g.	andiamo	andyamo

118

go to /a conference/	andare ad /un congresso/	andare ad /ōōn kongreso/
goal	gol (m)	gol
goalkeeper	portiere (m)	portyere
goat	capra	kapra
godfather	padrino	padrēēno
God/god	Dio/dio	dēēo/dēēo
godmother	madrina	madrēēna
goggles	occhialoni (mpl)	okyalonēē
underwater g.	maschera subacquea	maskera sōōbakwea
go-kart	go-kart –s	go kart go karts
gold (adj)	d'oro	doro
gold (n)	oro	oro
golf	golf (m)	golf
a round of g.	una partita a g.	ōōna partēēta a golf
g. ball	pallina da g.	palēēna da golf
g. club (=institution)	circolo di g.	chēērkolo dēē golf
g. club (=object)	mazza di g.	matsa dēē golf
g. course	campo di g.	kampo dēē golf
good	buono	bwono
good-looking	bello	belo
a g.-l. man	un bell' uomo	ōōn belwomo
a g.-l. woman	una bella donna	ōōna bela dona
goods (=merchandise)	merce (fs)	merche
goods train	treno merce	treno merche
goose	oca –che	oka oke
wild geese	oche selvagge	oke selvaje
government	governo	governo
grade (=level)	grado	grado
gradually	un po' alla volta	ōōn po ala volta
graduate of / /	laureato a / /	laōōreato a / /
grammar (=a g. book)	grammatica	gramatēēka
grammar (=language forms)	grammatica	gramatēēka
grams	grammi	gramēē
grandchild	nipote (m)	nēēpote
granddaughter	nipote (f)	nēēpote
grandfather	nonno	nono
grandmother	nonna	nona
grandson	nipote (m)	nēēpote
grant (for studies)	borsa di studio	borsa dēē stōōdyo

grapefruit (fresh)	pompelmo	pompelmo
tinned g.	p. in scatola	pompelmo ēēn skatola
grapes	uve (fpl)	ōōve
a bunch of g.	un grappolo d'u.	ōōn grapolo dōōve
grass	erba	eʀba
grateful	riconoscente (m & f)	ʀēēkonoshente
gravy	sugo	sōōgo
greasy (of food)	grasso	gʀaso
greasy (of hair)	unti (mpl)	ōōntee
green	verde (m & f)	veʀde
greengrocer's	fruttivendolo	fʀōōtēēvendolo
grey	grigio –gi	gʀēējo gʀēējēē
grey (=g.-haired)	grigio	gʀēējo
grill (vb)	arrostire	aʀostēēʀe
groceries	generi (mpl) alimentari	jeneʀēē alēēmentaʀēē
grocer's	droghiere (m)	dʀogyeʀe
ground (=the g.)	terra	teʀa
group	gruppo	gʀōōpo
g. ticket	biglietto collettivo	beelyeto koletēēvo
grow (=cultivate)	coltivare	koltēēvaʀe
grow (of person)	crescere – cresciuto	kʀeshere – kʀeshyōōto
guarantee (n)	garanzia	gaʀantsēēa
guarantee (vb)	*garantire	gaʀantēēʀe
guardian	guardiano	gwaʀdyano
guess	indovinare	ēēndoveēēnaʀe
guest	ospite (m & f)	ospēēte
guide (=person)	guida	gwēēda
guide (vb)	guidare	gwēēdaʀe
guide book	guida	gwēēda
guilty	colpevole (m & f)	kolpevole
guitar	chitarra	kēētaʀa
gum (of mouth)	gengiva	jenjēēva
chewing g.	ciunga	chōōnga
gun	fucile (m)	fōōchēēle
gymnasium	palestra	palestʀa

H

hair	capelli (mpl)	kapelēē
hairbrush	spazzola per capelli	spatsola peʀ kapelēē
	words ending in –o or marked (m)	words ending in –a or marked (f)
a	un/uno	una/un'
some	del/dell'/dello	della/dell'
some (plural)	dei/degl'/degli	delle

haircut	taglio dei capelli	talyo dey kapelee
hairdresser	parucchiere (m)	parookyere
	parucchiera (f)	parookyera
hair dryer	asciugacapelli (m)	ashyoogakapelee
hairgrip	molletta per capelli	moleta per kapelee
hair oil	brillantina	breelanteena
a bottle of h. o.	una bottiglia di b.	oona boteelya dee breelanteena
half	metà/mezzo	meta/medzo
h. a /litre/	mezzo /litro/	medzo /leetro/
h. a /slice/	mezza /feta/	medza /feta/
ham	prosciutto	proshooto
h. /sandwich/	/panino/ con p.	/paneeno/ kon proshooto
/six/ slices of h.	/sei/ fette di p.	/sey/ fete dee proshooto
hammer	martello	martelo
hand	mano (f) –i	mano manee
handbag	borsa	borsa
handcream	crema per le mani	krema per le manee
handkerchief	fazzoletto	fatsoleto
handle (eg of a case)	manico –ci	maneeko maneechee
hand luggage	bagaglio a mano	bagalyo a mano
handmade	fatto a mano	fato a mano
hang	appendere – appeso	apendere – apezo
hang gliding	deltaplano	deltaplano
happy	felice (m & f)	feleeche
harbour	porto	porto
h. master	capitano di p.	kapeetano dee porto
hard (=difficult)	difficile (m & f)	deefeecheele
hard (=not soft)	duro	dooro
hare	lepre (f)	lepre
harpoon gun	fiocina	fyocheena
harvest	raccolto	rakolto
hat	cappello	kapelo
hate (vb)	odiare	odyare
have	avere – avuto	avere – avooto
h. a rest	riposarmi	reepozarmee
h. fun	divertirmi	deeverteermee
hay fever	febbre (f) del fieno	febre del fyeno
he	lui	looee
head (part of body)	testa	testa
headache	mal (m) di t.	mal dee testa
headphones	cuffie (fpl)	koofye
a pair of h.	un paio di c.	oon payo dee koofye
headwaiter	capo camariere (m)	kapo kameryere

health	salute (f)	saloote
health certificate	certificato di salute	cherteefeeeekato dee saloote
healthy	sano	sano
hear	udire	oodeere
hearing aid	apparecchio acustico –chi acustichi	apaʀekyo akoosteeko apaʀekee akoosteekee
heart	cuore (m)	kwoʀe
h. attack	infarto	eenfaʀto
h. trouble	malattia di c.	malateea dee kwoʀe
heat	caldo	kaldo
heat wave	ondata di caldo	ondata dee kaldo
heater	riscaldatore (m)	ʀeeskaldatoʀe
heating	riscaldamento	ʀeeskaldamento
heavy	pesante	pezante
heel (=part of body)	tacco –chi	tako takee
heel (=part of shoe)	tacco –chi	tako takee
high heeled	tacchi alti	takee altee
low heeled	tacchi bassi	takee bassee
height	altezza	altetsa
helicopter	elicottero	eleekoteʀo
help (n)	aiuto	ayooto
help (vb)	aiutare	ayootaʀe
helpful	servizievole (m & f)	serveetsyevole
henna	henné (m)	ene
herbs	erbe (fpl)	eʀbe
here	qui	kwee
hero	eroe (m)	eʀoe
heroine	eroina	eʀoeena
herring	aringa	aʀeenga
high	alto	alto
h. chair	sedia alta	sedya alta
h. water	alta marea	alta maʀea
hijack (n)	dirottamento (m)	deeʀotamento
hill	collina	koleena
hilly	collinoso	koleenoso
hip	anca	anka
hire (vb)	noleggiare	nolejaʀe
history	storia	stoʀya
hit (vb)	*colpire	kolpeeʀe
hitchhike	fare l'autostop – fatto l'autostop	faʀe laootostop – fato laootostop
hobby	hobby (m) –	obee
hockey	hockey (m)	okee
a game of h.	una partita a h.	oona paʀteeta a okee

hole	buco –chi	bōōko bōōkēē
holiday	vacanza	vakantsa
h. camp	campeggio –ggi di vacanze	kampejo dēē vakantse kampejēē dēē vakantse
package h.	v. organizzata	vakantsa organēētsata
public h.	festa	festa
hollow (adj)	vuoto	vwoto
home	casa	kaza
at h.	a c.	a kaza
go h.	andare a c.	andare a kaza
homemade	fatto in casa	fato ēēn kaza
honest	onesto	onesto
honey	miele (m)	myele
a jar of h.	un vaso di m.	ōōn vaso dēē myele
honeymoon	luna di miele	lōōna dēē myele
hood (of a garment)	cappuccio –ci	kapōōcho kapōōchēē
hook	gancio –ci	gancho ganchēē
hoover (tdmk)	hoover (m)	ōōveʀ
hope (vb)	sperare	speʀaʀe
I h. not	spero di no	speʀo dēē no
I h. so	spero di sì	speʀo dēē sēē
horrific	orrendo	oʀendo
hors d'oeuvres	antipasti (pl)	antēēpastēē
horse	cavallo	kavalo
h. racing	corse (fpl) di c.	koʀse dēē kavalo
hose (=tube)	canna per innaffiare	kana peʀ ēēnafyaʀe
hospital	ospedale (m)	ospedale
hospitality	ospitalità	ospēētalēēta
host	ospite (m & f)	ospēēte
hostel (=youth h.)	albergo per la gioventù	albeʀgo peʀ la joventōō
hostess	padrona di casa	padʀona dēē kaza
hot	caldo	kaldo
I'm h.	ho c.	o kaldo
it's h. (of things/food)	è c.	e kaldo
it's h. (of the weather)	fa c.	fa kaldo
hotel	albergo –ghi	albeʀgo albeʀgēē
cheap h.	a. economico	albeʀgo ekonomēēko

	words ending in –o or marked (m)	words ending in –a or marked (f)
the	il/l'/lo	la/l'
the (plural)	i/gl'/gli	le/l'

123

first class h.	a. di prima classe	albeʀgo dēē pʀēēma klase
medium-priced h.	a. non troppo costoso	albeʀgo non tʀopo kostozo
hot-water bottle	bottiglia di acqua calda	botēēlya dēē akwa kalda
hour	ora	oʀa
house	casa	kaza
housewife	massaia	masaya
hovercraft	hovercraft (m)	oveʀkʀaft
by h.	in h.	ēēn oveʀkʀaft
how?	come?	kome
humid	umido	ōōmēēdo
humour	umorismo	ōōmoʀēēzmo
sense of h.	senso di u.	senso dēē ōōmoʀēēzmo
hundred	cento	chento
hundreds of / /	centinaia di / /	chentēēnaya dēē / /
hungry		
be h.	avere fame – avuto fame	aveʀ fame – avōōto fame
I'm h.	ho fame	o fame
hunting	caccia	kachya
go h.	andare a cacciare	andaʀe a kachyaʀe
hurry	fretta	fʀeta
I'm in a h.	ho f.	o fʀeta
hurry (vb)	fare presto – fatto presto	faʀe pʀesto – fato pʀesto
please h.!	faccia presto per favore!	facha pʀesto peʀ favoʀe
hurt (adj)	offeso	ofezo
husband	marito	maʀēēto
hut	capanna	kapana
hydrofoil	idrogetto	ēēdʀojeto
by h.	in i.	ēēn ēēdʀojeto

I

ice	ghiaccio	gyacho
ice hockey	disco sul ghiaccio	dēēsko sōōl gyacho
a game of i. h.	una partita a d. sul g.	ōōna paʀtēēta a dēēsko sōōl gyacho

ice skating	pattinaggio sul ghiaccio	pateenajo sool gyacho
go i. s.	fare il p. sul g. – fatto il p. sul g	fare eel pateenajo sool gyacho – fato eel pateenajo sool gyacho
ice cream	gelato	jelato
iced (drink/water)	ghiacciato	gyachato
icy	gelido	jeleedo
idea	idea	eedea
ideal (adj)	ideale (m & f)	eedeale
identification	identificazione (f)	eedenteefeekatsyone
identify	identificare	eedenteefeekare
identity card	carta d'identità	karta deedenteeta
if	se	se
i. you can	s. può	se pwo
i. possible	s. possibile	se poseebeele
ill (=not well)	malato	malato
he's i.	è m.	e malato
illegal	illegale (m & f)	eelegale
illustration (in book)	illustrazione (f)	eeloostratsyone
immediate	immediato	eemedyato
immediately	subito	soobeeto
immigration	immigrazione (f)	eemeegratsyone
i. control	controllo i.	kontrolo eemeegratsyone
immune	immune (m & f)	eemoone
immunisation	immunizzazione (f)	eemooneedzatsyone
immunise	immunizzare	eemooneedzare
immunity	immunità	eemooneeta
diplomatic i.	i. diplomatica	eemooneeta deeplomateeka
impatient	impaziente (m & f)	eempatsyente
imperfect (goods)	diffettoso	deefetozo
important	importante (m & f)	eemportante
impossible	impossibile (m & f)	eemposeebeele
improve	migliorare	meelyorare
in	in	een
i. the morning	nella mattina	nela mateena
i. the park	nel parco	nel parko
i. summer	d'estate	destate
i. /July/	in /luglio/	een /loolyo/
be i. (adv)	essere in casa – stato in casa	esere een kaza – stato een kaza
in case of /fire/	in caso di /incendio/	een kazo dee /eenchendyo/

125

in front of	di fronte a/davanti a	dēē fʀonte a/ davantēē a
inch	pollice (m)	poleeche
include	comprendere – compreso	kompʀendere – kompʀezo
including	compreso	kompʀezo
incredible	incredibile (m & f)	ēēnkʀedeebēēle
independent	independente (m & f)	ēēndependente
indigestion	indigestione (f)	ēēndēējestyone
i. tablet	pastiglia per l'i.	pastēēlya peʀ leendēējestyone
individual (adj)	individuale (m & f)	ēēndeeveedwale
indoors	all'interno	aleenteʀno
indoor /swimming pool/	/piscina/ all'i.	/pēēsheena/ aleenteʀno
industry	industria	ēēndoostʀya
inefficient	inefficiente (m & f)	ēēnefeechente
inexperienced	inesperto	ēēnespeʀto
infected	infettato	ēēnfetato
infectious	contagioso	kontajoso
inflatable	gonfiabile (m & f)	gonfyabēēle
inflate	gonfiare	gonfyaʀe
inform	informare	ēēnfoʀmaʀe
i. /the police/ of / /	i. /la polizia/ di / /	ēēnfoʀmaʀe /la poleetsēēa/ dēē / /
informal	informale (m & f)	ēēnfoʀmale
information	informazione (f)	ēēnfoʀmatsyone
i. desk	ufficio d'informazioni	oofeecho deenfoʀmatsyonēē
i. office	ufficio d'informazioni	oofeecho deenfoʀmatsyonēē
initials	iniziali (mpl)	ēēneetsyalēē
injection	iniezione (f)	ēēnyetsyone
I'd like a /tetanus/ i.	vorrei un'i. contro /il tetano/	voʀey ōōn ēēnyetsyone kontʀo /eel tetano/
injury	danno	dano
ink	inchiostro	ēēnkyostʀo
a bottle of i.	una bottiglia di i.	ōōna botēēlya dēē ēēnkyostʀo

	words ending in –o or marked (m)	words ending in –a or marked (f)
a	un/uno	una/un'
some	del/dell'/dello	della/dell'
some (plural)	dei/degl'/degli	delle

innocent (=not guilty)	innocente (m & f)	ēēnochente
inoculate	inoculare	ēēnokōōlare
inoculation	inoculazione (f)	ēēnokōōlatsyone
inquiry	richiesta di informazione	rēēkyesta dēē ēēnformatsyone
make an i. about / /	richiedere informazioni sul / /	rēēkyedere ēēnformatsyonēē sōōl / /
insect	insetto	ēēnseto
i. bite	puntura d'i.	pōōntōōra dēēnseto
i. repellent	sprai (m) contro gli insetti	spray kontro ly ēēnsetēē
insecticide	insetticida	ēēnsetēēchēēda
a bottle of i.	una bottiglia di i.	ōōna botēēlya dēē ēēnsetēēchēēda
inside (adv)	dentro	dentro
inside (prep)	dentro a	dentro a
insomnia	insonnia	ēēnsonya
instead	invece	ēēnveche
i. of /coffee/	i. di /caffè/	ēēnveche dēē /kafe/
instructions	istruzioni (fpl)	ēēstrōōtsyonēē
i. for use	i. per uso	ēēstrōōtsyonēē per ōōzo
instrument	strumento	strōōmento
musical i.	s. musicale	strōōmento mōōzēēkale
insulin	insulina	ēēnsōōlēēna
insurance	assicurazione (f)	asēēkōōratsyone
i. certificate	certificato di a.	chertēēfēēkato dēē asēēkōōratsyone
i. policy	polizza di a.	polēētsa dēē asēēkōōratsyone
insure /my life/	assicurare /mia vita/	asēēkōōrare /mēēa vēēta/
intelligent	intelligente (m & f)	ēēntelēēējente
intensive	intensivo	ēēntensēēvo
intercontinental (flight)	intercontinentale	ēēnterkontēēnentale
interested in / /	appassionato di / /	apasyonato dēē / /
interesting	interessante (m & f)	ēēnteresante
internal	interno	ēēnterno
international	internazionale (m & f)	ēēnternatsyonale
interpret	interpretare	ēēnterpretare
interpreter	interprete (m & f)	ēēnterprete

127

interval (=break)	intervallo	ēēnterˈvalo
interval (in theatre)	pausa	paōōza
into	dentro	dentro
introduce	presentare	prezentare
introduction	presentazione (f)	prezentatsyone
letter of i.	lettera di p.	letera dēē prezentatsyone
invalid (n)	invalido	ēēnvaleēdo
invitation	invito	ēēnvēēto
invite	invitare	ēēnvēētare
iodine	iodio	yodyo
a bottle of i.	una bottiglia di i.	ōōna botēēlya dēē yodyo
iron (n) (object)	ferro a stiro	fero a stēēro
travelling i.	f. da viaggio	fero da vyajo
iron (vb) (clothing)	stirare	stēērare
ironmonger's	negozio di ferramento	negotsyo dēē feramento
irregular	irregolare (m & f)	ēēregolare
irritation (medical)	irritazione (f)	ēērēētatsyone
island	isola	ēēzola
itch	prurito	prōōrēēto

J

jacket	giacca –che	jaka jake
/tweed/ j.	g. /di tweed/	jaka /dēē twēēd/
jam	marmellata	marmelata
January	gennaio	jenayo
jar	vaso	vazo
a j. of /jam/	un v. di /marmellata/	ōōn vazo dēē /marmelata/
jaw	mascella	mashela
jazz	jazz (m)	jadz
jealous	geloso	jelozo
he's j. of /me/	è g. di /me/	e jelozo dēē /me/
jeans	jeans (mpl)	jēēnz
a pair of j.	un paio di j.	ōōn payo dēē jēēnz
jelly (see under flavour)	gelatina	jelatēēna
jellyfish	medusa	medōōza
Jew	ebreo	ebreo
jeweller's	gioielliere (m)	jyoyelyere
jewellery	gioielli (mpl)	jyoyelēē
jigsaw puzzle	puzzle (m)	pōōdzle
job	impiego	ēēmpyego
jockey	fantino	fantēēno

joke	barzelletta	ba<u>r</u>dzeleta
journey	viaggio –ggi	vyajo vyaj<u>ee</u>
judo	judo	j<u>oo</u>do
do some j.	fare un po' di j. – fatto un po' di j.	fa<u>r</u>e <u>oo</u>n po d<u>ee</u> j<u>oo</u>do – fato <u>oo</u>n po d<u>ee</u> j<u>oo</u>do
jug	brocca	b<u>r</u>oka
a j. of / /	una b. di / /	<u>oo</u>na b<u>r</u>oka d<u>ee</u> / /
juice	succo	s<u>oo</u>ko
grapefruit j.	s. di pompelmo	s<u>oo</u>ko d<u>ee</u> pompelmo
lemon j.	s. di limone	s<u>oo</u>ko d<u>ee</u> l<u>ee</u>mone
orange j.	s. di arancio	s<u>oo</u>ko d<u>ee</u> a<u>r</u>ancho
pineapple j.	s. di ananas	s<u>oo</u>ko d<u>ee</u> ananas
tomato j.	s. di pomodoro	s<u>oo</u>ko d<u>ee</u> pomod<u>or</u>o
juicy	succoso	s<u>oo</u>kozo
July	luglio	l<u>oo</u>lyo
jump (vb)	saltare	salta<u>r</u>e
junction	incrocio –ci	<u>ee</u>nk<u>r</u>ochyo <u>ee</u>nk<u>r</u>och<u>ee</u>
June	giugno	j<u>oo</u>nyo
junk shop	negozio di articoli di seconda mano	negotsyo d<u>ee</u> a<u>r</u>t<u>ee</u>kol<u>ee</u> d<u>ee</u> sekonda mano

K

keep (vb)	tenere	tene<u>r</u>e
kettle	bricco	b<u>r</u><u>ee</u>ko
key	chiave (f)	kyave
key ring	portachiavi (m)	po<u>r</u>takyav<u>ee</u>
khaki (colour)	cacchi (inv)	kak<u>ee</u>
kick (vb)	dare un calcio – dato un calcio	da<u>r</u>e <u>oo</u>n kalcho – dato <u>oo</u>n kalcho
kidneys	reni (mpl)	<u>r</u>en<u>ee</u>
kill (vb)	uccidere – ucciso	<u>oo</u>ch<u>ee</u>de<u>r</u>e – <u>oo</u>ch<u>ee</u>zo
kilogramme/kilo	chilogramma (m)/chilo	k<u>ee</u>log<u>r</u>ama/k<u>ee</u>lo
kilometre	chilometro	k<u>ee</u>lomet<u>r</u>o

	words ending in –o or marked (m)	words ending in –a or marked (f)
the	il/l'/lo	la/l'
the (plural)	i/gl'/gli	le/l'

KIND

kind (adj) (=friendly)	gentile	jent__ee__le
it's very k. of you	è g. da parte sua	e jent__ee__le da **parte** s__oo__a
kind (n) (=type)	tipo	t__ee__po
a k. of /beer/	un t. di /birra/	__oo__n t__ee__po d__ee__ /b__ee__Ra/
kindness	gentilezza	jent__ee__letsa
king	re (m) –	Re
kiss (n)	bacio –ci	bacho bach__ee__
kiss (vb)	baciare	bach__are__
kit	equippagiamento	ekw__ee__pajamento
first aid k.	e. di pronto soccorso	ekw__ee__pajamento d__ee__ **pronto** so**korso**
kitchen	cucina	k__oo__ch__ee__na
kite	aquilone (m)	akw__ee__lone
Kleenex (tissues) (tdmk)	fazzoletti (mpl) di carta	fatsolet__ee__ d__ee__ **karta**
a box of K.	una scatola di f. di c.	__oo__na **skatola** d__ee__ fatsolet__ee__ d__ee__ **karta**
knee	ginocchio –chia	j__ee__nokyo j__ee__nokya
knife	coltello	koltelo
carving k.	c. per tagliare la carne	koltelo peR talyaRe la **karne**
knit	lavorare a maglia	lavoraRe a **malya**
knitting	lavoro a maglia	lavoRo a **malya**
do some k.	lavorare a maglia	lavoraRe a **malya**
k. needles	aghi (mpl) da maglia	ag__ee__ da **malya**
k. pattern	campione (m) di l. a m.	kampyone d__ee__ lavoRo a **malya**
knitwear	maglieria	malyeR__ee__a
knob (door)	pomo	**pomo**
knob (radio)	manopola	manopola
know (a fact)	sapere	sapeRe
I k.	lo so	lo so
know (a person)	conoscere – conosciuto	konosheRe – konoshy__oo__to
I k. him	lo conosco	lo konosko
Kosher	Kosher	**kosher**

L

label (=luggage l.)	etichetta	et__ee__keta
stick-on l.	e. da incollare	et__ee__keta da __ee__nkolaRe

130

lace (=material)	pizzo	pēetso
laces	lacci (mpl)	lachee
ladder	scala	skala
Ladies' (=lavatory)	gabinetto per le donne	gabēeneto peʀ le done
lady	signora	seenyoʀa
lake	lago –ghi	lago lagee
lamb	agnello	anyelo
a leg of l.	una coscia di a.	ōona kosha dee anyelo
l. chop	costoletta di a.	kostoleta dee anyelo
lamp	lampada	lampada
bicycle l.	lampadina di bicicletta	lampadeena dee beecheekleta
lampshade	paralume (m)	paʀalōome
land	terra	teʀa
landed (of a plane)	atterrato	ateʀato
landlady	padrona di casa	padʀona dee kaza
landlord	padrone (m) di casa	padʀone dee kaza
lane (=small road)	vicolo	veekolo
lane (=traffic l.)	corsia	koʀseea
language	lingua	leengwa
large (size)	grande (m & f)	gʀande
last (= final)	ultimo	ōolteemo
late	in ritardo	een ʀeetaʀdo
he's l.	lui è in r.	looee e een ʀeetaʀdo
it's l. (= time of day)	è tardi	e taʀdee
later (= at a later time)	più tardi	pyōo taʀdee
laugh (vb)	ridere – riso	ʀeedeʀe – ʀeeso
launder	lavare e stirare	lavaʀe e steeʀaʀe
launderette	lavanderia self-service	lavandeʀeea self-servees
laundry (place)	lavanderia	lavandeʀeea
laundry (washing)	biancheria	byankeʀeea
lavatory	gabinetto	gabēeneto
Gent's	g. per gli uomini	gabēeneto peʀ ly womēenee
Ladies'	g. per le donne	gabēeneto peʀ le done
law	legge (f)	leje
lawyer	avvocato	avokato
laxative	lassativo	lasatēevo
mild l.	l. debole	lasatēevo debole
strong l.	l. forte	lasatēevo foʀte

suppository	supposta	sōoposta
lay-by	piazzuola	pyatswola
lazy	pigro	pēēgʀo
leaflet	opuscolo	opōoskolo
leak (n)	perdita	peʀdēēta
leak (vb)	spandere	spandeʀe
it's leaking	spande	spande
learner (driver)	uno che impara a guidare	ōono ke ēēmpaʀa a gwēēdaʀe
learn /Italian/	imparare /l'italiano/	ēēmpaʀaʀe /lēētalyano/
leather	pelle (f)	pele
l. goods shop	negozio di articoli di p.	negotsyo dēē aʀtēēkolēē dēē pele
leave	lasciare	lashaʀe
l. /my luggage/	l. /le mie valigie/	lashaʀe /le mēēe valēēje/
l. me alone	mi lasci stare	mēē lashēē staʀe
I've left /my suitcase/ behind	ho dimenticato /la mia valigia/	o dēēmentēēkato /la mēēa valēēja/
leave (=depart)	partire	paʀtēēre
l. /at 4.30 p.m./	p. /alle 4.30/	paʀtēēre /ale kwatʀo e medzo/
l. in /July/	p. in /luglio/	paʀtēēre ēēn /lōolyo/
l. on /Monday/	p. /lunedì/	paʀtēēre /lōonedēē/
left (= not right)	sinistra	sēēnēēstra
left-handed	mancino	manchēēno
left-luggage office	deposito bagagli	depozēēto bagaly
leg	gamba	gamba
legal	legale (m & f)	legale
lemon	limone (m)	lēēmone
a slice of l.	una fetta di l.	ōona feta dēē lēēmone
l. juice	succo di l.	sōoko dēē lēēmone
lemonade	limonata	lēēmonata
a bottle of l.	una bottiglia di l.	ōona botēēlya dēē lēēmonata
a can of l.	un barattolo di l.	ōon baʀatolo dēē lēēmonata

	words ending in –o or marked (m)	words ending in –a or marked (f)
a	un/uno	una/un'
some	del/dell'/dello	della/dell'
some (plural)	dei/degl'/degli	delle

English	Italian	Pronunciation
a glass of l.	un bicchiere di l.	ōon beekyere dee leemonata
lend	prestare	prestare
could you l. me some /money/?	mi potrebbe p. un po' di /soldi/?	mee potrebe prestare ōon po dee /soldee/
length	lunghezza	lōongetsa
full l.	lungo	lōongo
knee l.	a ginocchio	a jeenokyo
lengthen	allungare	alōongare
lens (of camera)	lente (f)	lente
l. cap	coperchino l.	koperkeeno lente
wide-angle l.	obiettivo grandangolare	obyeteevo grandangolare
zoom l.	l. zoom	lente dsoom
less	meno	lente dzōom
lesson	lezione (f)	letsyone
driving l.	l. di guida	letsyone dee gweeda
/Italian/ l.	l. /d'italiano/	letsyone /deetalyano/
let (=allow)	lasciare	lashare
let /me/ try	/mi/ lasci provare	/mee/ lashee provare
letter (correspondence)	lettera	letera
air-l.	l. aerea	letera aerea
express l.	l. espresso	letera espreso
l. box	cassetta delle lettere	kaseta dele letere
registered l.	l. raccomandata	letera rakomandata
letter (= of the alphabet)	lettera	letera
lettuce	insalata	eensalata
level (adj)	piano	pyano
level (n) (=grade)	livello	leevelo
level crossing	passaggio a livello	pasajo a leevelo
library	biblioteca –che	beeblyoteka beeblyoteke
licence	permesso	permeso
lid (of eye)	palpebra	palpebra
lid (of pot)	coperchio	koperkyo
lie (n) (=untruth)	bugia	boojeea
lie (vb) (=l. down)	sdraiarmi	zdrayarmee
lie (vb) (=tell an untruth)	dire una bugia – detto una bugia	deere ōona boojeea – deto ōona boojeea

lifebelt	cintura di sicurezza	chēēntōōra dēē sēēkōōretsa
lifeboat	scialuppa di salvataggio	shalōōpa dēē salvatajo
lifeguard	guardia di salvataggio	gwaʀdya dēē salvatajo
life jacket	cintura di salvataggio	chēēntōōra dēē salvatajo
lift (n) (= elevator)	ascensore (m)	ashensoʀe
lift (n) (=ride)	passaggio	pasajo
could you give me a l. to / /?	mi potrebbe dar un passaggio a / /?	mēē potʀebe daʀ ōōn pasajo a / /
lift (vb)	alzare	altsaʀe
light switch	interruttore (m)	ēēnteʀōōtoʀe
light (adj) (= not dark)	luminoso	lōōmēēnozo
light (adj) (= not heavy)	leggero	lejeʀo
light (n) (electric l.)	luce (f)	lōōche
can I have a l.?	mi accende la sigaretta?	mēē achende la sēēgaʀeta
light /a fire/	accendere /un fuoco/ – acceso /un fuoco/	achendeʀe /ōōn fwoko/ – achezo /ōōn fwoko/
light bulb	lampadina	lampadēēna
/40/ watt	/quaranta/ watt	/kwaʀanta/ vat
lighter (=cigarette l.)	accendino	achendēēno
disposable l.	a. da buttare	achendēēno da bōōtaʀe
lighter fuel	gas per accendini	gaz peʀ achendēēnēē
like (prep)	come	kome
what's it l.?	com'è?	kome
like (vb)	piacere	pyacheʀe
do you l. /swimming/?	le piace /nuotare/?	le pyache /nwotaʀe/
I l. it	mi piace	mēē pyache
likely	probabile	pʀobabēēle
lime	limetta	lēēmeta
l. juice	succo di l.	sōōko dēē lēēmeta
limit (n)	limite (m)	lēēmēēte
height l.	l. de altezza	lēēmēēte dēē altetsa
speed l.	l. de velocità	lēēmēēte dēē velochēēta
weight l.	l. di peso	lēēmēēte dēē pezo

134

line	linea	lēēnea
outside l.	l. esterna	lēēnea esterna
telephone l.	l. telefonica	lēēnea telefonēēka
linen	biancheria	byankerēēa
liner	transatlantico	transatlantēēko
lingerie department	reparto maglieria femminile	reparto malyerēēa femēēneele
lining	fodera	fodera
/fur/ l.	f. di /pelo/	fodera dēē /pelo/
lip	labbro (m) labbra (fpl)	labro labra
lower l.	l. inferiore	labro ēēnferyore
upper l.	l. superiore	labro soōperyore
lipstick	rosetto	rozeto
liqueur	liquore (m)	lēēkwore
liquid	liquido	lēēkwēēdo
list	elenco –chi	elenko elenkēē
shopping l.	lista per le spese	lēēsta per le speze
wine l.	lista di vini	lēēsta dēē vēēnēē
listen to /some music/	ascoltare /un po' di musica/	askoltare /oōn po dēē moōzeēēka/
litre	litro	lēētro
litter	rifiuti (mpl)	rēēfyoōtēē
little (adj)	piccolo	pēēkolo
a l. boy	un bambino p.	oōn bambēēno pēēkolo
smaller	più p.	pyoō pēēkolo
smallest	il più p.	eēl pyoō pēēkolo
little (n)	po'	po
a l. money	un po' di soldi	oōn po dēē soldēē
live (= be alive)	vivere	vēēvere
live (=reside)	abitare	abēētare
liver	fegato	fegato
load	caricare	karēēkare
loaf (of bread)	pagnotta	panyota
a large l.	una p. grande	oōna panyota grande
a small l.	una p. piccola	oōna panyota pēēkola
lobster	aragosta	aragosta
local (adj)	locale	lokale
l. crafts	artigianato (ms) regionale	artēējēēnato rejonale

	words ending in –o or marked (m)	words ending in –a or marked (f)
the	il/l'/lo	la/l'
the (plural)	i/gl'/gli	le/l'

lock (n)	serratura	seraTOOra
lock (vb)	chiudere a chiave – chiuso a chiave	kyOOdere a kyave – kyOOzo a kyave
locker	armadietto	aRmadYeto
left-luggage l.	a. deposito	aRmadYeto depozEEto
logbook (car)	libretto	leEbReto
lonely	solitario –ri	soleEtaRyo soleEtaREE
long	lungo	lOOngo
look after /the baby/	badare /al bambino/	badaRe /al bambEEno/
look at /this/	guardare /questo/	gwaRdEE /kwesto/
look for /my passport/	cercare /il mio passaporto/	cheRkaRe /eEl mEEo pasapoRto/
look /smart/	essere /elegante/ – stato /elegante/	eseRe /elegante/ – stato /elegante/
lorry	camion (m) –	kamyon
lorry driver	camionista (m) –isti	kamyonEEsta kamyonEEstEE
lose	perdere – perso	peRdere – peRso
I've lost /my wallet/	ho perso /il mio portafoglio/	o peRso /eEl mEEo poRtafolyo/
lost	perso	peRso
I'm l.	sono p.	sono peRso
lost property office	ufficio –ci oggetti smarriti	oofeEcho ojetEE zmaREEtEE oofeEchEE ojetEE zmaREEtEE
lot	molto	molto
a l. of money	molti soldi	moltEE soldEE
loud	forte (m & f)	foRte
loudly	fortemente	foRtemente
lounge (in hotel)	sala	sala
departure l.	s. di partenza	sala dEE paRtentsa
TV l.	s. di televisione	sala dEE televeEzyone
love (n)	amore (m)	amoRe
make l.	fare l'a. – fatto l'a.	faRe lamoRe – fato lamoRe
love (vb)	amare	amaRe
low (=not high)	basso	baso
l. water	bassa marea	basa maRea
low (=not loud)	basso	baso
lower (vb)	abbassare	abasaRe
LP (=long playing record)	long playing (m)	long playing

lucky	fortunato	fortoonato
be l.	essere f.	esere fortoonato
he's l.	è fortunato	e fortoonato
luggage	bagaglio –gli	bagalyo bagaly
cabin l.	b. in cabina	bagalyo een kabeena
hand l.	b. a mano	bagalyo a mano
l. rack (in train)	portabagagli (m)	portabagaly
l. van (on train)	bagagliaio	bagalyayo
lump (body)	gonfiore (m)	gonfyore
a l. of sugar	una zolletta di zucchero	oona tsoleta dee tsookero
lunch	colazione (f)	kolatsyone
have l.	fare c. – fatto c.	fare kolatsyone – fato kolatsyone
packed l.	c. a sacco	kolatsyone a sako
luxury	lusso	looso

M

machine	macchina	makeena
mad	matto	mato
made in / /	fatto in / /	fato een / /
magazine	rivista	reeveesta
magnifying glass	lente (f) d'ingrandimento	lente deengrandeemento
mahogany (wood)	mogano	mogano
maid	cameriera	kameryera
m. service	servizio di c.	serveetsyo dee kameryera
mail	posta	posta
by air-m.	p. aerea	posta aerea
express m.	p. espressa	posta espresa
send it by / / m.	spedirlo per p. / /	spedeerlo per posta / /
surface m.	p. normale	posta normale
main	principale (m & f)	preencheepale
m. road	strada p.	strada preencheepale
make (n) (eg of a car)	marca –che	marka marke
make (vb)	fare – fatto	fare – fato
m. /a complaint/	protestare	protestare
m. /money/	fare /soldi/	fare /soldee/

make-up (= face m.-u.)	trucco	trōoko
eye m.-u.	t. per gli occhi	trōoko peʀ ly okēē
male (adj)	maschile	maskēēle
mallet	martello di legno	maʀtelo dēē lenyo
man	uomo –mini	womo womēēnēē
young m.	giovanotto	jovanoto
manager	direttore (m)	dēēʀetore
manicure	manicure (f)	manēēkōōʀe
m. set	necessaire per m.	nechesayʀe peʀ manēēkōōʀe
man-made (adj)	artificiale (m & f)	aʀtēēfēēchale
m.-m. fibre	fibra a.	fēēbʀa aʀtēēfēēchale
many	molti (mpl) –te (fpl)	moltēē molte
map	mappa	mapa
large-scale m.	m. dettagliata	mapa detalyata
m. of /Italy/	m. /d'Italia/	mapa /dēētalya/
road m.	carta automobilistica	kaʀta aōotomobeeleestēēka
street m.	carta stradale	kaʀta stʀadale
marble (material)	marmo	maʀmo
March	marzo	maʀtso
margarine	margarina	maʀgaʀēēna
mark (=spot/stain)	macchia	makya
market	mercato	meʀkato
fish m.	m. di pesce	meʀkato dēē peshe
fruit & vegetable m.	m. di frutta e verdura	meʀkato dēē frōota e veʀdōōra
m. place	piazza del m.	pyatsa del meʀkato
meat m.	m. della carne	meʀkato dela kaʀne
marmalade	marmellata di arancio	maʀmelata dēē aʀancho
a jar of m.	un vaso di m. di a.	ōon vazo dēē maʀmelata dēē aʀancho
maroon (colour)	castano	kastano
married	sposato	spozato
mascara (for eyelashes)	rimel (m)	ʀēēmel
masculine	maschile	maskēēle

	words ending in –o or marked (m)	words ending in –a or marked (f)
a	un/uno	una/un'
some	del/dell'/dello	della/dell'
some (plural)	dei/degl'/degli	delle

mask	maschera	maskeʀa
snorkel m.	snorkel (m)	znoʀkel
mass (=Catholic service)	messa	mesa
massage	massaggio –ggi	masajo masajēē
mast	albero	albeʀo
mat	stuoia	stwoya
bath m.	s. da bagno	stwoya da banyo
door m.	zerbino	tseʀbēēno
match	fiammifero	fyamēēfeʀo
a box of matches	una scatola di fiammiferi	ōōna skatola dēē fyamēēfeʀēē
wax matches	cerini (mpl)	cheʀēēnēē
match (=competition)	partita	paʀtēēta
football m.	p. di calcio	paʀtēēta dēē kalcho
material (=cloth)	stoffa	stofa
checked m.	s. a. quadretti	stofa a kwadʀetēē
heavy m.	s. pesante	stofa pezante
lightweight m.	s. leggera	stofa lejeʀa
plain m.	s. a tinta unita	stofa a tēēnta ōōnēēta
mattress	materasso	mateʀaso
mauve	malva (m, f & pl)	malva
maximum (adj)	massimo	masēēmo
May	maggio	majo
may	potere	poteʀe
mayonnaise	maionese (m)	mayoneze
me	me	me
meal	pasto	pasto
light m.	p. leggiero	pasto lejeʀo
mean (=not generous)	avaro	avaʀo
mean (vb) (of a word)	voler dire	voleʀ dēēʀe
what does it m.?	che cosa vuol dire?	ke koza vwol dēēʀe
measles	morbillo (s)	moʀbēēlo
measure (vb)	misurare	mēēzōōʀaʀe
meat	carne (f)	kaʀne
cold m.	c. fredda	kaʀne fʀeda
beef	manzo	mandzo
lamb	agnello	anyelo
mutton	castrato	kastʀato
pork	maiale	mayale
mechanic	meccanico	mekanēēko
mechanism	meccanismo	mekanēēzmo
medical	medico	medēēko

139

English	Italian	Pronunciation
medicine	medicina	medeēcheēna
a bottle of m.	una bottiglia di m.	ōōna boteēlya dee medeēcheēna
medium (size)	medio	medyo
m.-dry (of sweetness)	mezzo seco	medzo seko
m.-rare (eg of steak)	poco cotto	poko koto
m.-sweet (of sweetness)	amabile	amabeēle
meet /your family/	incontrare /la sua famiglia/	eēnkontraʀe /la sōōa fameēlya/
meeting (business)	riunione (f)	ʀyōōnyone
melon	melone (m)	
half a m.	mezzo m.	medzo melone
a slice of m.	una fetta di m.	ōōna feta deē melone
member (of a group)	membro	membʀo
memory	memoria	memoʀya
a good/bad m.	una buona/cattiva m.	ōōna bwona/kateēva memoʀya
happy memories	bel ricordo (ms)	bel ʀeēkoʀdo
mend	aggiustare	ajōōstaʀe
men's outfitter's	negozio di vestiti da uomo	negotsyo deē vesteētee da womo
menu	menu (m)	menōō
à la carte m.	m. alla carta	menōō a la kaʀta
set m.	m. fisso	menōō feēso
mess	confusione (f)	konfōōzyone
message	messaggio –ggi	mesajo mesajeē
metal	metallo	metalo
meter	contatore (m)	kontatoʀe
electricity m.	c. dell'eletricittà	kontatoʀe deleletʀeēcheēta
gas m.	c. del gas	kontatoʀe del gaz
method	metodo	metodo
methylated spirit	alcool (m) denaturato	alko-ol denatōōʀato
a bottle of m. s.	una bottiglia di a. d.	ōōna boteēlya deē alko-ol denatōōʀato
metre (=length)	metro	metʀo
microphone	microfono	meēkʀofono
midday	mezzogiorno	medzojoʀno
middle	mezzo	medzo
in the m. of / /	nel m. di / /	nel medzo deē / /

middle-aged	di mezz'età	dēē medzeta
midnight	mezzanotte	medzanote
migraine	emicrania	emēēkranya
mild (of antibiotic)	leggiero	lejeʀo
mild (of tobacco)	leggiero	lejeʀo
mild (of weather)	mite	mēēte
mile	miglio	mēēlyo
milk	latte (m)	late
a bottle of m.	una bottiglia di l.	ōōna botēēlya dēē late
a glass of m.	un bicchiere di l.	ōōn bēēkyeʀe dēē late
powdered m.	l. in polvere	late ēēn polveʀe
tinned m.	l. in scatola	late ēēn skatola
milk shake (see under flavour)	frullato di latte	fʀōōlato dēē late
million	milione (m)	mēēlyone
millions of / /	milioni di / /	mēēlyonēē dēē / /
mince (vb)	macinare	machēēnaʀe
minced meat	carne macinata	kaʀne machēēnata
mine (n)	miniera	mēēnyeʀa
coal m.	m. di carbone	mēēnyeʀa dēē kaʀbone
miner	minatore (m)	mēēnatoʀe
mineral water	acqua minerale	akwa mēēneʀale
a bottle of m. w.	una bottiglia di a. m.	ōōna botēēlya dēē akwa mēēneʀale
a glass of m. w.	un bicchiere di a. m.	ōōn bēēkyeʀe dēē akwa mēēneʀale
fizzy m. w.	a. m. gassata	akwa mēēneʀale gasata
plain m. w.	a. m. naturale	akwa mēēneʀale natōōrale
minibus	minibus (m)	mēēneēbōōs
minimum (adj)	minimo	mēēnēēmo
mink	visone (m)	vēēzone
m. coat	pellicia di v.	pelēēcha dēē vēēzone
minus	meno	meno
minute (time)	minuto	mēēnōōto
mirror	specchio –chi	spekyo spekēē
hand-m.	s. a mano	spekyo a mano
Miss / /	Signorina / /	sēēnyoʀēēna / /

	words ending in −o or marked (m)	words ending in −a or marked (f)
the	il/l'/lo	la/l'
the (plural)	i/gl'/gli	le/l'

miss /the train/	perdere /il treno/ – perso /il treno/	pɛʀdeʀe /ēēl tʀeno/ – pɛʀzo /ēēl tʀeno/
mist	foschia	foskya
mistake (n)	sbaglio –gli	zbalyo zbaly
mix (vb)	mescolare	meskolaʀe
mixer (of food)	frullatore (m)	fʀōōlatoʀe
mixture	miscuglio –gli	mēēskōōlyo mēēskōōly
model (object)	modello	modelo
latest m.	ultimo m.	ōōltēēmo modelo
m. /aeroplane/	/aeroplano/ m.	/aeʀoplano/ modelo
model (profession)	modella	modela
modern	moderno	modeʀno
moment	momento	momento
Monday	lunedì (m)	lōōnedēē
on Monday	l.	lōōnedēē
on Mondays	di l.	dēē lōōnedēē
money	soldi (mpl)	soldēē
make m.	fare s.	faʀe soldēē
mono (adj)	mono	mono
month	mese (m)	meze
last m.	il m. scorso	ēēl meze skoʀso
next m.	il m. prossimo	ēēl meze pʀosēēmo
this m.	questo m.	kwesto meze
monthly	mensilmente	mensēēlmente
monument	monumento	monōōmento
mood	umore (m)	ōōmoʀe
in a good/bad m.	di buono/cattivo u.	dēē bwono/katēēvo ōōmoʀe
moon	luna	lōōna
mop (n)	scopa	skopa
moped	micromotore (m)	mēēkʀomotoʀe
more	più	pyōō
m. /cake/ please	ancora /del dolce/ per favore	ankoʀa /del dolche/ peʀ favoʀe
morning	mattina	matēēna
this m.	questa m.	kwesta matēēna
tomorrow m.	domani m.	domanēē matēēna
yesterday m.	ieri m.	yeʀēē matēēna
mortgage (n)	ipoteca –che	ēēpoteka ēēpoteke
mosque	moschea	moshea
mosquito	zanzara	dzandzaʀa
m. net	zanzariera	dzandzaʀyeʀa

142

most	la maggior parte	la majoʀ paʀte
m. /money/	la m. p. /dei soldi/	la majoʀ paʀte /dey soldēē/
m. /people/	la m. p. /della gente/	la majoʀ paʀte /dela jente/
motel	motel (m)	motel
mother	madre (f)	madʀe
mother-in-law	suocera	swocheʀa
motor	motore (m)	motoʀe
outboard m.	fuoribordo	fwoʀēēbordo
motor racing	corse (fpl) di macchina	koʀse dēē makēēna
go m. r.	fare le c. di m.	faʀe le koʀse dēē makēēna
motorail (ie car on a train)	treno-macchine (m)	tʀeno-makēēne
motorbike	motocicletta	motochēēkleta
motorboat	motoscafo	motoskafo
motorist	autista (m & f) –i	aōōtēēsta aōōtēēstēē
motorway	autostrada	aōōtostrada
mouldy	ammuffito	amōōfēēto
mountain	montagna	montanya
mountaineer	alpinista (m) –sti	alpēēnēēsta alpēēnēēstēē
mountaineering	alpinismo	alpēēnēēzmo
go m.	fare l'a.	faʀe lalpēēnēēzmo
mountainous	montuoso	montwozo
mouse	topo	topo
mousetrap	trappola per topi	tʀapola peʀ topēē
moustache	baffi (mpl)	bafēē
mouth	bocca –che	boka boke
mouthwash	sciacquo per la boca	shyakwo peʀ la boka
a bottle of m.	una bottiglia di s. per la b.	ōōna botēēlya dēē shyakwo peʀ la boka
move (vb)	muovere –mosso	mwoveʀe – moso
movement	movimento	movēēmento
Mr / /	Signor / /	sēēnyoʀ / /
Mrs / /	Signora / /	sēēnyoʀa / /
much	molto	molto
mud	fango	fango
muddy	fangoso	fangozo
mug	boccale (m)	bokale
mumps	orecchioni (mpl)	oʀekyonēē
murder (n)	assassinio	asasēēnyo
murder (vb)	assassinare	asasēēnaʀe
muscle	muscolo	mōōskolo
museum	museo	mōōzeo

143

mushrooms	funghi (mpl)	fōōngee
mushroom /soup/	/zuppa/ di f.	/tsōōpa/ dee fōōngee
music	musica	mōōzeeka
classical m.	m. classica	mōōzeeka klaseeka
folk m.	m. folk	mōōzeeka folk
light m.	m. leggera	mōōzeeka lejeRa
pop m.	m. pop	mōōzeeka pop
musical (=an entertainment)	musicale (m)	mōōzeekale
musician	musicista (m) –sti	mōōzeecheesta mōōzeecheestee
Muslim	mussola (m) mussolina (f)	mōōsola mōōsoleena
mussels	cozze (fpl)	kotse
must	dovere	doveRe
mustard	senape (m)	senape

N

nail (finger/toe)	unghia	ōōngya
nailbrush	spazzolino per le unghie	spatsoleeno peR le ōōngye
n. file	lima per le unghie	leema peR le ōōngye
n. scissors	forbicine per le unghie	foRbeecheene peR le ōōngye
n. varnish	smalto per le unghie	zmalto peR le ōōngye
nail (metal)	chiodo	kyodo
naked	nudo	nōōdo
name	nome (m)	nome
first n.	n.	nome
surname	cognome (m)	konyome
napkin	tovagliolo	tovalyolo
n. ring	anello per t.	anelo peR tovolyolo
paper n.	t. di carta	tovalyolo dee kaRta
nappy	pannolina	panoleena
disposable nappies	pannoline a buttar via	panoleene da bōōtaR veea
narrow	stretto	stReto
nasty (infml)	brutto	bRōōto

	words ending in –o or marked (m)	words ending in –a or marked (f)
a	un/uno	una/un'
some	del/dell'/dello	della/dell'
some (plural)	dei/degl'/degli	delle

nation	nazione (f)	natsyone
national	nazionale (m & f)	natsyonale
nationality	nazionalità	natsyonaleeta
natural	naturale	natoorale
nature	natura	natoora
naughty (usually of young children)	cattivo	kateevo
nausea	nausea	naoozea
navigate	navigare	naveegare
navy	marina	mareena
near (adv)	vicino	veecheeno
near (prep) /the station/	vicino /alla stazione/	veecheeno /ala statsyone/
neat (of a drink)	liscio	leeshyo
necessary	necessario –ri	nechesaryo nechesaree
necessity	necessità –	necheseeta
neck	collo	kolo
necklace	collana	kolana
née	nata	nata
need (vb)	aver bisogno di – avuto bisogno di	aver beezonyo dee – avooto beezonyo dee
I n. /more money/	ho b. di /più soldi/	o beezonyo dee /pyoo soldee/
needle	ago –ghi	ago agee
knitting needles	aghi da maglia	agee da malya
negative (=film n.)	negativo	negateevo
nephew	nipote (m)	neepote
nervous (=apprehensive)	apprensivo	aprenseevo
nervous breakdown	esaurimento nervoso	ezaooreemento nervozo
Nescafe (tdmk)	nescaffè (m)	neskafe
net (=fishing n.)	rete (f)	rete
hair net	retina per capelli	reteena per kapelee
net weight	peso netto	pezo neto
never	mai	maee
new (of things)	nuovo	nwovo
news	notizie (fpl)	noteetsye
newsagent's	giornalaio	jornalayo
newspaper	giornale (m)	jornale
/English/ n.	g. /inglese/	jornale /eengleze/
evening p.	g. della sera	jornale dela sera
local n.	g. locale	jornale lokale
morning p.	quotidiano	kwoteedyano
next	prossimo	proseemo

145

next door	vicino	veecheeno
n. d. /to the station/	v. /alla stazione/	veecheeno /ala statsyone/
the house n. d.	la casa vicina	la kaza veecheena
next of kin	parente (m) prossimo	parente proseemo
next to / /	vicino a / /	veecheeno a / /
nib (of pen)	pennino	peneeno
nice	bello	belo
niece	nipote (f)	neepote
night	notte (f)	note
last n.	la n. scorsa	la note skorsa
tomorrow n.	domani n.	domanee note
tonight	stanotte	stanote
nightclub	night (m)	nayt
nightdress	camicia da notte	kameecha da note
night life	vita notturna	veeta notoorna
no money	nessun denaro	nesoon denaro
no one	nessuno	nesoono
noisy	rumoroso	roomorozo
nonsense	sciocchezze (fpl)	shyoketse
nonstick	non attacca	non ataka
n. /frying-pan/	/padella/ che n. a.	/padela/ ke non ataka
nonstop	senza fermate	sentsa fermate
normal	normale (m & f)	normale
north	nord (m)	nord
northeast	nordest (m)	nordest
northwest	nordovest (m)	nordovest
nose	naso	nazo
nosebleed	sangue (m) al naso	sangwe al nazo
not	non	non
note (=money)	biglietto	beelyeto
/10,000/ lire n.	b. a /10,000/ lire	beelyeto a /dyechemeela/ leere
note (written)	bigliettino	beelyeteeno
notebook	agenda	ajenda
nothing	niente	nyente
notice	avviso	aveezo
n. board	cartello per gli avvisi	kartelo per ly aveezee
November	novembre (m)	novembre
now	adesso	adeso
nowhere	da nessuna parte	da nesoona parte
nude	nudo	noodo
n. show	spettacolo di nudi	spetakolo dee noodee

number	numero	nōōmero
n. /7/	n. /sette/	nōōmero /sete/
telephone n.	n. telefonico	nōōmero telefoneeko
wrong n.	n. sbagliato	nōōmero zbalyato
nurse	infermiera	eenfermyera
nursery (=day n. for children)	asilo	aseelo
nut	noce	noche
almonds	mandorle (fpl)	mandorle
peanuts	arachidi (fpl)	arakeedee
nut (metal)	dado	dado
a n. and bolt	un d. e un bullone	ōōn dado e ōōn bōōlone
nutcrackers	schiaccionoci (ms)	skyachanochee
nylon	nailon (m)	naylon
a pair of nylons (stockings)	un paio di calze	ōōn payo dee kaltse

O

oak (wood)	quercia	kwercha
oar (for rowing)	remo	remo
October	ottobre (m)	otobre
of	di	dee
off (of light etc)	spento	spento
offence	infrazione (f)	eenfratsyone
parking offence	i. di parcheggio	eenfratsyone dee parkejo
offer (n)	offerta	oferta
make an o.	fare un'o. – fatto un'o.	fare ōōn oferta – fato ōōn oferta
office	ufficio –ci	ōōfeecho ōōfeechee
office worker	impiegato in un ufficio (m)/impiegata in un ufficio (f)	eempyegato een ōōn ōōfeecho eempyegata een ōōn ōōfeecho
official (adj)	ufficiale	ōōfeechale
official (n)	funzionario –ri	fōōntsyonaryo fōōntsyonaree
often	spesso	speso
oil (lubricating)	olio	olyo
	words ending in –o or marked (m)	words ending in –a or marked (f)
the	il/l'/lo	la/l'
the (plural)	i/gl'/gli	le/l'

oil (salad)	olio	olyo
olive o.	o. di olivo	olyo dēē olēēvo
vegetable o.	o. di seme	olyo dēē seme
oil painting	pittura a olio	pēētōōʀa a olyo
oily	unto	ōōnto
ointment	pomata	pomata
a jar of o.	un vaso di p.	ōōn vazo dēē pomata
a tube of o.	un tubo di p.	ōōn tōōbo dēē pomata
old (of people and things)	vecchio –chi	vekyo vekēē
he is /six/ years o.	ha /sei/ anni	a /sey/ anēē
old-fashioned	antiquato	antēēkwato
olives	olive (fpl)	olēēve
black o.	o. nere	olēēve neʀe
green o.	o. verdi	olēēve veʀdēē
omelette	omelette (f)	omelet
on	su	sōō
o. Monday	lunedì	lōōnedēē
o. the table	sulla tavola	sōōla tavola
o. the bed	sul letto	sōōl leto
on (of light etc)	acceso	achezo
once (=one time)	una volta	ōōna volta
one-way	senso unico	senso ōōnēēko
onion	cipolla	chēēpola
spring onion	cipollina	chēēpolēēna
only	solo	solo
open (adj)	aperto	apeʀto
open (vb)	aprire – aperto	apʀēēʀe – apeʀto
open-air restaurant	ristorante all'aperto	ʀēēstoʀante alapeʀto
o.-a. swimming pool	piscina all'aperto	pēēshēēna alapeʀto
opening times	orario	oʀaʀyo
opera	opera	opeʀa
o. house	teatro dell'o.	teatʀo delopeʀa
operate (surgically)	operare	opeʀaʀe
operation (surgical)	operazione (f)	opeʀatsyone
opposite (adv)	di fronte	dēē fʀonte
o. /the station/	di f. /alla stazione/	dēē fʀonte /ala statsyone/
optician	ottico	otēēko
or	o	o
orange (colour)	arancio –ce	aʀancho aʀanchēē
orange (fruit)	arancia –ce	aʀancha aʀanche
fizzy o,	aranciata	aʀanchata
o. juice	succo d'a.	sōōko daʀancha

148

English	Italian	Pronunciation
a bottle of o. juice	una bottiglia d'aranciata	$\overline{oo}$na bot$\overline{ee}$lya daranchata
a glass of o. juice	un bicchiere d'aranciata	$\overline{oo}$n b$\overline{ee}$kyere daranchata
orchestra	orchestra	orkestra
order /a steak/	ordinare /una bistecca/	ord$\overline{ee}$nare /$\overline{oo}$na b$\overline{ee}$steka/
ordinary	normale (m & f)	normale
organisation	organizzazione (f)	organ$\overline{ee}$dzatsyone
organise	organizzare	organ$\overline{ee}$dzare
original	originale (m & f)	or$\overline{ee}$j$\overline{ee}$nale
ornament	decorazione (f)	dekoratsyone
other	altro	altro
the o. /train/	l'a. /treno/	laltro /treno/
out	fuori	fwor$\overline{ee}$
he's o.	è f.	e fwor$\overline{ee}$
out of date (eg clothes)	fuori moda	fwor$\overline{ee}$ moda
out of date (eg passport)	scaduto	skad$\overline{oo}$to
out of order	non funziona	non f$\overline{oo}$ntsyona
outside (adv)	fuori	fwor$\overline{ee}$
outside (prep)	fuori da	fwor$\overline{ee}$ da
oven	forno	forno
over (=above)	sopra	sopra
overcoat	cappotto	kapoto
overcooked	troppo cotto	tropo koto
overland	via terra	v$\overline{ee}$a tera
overseas	all'estero	alestero
overtake	sorpassare	sorpasare
overweight (people)	grosso	groso
be o.	essere troppo g.	esere tropo groso
he's o.	è troppo g.	e tropo groso
be overweight (things)	pesare troppo	pezare tropo
owe	dovere	dovere
how much do I o. you?	quanto le devo?	kwanto le devo
you o. me / /	mi deve / /	m$\overline{ee}$ deve / /
owner	padrone (m) padrona (f)	padrone padrona
oxygen	ossigeno	os$\overline{ee}$jeno
oysters	ostriche (fpl)	ostr$\overline{ee}$ke
a dozen o.	dodici o.	dod$\overline{ee}$ch$\overline{ee}$ ostr$\overline{ee}$ke

pack (vb)	impacchettare	ēempaketaᴙe
p. /my suitcase/	fare la valigia	faᴙe la valēeja
package holiday	vacanza organizzata	vakantsa organēetsata
packet	pacchetto	paketo
a p. of /cigarettes/ (=20)	un p. di /sigarette/	ōōn paketo dēe /sēegaᴙete/
packing materials (to prevent breakages)	imballaggio –ggi	ēembalajo ēembalajēe
pad (of writing paper)	carta da lettere	kaᴙta da leteᴙe
sketch-p.	blocco di carta da disegno	bloko dēe kaᴙta da dēezenyo
paddle (for canoe)	pagaia	pagaya
padlock (n)	lucchetto	lōoketo
page (of a book)	pagina	pajēena
pain	dolore (m)	doloᴙe
p. /in the arm/	d. /al braccio/	doloᴙe /al bᴙacho/
painful	doloroso	doloᴙoso
painkiller	analgesico	analjezēeko
paint	vernice (f)	veᴙnēeche
a tin of p.	un barattolo di v.	ōōn baᴙatolo dēe veᴙnēeche
paintbrush	pennello	penelo
painting	quadro	kwadᴙo
oil p.	q. a olio	kwadᴙo a olyo
watercolour	q. a acquarelle	kwadᴙo a akwaᴙele
paints	colori (mpl)	koloᴙēe
a box of p.	una scatola di c.	ōōna skatola dēe koloᴙēe
pair	paio	payo
a p. of / /	un p. di / /	ōōn payo dēe / /
palace	palazzo	palatso
pale (of people & things)	pallido	palēedo
pants	mutande (fpl)	mōōtande
a pair of p.	un paio di m.	ōōn payo dēe mōōtande
panty-girdle	busto	bōosto
paper	carta	kaᴙta
airmail p.	c. aerea	kaᴙta aeᴙea

	words ending in –o or marked (m)	words ending in –a or marked (f)
a	un/uno	una/un'
some	del/dell'/dello	della/dell'
some (plural)	dei/degl'/degli	delle

a sheet of p.	un foglio di c.	ōon folyo dēē kaRta
drawing p.	c. da disegnare	kaRta da dēēzenyaRe
wrapping p.	c. da imballaggio	kaRta da ēēmbalajo
writing p.	c. da scrivere	kaRta da skRēēveRe
paperback	edizione (f) economica	edēētsyone ekonomēēka
paper clip	fermaglio –gli per carta	feRmalyo peR kaRta
parcel	pacco –chi	pako pakēē
by p. post	servizio dei pacchi postali	seRvēētsyo dey pakēē postalēē
parent	genitore (m & f)	jenēētoRe
park (n)	parco –chi	paRko paRkēē
park (vb)	parcheggiare	paRkejaRe
parking	parcheggio	paRkejo
no p.	p. vietato	paRkejo vyetato
parliament	parlamento	paRlamento
part	parte (f)	paRte
p. of / /	p. di / /	paRte dēē / /
partner (business)	socio –ci	socho sochēē
partridge	pernice (f)	peRnēēche
part-time work	impiego a mezza giornata	impyego a medza joRnata
party	festa	festa
birthday p.	f. di compleanno	festa dēē kompleano
party of /people/	gruppo di /persone/	grōōpo dēē /peRsone/
pass (n) (=p. to enter building)	lasciapassare (m)	lashapasaRe
mountain p.	valico	valēēko
passage (on a boat)	passaggio –ggi	pasajo pasajēē
passenger (in boat)	passeggero	pasejeRo
passenger (in train)	viaggiatore (m)	vyajatoRe
transit p.	v. di transito	vyajatoRe dēē tranzēēto
passport	passaporto	pasapoRto
past (prep)	passato	pasato
go p. /the station/	passare per /la stazione/	pasaRe peR /la statsyone/
pastilles	pastiglie (fpl)	pastēēlye
throat p.	p. per la gola	pastēēlye peR la gola
pastries (=cakes)	pasticcine (fpl)	pastēēchēēne
patch (n)	toppa	topa
patch (vb)	ratoppare	ratopaRe

151

pâté	paté (m)	pate
liver p.	p. di fegato	pate dēē fegato
path	sentiero	sentyeRo
patient (adj)	paziente (m & f)	patsyente
patient (n)	paziente (m)	patsyente
outp.	p. non residente	patsyente non rezēēdente
pattern	disegno	deezenyo
dress p.	d. per vestito	dēēzenyo peR vestēēto
knitting p.	d. per maglia	dēēzenyo peR malya
pavement	marciapiede (m)	maRchapyede
pay	pagare	pagaRe
by /credit card/	con /carta di credito/	kon /kaRta dēē kRedēēto/
in advance	in anticipo	ēēn antēēcheepo
in cash	in contanti	ēēn kontantēē
in /pounds/	in /sterline/	ēēn /steRlēēne/
the bill	il conto	ēēl konto
peach	pesca –che	peska peska
peanuts	arachidi (fpl)	aRakēēdēē
a packet of p.	un pacchetto di a.	ōōn paketo dēē aRakēēdēē
pear	pera	peRa
pearl	perla	peRla
peas	piselli (mpl)	pēēselēē
pedestrian	pedone (m)	pedone
p. crossing	passaggio pedonale	pasajo pedonale
peel (vb)	sbucciare	sbōōchaRe
peg (=clothes p.)	attaccapanni (m) –	atakapanēē
pen (=fountain p.)	penna	pena
ballpoint p.	penna a sfera	pena a sfeRa
pencil	matita	matēēta
p. sharpener	temperino	tempeRēēno
pen friend	amico –ci per corrispondenza	amēēko amēēchēē peR koRēēspondentsa –
	amica –che per corrispondenza	amēēka amēēke peR koRēēspondentsa
penicillin	penicillina	penēēchēēlēēna
I'm allergic to p.	sono allergico alla p.	sono aleRjēēko alla penēēchēēlēēna
penknife	temperino	tempeRēēno
people	gente (fs)	jente
pepper	pepe (m)	pepe

pepper (=vegetable)	peperone (m)	peperone
green p.	p. verde	peperone verde
red p.	p. rosso	peperone roso
peppermint (=flavour/drink)	menta	menta
p. (sweet)	mentina	menteena
per annum	all'anno	alano
per cent	per cento	per chento
percolator	macchina per il caffè	makeena per eel kafe
perfect (adj)	perfetto	perfeto
performance	spettacolo	spetakolo
perfume	profumo	profoomo
a bottle of p.	una bottiglia di p.	oona boteelya dee profoomo
period (=menstrual p.)	mestruazioni (fpl)	mestrwatsyonee
period (of time)	periodo	pereeodo
perm (=permanent wave)	permanente (m)	permanente
permanent	permanente (m & f)	permanente
permission	permesso	permeso
p. to /enter/	p. di /entrare/	permeso dee /entrare/
permit (n)	permesso	permeso
permit (vb)	permettere – permesso	permetere – permeso
person	persona	persona
personal	personale (m & f)	personale
pet	animale (m) domestico	aneemale domesteeko
petrol	benzina	bendzeena
petrol station	distributore (m)	deestreebootore
petticoat	sottoveste (m)	sotoveste
photograph /photo	fotografia	fotografeea
black and white p.	f. in bianco e nero	fotografeea een byanko e nero
colour p.	f. a colore	fotografeea a kolore
take a p.	fare una f. – fatto una f.	fare oona fotografeea – fato oona fotografeea
photographer	fotografo	fotografo

	words ending in –o or marked (m)	words ending in –a or marked (f)
the	il/l'/lo	la/l'
the (plural)	i/gl'/gli	le/l'

153

photographer's studio	studio fotografico	st$\overline{oo}$dyo fotog**r**afeeko
phrase	frase (f)	f**r**aze
phrase book	frasario –ri	f**r**aza**r**yo f**r**aza**r**ee
piano	pianoforte (m)	pyano**fo**rte
pick (=gather flowers etc)	raccogliere – raccolto	**r**akolye**r**e – **r**akolto
picnic	picnic (m)	**pee**knee**k**
go on a p.	fare un p. – fatto un p.	fa**r**e $\overline{oo}$n **pee**knee**k** – **fa**to $\overline{oo}$n **pee**knee**k**
picture (drawing or painting)	quadro	kwad**r**o
piece	pezzo	**pe**tso
a p. of / /	un p. di / /	$\overline{oo}$n **pe**tso dee / /
pig	maiale (m)	ma**ya**le
pigeon	piccione (m)	pee**chyo**ne
piles (illness)	emorroidi (fpl)	emo**r**oy**dee**
pill	pillola	**pee**lola
a bottle of pills	una bottiglia di pillole	$\overline{oo}$na bot**ee**lya dee **pee**lole
sleeping pills	pillole per dormire	**pee**lole pe**r** do**r**me**e**re
the Pill	la p.	la **pee**lola
pillow	cuscino	k$\overline{oo}$**shee**no
p. case	federa	**fe**de**r**a
pilot	pilota (m) –i	pee**lo**ta peelo**tee**
pin	spillino	spee**lee**no
pine (wood)	pino	**pee**no
pineapple	ananas (m) –	**a**nanas
a slice of p.	una fetta di a.	$\overline{oo}$na **fe**ta dee **a**nanas
p. juice	succo di a	s$\overline{oo}$ko dee **a**nanas
pink	rosa	**r**oza
pint	pinta	**pee**nta
pip (=seed of citrus fruit)	semino	se**mee**no
pipe (smoker's)	pipa	**pee**pa
p. cleaner	pulisci-p. (m) –	p$\overline{oo}$lee**shee**-**pee**pa
place (eg on a plane)	posto	**po**sto
place (exact location)	luogo	**lwo**go
p. of birth	l. di nascita	**lwo**go dee na**shee**ta
p. of work	posto di lavoro	**po**sto dee la**vo**ro
plain (adj) (=not coloured)	tinta smorta	**tee**nta **smo**rta
plain (adj) (=not flavoured)	insaporo	$\overline{ee}$nsa**po**ro
plain (adj) (=simple)	semplice	sem**plee**che

plan (n)	piano	**py**ano
plan (vb)	organizzare	organ**eedza**re
plane (n) (infml)	aereo	ae**re**o
by p.	in a.	**een** ae**re**o
plant (n)	pianta	**pyanta**
plant (vb)	piantare	pyant**a**re
plaster (for walls)	intonaco	**een**tonako
sticking p. (for cuts)	cerotto	che**ro**to
plastic	plastica	**plast**eeka
plate (=dental p.)	dentiera	dent**ye**ra
plate (=dinner p.)	piatto	**py**ato
platform /8/	binario /otto/	bee**na**ryo /oto/
platinum	piatino	pyat**ee**no
play (n) (at theatre)	commedia	ko**me**dya
play (vb)	giocare	jok**a**re
p. a game of / /	g. a / /	jok**a**re a / /
play (vb) (an instrument)	suonare	swo**na**re
playground	campo giochi (m)	**kam**po jok**ee**
pleasant	piacevole (m & f)	pya**che**vole
pleased	contento	kon**ten**to
p. with / /	c. di / /	kon**ten**to dee / /
plenty	molto	**mol**to
p. of / /	m. / /	**mol**to / /
pliers	pinze (fpl)	**pin**tse
a pair of p.	un paio di p.	**oon payo** dee **pin**tse
plimsolls	scarpe (fpl) di ginnastica	**skar**pe dee jeenast**ee**ka
a pair of p.	un paio di s. di g.	**oon payo** dee **skar**pe dee jeenast**ee**ka
plug (electric)	spina (f)	**spee**na
adaptor p.	raccordo elettrico	ra**kor**do elet**ree**ko
plug (for sink)	tappo	**ta**po
plug in	attacare	ata**ka**re
plum	prugna	**proo**nya
plumber	idraulico	eedra**oolee**ko
plus	più	**pyoo**
p.m.	di pomeriggio	dee pome**ree**jo
pneumonia	polmonite (f)	polmon**ee**te
poach	cuocere in camicia	**kwoche**re **een** kam**ee**cha – koto **een** kam**ee**cha
pocket	tasca	**tas**ka
pocket dictionary	vocabolario tascabile	vokabo**lar**yo taska**bee**le
pocketknife	temperino	temper**ee**no

pocket money	paga settimanale dei ragazzi	paga setēēmanale dey ʀagatsēē
point (n) (=a sharpened p.)	punta	pōōnta
point (vb) (=indicate)	indicare	ēendēēkaʀe
pointed	appuntito	apōōntēēto
poison	veleno	veleno
poisoning	avvelenamento	avelenamento
food p.	a. da cibo	avelenamento da chēēbo
poisonous	velenoso	velenozo
poker (=game)	poker (m)	pokeʀ
a game of p.	una partita di p.	ōōna paʀtēēta dēē pokeʀ
police	polizia	polēētsēēa
police station	stazione (f) di polizia	statsyone dēē polēētsēēa
policeman	poliziotto	polēētsyoto
polish (n)	lucido	lōōchēēdo
shoe p.	l. per le scarpe	lōōchēēdo peʀ le skaʀpe
polish (vb)	lucidare	lōōchēēdaʀe
polite	cortese	koʀteze
politician	uomo politico –mini politici	womo polēētēēko womēēnēē polēētēēchēē
politics	politica (s)	polēētēēka
polo neck sweater	argentina	aʀjentēēna
pond	stagno	stanyo
pony	pony (m) –	ponēē
pool (=swimming pool)	piscina	pēēshēēna
poor (=not rich)	povero	poveʀo
poor (p. quality)	scadente (m & f)	skadente
pop (music)	pop (m)	pop
popcorn	pop-corn (m)	popkoʀn
popular	in voga	ēēn voga
population	popolazione (f)	popolatsyone
pork	maiale (m)	mayale
pornographic	pornografico	poʀnogʀafēēko
port (=harbour)	porto	poʀto

	words ending in –o or marked (m)	words ending in –a or marked (f)
a	un/uno	una/un'
some	del/dell'/dello	della/dell'
some (plural)	dei/degl'/degli	delle

portable	portabile (m & f)	portabeele
p. /radio/	/radio/ (f) p.	/radyo/ portabeele
porter (hotel)	portiere (m)	portyere
porter (railway)	facchino	fakeeno
portion	porzione (f)	portsyone
a p. of / /	una p. di / /	oona portsyone dee / /
portrait	ritratto	reetrato
position	posizione (f)	pozeetsyone
possible	possibile (m & f)	poseebeele
post (vb)	impostare	eempostare
p. this airmail	i. questa per via aerea	eempostare kwesta per veea aerea
as printed matter	come stampa	kome stampa
express	espresso	espreso
parcel post	come pacco	kome pako
registered	raccomandato	rakomandato
surface mail	posta normale	posta normale
postage	spese (fpl) postali	speze postalee
postal order	vaglia	valya
postbox	cassetta delle lettere	kaseta dele letere
postcard	cartolina	kartoleena
postcode	codice (m) postale	kodeeche postale
poster	poster (m)	poster
post office	ufficio postale	oofeecho postale
pot	teiera	teyera
a p. of tea	una t. di tè	oona teyera dee te
potatoes	patate (fpl)	patate
potato peeler	sbuccia –ce patate	sboocha patate sbooche patate
pottery (substance)	terraglia	teralya
poultry	pollame	polame
chicken	pollo	polo
duck	anitra	aneetra
turkey	tacchino	takeeno
pound (money)	sterlina	sterleena
pound (weight)	libbra	leebra
pour	versare	versare
powder (face p.)	cipria	cheeprya
baby p.	talco	talko
talcum p.	talco	talko
practice (=custom)	abitudine (f)	abeetoodeene
practice (=training)	pratica	prateeka
practise (=train)	esercitarmi	ezercheetarmee
pram	carrozzina	karotseena
prawns	gamberi (mpl)	gamberee

precious	prezioso	pretsyozo
p. stone	pietra preziosa	pyetra pretsyoza
prefer	*preferire	prefereere
pregnant	incinta	eencheenta
prepare	preparare	preparare
prescribe	prescrivere – prescritto	preskreevere – preskreeto
prescription	ricetta	reecheta
present (adj)	presente (m & f)	prezente
present (n) (=gift)	regalo	regalo
present (n) (time)	presente (m)	prezente
present (vb)	presentare	prezentare
president (of company)	presidente (m)	prezeedente
press (vb) (eg button)	premere – preso	premere – preso
press (vb) (ironing)	stirare	steerare
pressure	pressione (f)	presyone
b. pressure	p. del sangue	presyone del sangwe
pressure cooker	pentola a pressione	pentola a presyone
pretty	grazioso	gratsyozo
price	prezzo	pretso
priest	prete (m)	prete
prince	principe (m)	preencheepe
princess	principessa	preencheepesa
print (n) (photographic)	copia	kopya
print (vb)	stampare	stampare
printer	stampatore (m)	stampatore
prison	prigione (f)	preejone proteteevo
private	privato	preevato
p. /bath/	/bagno/ p.	/banyo/ preevato
prize	premio –mi	premyo premee
probable	probabile (m & f)	probabeele
problem	problema (m) –i	problema problemee
procession	processione (f)	prochesyone
produce (vb)	produrre – prodotto	prodoore – prodoto
product	prodotto	prodoto
programme (of events)	programma (m) –i	programa programee
promise (n)	promessa	promesa
promise (vb)	promettere – promesso	prometere – promeso
pronounce	pronunciare	pronoonchare
proof	prova	prova
property (=belongings)	roba	roba

prospectus	opuscolo	opōōskolo
prostitute	prostituta	prosteetoota
protect	proteggere – protetto	protejere – proteto
p. me from / /	mi p. da / /	mee protejere da / /
protection	protezione (f)	protetsyone
protective	protettivo	proteteevo
Protestant (adj)	protestante (m & f)	protestante
prove	dimostrare	deemostrare
provisions	provviste (fpl)	proveeste
prunes	prugne (fpl) secche	proonye seke
pub	bar (m) inglese	bar eengleze
public	pubblico –ci	poobleeko poobleechee
p. buildings	edifici pubblici	edeefeechee poobleechee
p. convenience	gabinetto pubblico	gabeeneto poobleeko
p. /garden/	/giardini/ pubblici	/jardeenee/ poobleechee
pull	tirare	teerare
pump	pompa	pompa
bicycle p.	p. per bicicletta	pompa per beecheekleta
foot p.	p. a piede	pompa a pyede
water p.	p. per acqua	pompa per akwa
puncture	foratura	foratoora
punish	*punire	pooneere
punishment	castigo –ghi	kasteego kasteegee
pupil	alunno	aloono
pure	puro	pooro
purple	porpora (inv)	porpora
purse	borsellino	borseleeno
pus	pus (m)	poos
push (vb)	spingere –spinto	speenjere – speento
pushchair	sedia a rotelle	sedya a rotele
put	mettere – messo	metere – meso
p. on /my coat/	m. /il mio cappotto/	metere /eel meeo kapoto/
puzzle	puzzle (m)	poodzle
jigsaw p.	puzzle (m)	poodzle
pyjamas	pigiama (ms)	peejama
a pair of p.	un p.	oon peejama
	words ending in –o or marked (m)	words ending in –a or marked (f)
the	il/l'/lo	la/l'
the (plural)	i/gl'/gli	le/l'

159

Q

quail (=bird)	quaglia	**kwal**ya
qualifications	qualificazioni (fpl)	kwal<u>ee</u>f<u>ee</u>katsyon<u>ee</u>
qualified	qualificato	kwal<u>ee</u>f<u>ee</u>kato
quality	qualità –	kwal<u>ee</u>ta
quarrel (n)	litigio –gi	l<u>ee</u>t<u>ee</u>jo l<u>ee</u>t<u>ee</u>jee
quarter	quarto	**kwar**to
a q. /of an hour/	un q. /d'ora/	<u>oo</u>n **kwar**to /**do**ra/
queen	regina	ʀej<u>ee</u>na
query (vb)	fare una domanda	faʀe <u>oo</u>na domanda
I would like to q. /the bill/	vorrei fare una domanda /sul conto/	voʀey faʀe <u>oo</u>na domanda /s<u>oo</u>l **kon**to/
question (n)	domanda	domanda
question (vb)	domandare	doman**da**ʀe
queue (n)	coda	koda
queue (vb)	fare la coda – fatto la coda	faʀe la koda – **fa**to la koda
quick	veloce (m & f)	veloche
quickly	velocemente	veloche**men**te
quiet (adj)	silenzioso	s<u>ee</u>len**tsyo**zo
q. pleasel	silenzio, per favore!	s<u>ee</u>lentsyo peʀ favoʀe
quinine	chinino	k<u>ee</u>n<u>ee</u>no
quite	abbastanza	abas**tan**tsa

R

rabbi	rabbino	ʀab<u>ee</u>no
rabbit	coniglio	kon<u>ee</u>lyo
rabies	rabbia	ʀabya
race (n) (=contest)	corsa	koʀsa
horse r.	c. di cavalli	koʀsa d<u>ee</u> kaval<u>ee</u>
motor r.	c. di macchine	koʀsa d<u>ee</u> mak<u>ee</u>ne
race (vb)	correre – corso	koʀeʀe – koʀso
racecourse	ippodromo	<u>ee</u>podʀomo
racehorse	cavallo da corsa	kavalo da koʀsa
races (=the r.)	corse (fpl)	koʀse
racing	corsa	koʀsa
horse r.	corse di cavalli	koʀse d<u>ee</u> kaval<u>ee</u>
motor r.	corse di macchine	koʀse d<u>ee</u> mak<u>ee</u>ne
racquet	racchetta	ʀaketa
tennis r.	r. da tennis	ʀaketa da ten<u>ee</u>s
squash r.	r. da squash	ʀaketa da skwosh
radio	radio (f)	ʀadyo
car r.	autoradio (f)	a<u>oo</u>toʀadyo

portable r.	r. portatile	ʀadyo poʀtatēēle
transistor r.	r. transistor	ʀadyo tʀansēēstor
radishes	ravanelli (mpl)	ʀavanelēē
raft	zattera	tsateʀa
life r.	z. di salvataggio	tsateʀa dēē salvatajo
rag (for cleaning)	panno	pano
railway	ferrovia	feʀovēēa
r. station	stazione (f) ferroviaria	statsyone feʀovyaʀya
underground r.	metropolitana	metʀopolēētana
rain (n)	pioggia	pyoja
rain (vb)	piovere	pyoveʀe
it's raining	piove	pyove
raincoat	impermeabile (m)	ēēmpeʀmeabēēle
raisins	uve passe (fpl)	ōōve pase
rally	rally (m) –	ʀalēē
motor r.	r. automobilistico	ʀalēē aōotomobēēlēēstēēko
range (=mountain r.)	catena di montagne	katena dēē montanye
range (=r. of goods)	varietà	vaʀyeta
rare (eg of steak)	al sangue	al sangwe
medium-rare	poco cotto	poko koto
rare (=unusual)	raro	ʀaʀo
rash	esantema (m) –mi	ezantema ezantemēē
rasher of bacon	fetta	feta
raspberry	lampone (m)	lampone
a punnet of raspberries	un cestino di lamponi	ōōn chestēēno dēē lamponēē
rat	topo	topo
rate (n)	tariffa	taʀēēfa
cheap r. (mail, telephone)	t. ridotta	taʀēēfa ʀēēdota
exchange r.	tasso di cambio	taso dēē kambyo
postal r.	t. postale	taʀēēfa postale
r. per day	t. giornaliera	taʀēēfa jyoʀnalyeʀa
rates (charges)	tariffe (fpl)	taʀēēfe
rattle (baby's r.)	raganetta	ʀaganeta
rattle (noise)	tintinnio	tēēntēēnēēo
raw	crudo	kʀōōdo
razor	rasoio	ʀazoyo
electric r.	r. elettrico	ʀazoyo eletʀēēko
r. blade	lamatta per r.	lamata peʀ ʀazoyo
a packet of r. blades	un pacchetto di lamatte	ōōn paketo dēē lamate

reach (vb)	raggiungere – raggiunto	ʀaj**oo**njeʀe – ʀaj**oo**nto
reach /Milan/	arrivare a /Milano/	aʀ**ee**vaʀe a /m**ee**lano/
read /a magazine/	leggere /una rivista/	lejeʀe /**oo**na ʀeev**ee**sta/
ready	pronto	**pro**nto
real	vero	ve**ro**
rear /coach/	/carrozza/ di coda	/kaʀotsa/ d**ee** koda
reason (n)	ragione (f)	ʀaj**o**ne
reasonable	ragionevole (m & f)	ʀaj**o**nevole
receipt	ricevuta	ʀ**ee**chev**oo**ta
receive	ricevere	ʀ**ee**cheveʀe
recent	recente (m & f)	ʀechente
Reception (eg in a hotel)	ufficio –ci ricevimento	**oo**fe**e**cho ʀ**ee**chevee**me**nto **oo**fee**ch**ee ʀ**ee**chevee**me**nto
recharge (battery)	ricaricare	ʀ**ee**kaʀ**ee**kaʀe
recipe	ricetta di cucina	ʀ**ee**cheta d**ee** ko**och**eena
recognise	riconoscere – riconosciuto	ʀ**ee**konoshere – ʀ**ee**konosh**oo**to
recommend	raccomandare	ʀakomandaʀe
record (n)	disco	d**ee**sko
33 r.p.m. r.	d. a 33 giri	d**ee**sko a tʀenta tʀe j**ee**ʀee
45 r.p.m. r.	d. a 45 giri	d**ee**sko a kwaʀanta ch**ee**nkwe j**ee**ʀee
classical r.	d. classico	d**ee**sko klas**ee**ko
jazz r.	d. jazz	d**ee**sko jas
light music r.	d. di musica leggera	d**ee**sko d**ee** m**oo**zeeka lejeʀa
pop r.	d. pop	d**ee**sko pop
record (vb)	registrare	ʀej**ee**straʀe
record player	giradischi (m) –	j**ee**ʀad**ee**skee
record shop	negozio –zi di dischi	negotsyo d**ee** d**ee**skee negotse**e** dee d**ee**skee
rectangular	rettangolare (m & f)	ʀetangolaʀe
red	rosso	ʀoso

	words ending in –o or marked (m)	words ending in –a or marked (f)
a	un/uno	una/un'
some	del/dell'/dello	della/dell'
some (plural)	dei/degl'/degli	delle

162

REPLACE

reduce	ridurre – ridotto	rēedōōre – rēedoto
r. the price	r. il prezzo	rēedōōre ēel pretso – rēedoto ēel pretso
reduction	riduzione (f)	rēedōōtsyone
reel (of cotton)	rotolo	rotolo
reel (recording tape)	rotolo	rotolo
refill (for a ballpoint)	refill (m) –	refēel
refill (for a lighter)	refill (m) –	refēel
refrigerator/fridge (infml)	frigorifero/frigo	frēegorēefero/frēego
refund (n)	rimborso	rēemborso
refund (vb)	rimborsare	rēemborsare
registered (mail)	raccomandata	rakomandata
registration number	numero di targa	nōōmero dēe targa
regret (vb)	rincrescere – rincresciuto	rēenkreshere – rēenkreshōōto
regular /service/	/servizio/ normale	/servēetsyo/ normale
regulations	regolamenti (mpl)	regolamentēe
relations	parenti (mpl)	parentēe
relative (n)	parente (m & f)	parente
reliable	di fiducia	dēe feedōōcha
religion	religione (f)	relēejone
religious	religioso	relēejozo
remedy	rimedio –i	rēemedyo rēemedēe
remember	ricordare	rēekordare
I don't r.	non mi ricordo	non mēe rēekordo
I r. /the name/	mi ricordo /il nome/	mēe rēekordo /eel nome/
remove	togliere – tolto	tolyere – tolto
renew	rinnovare	rēenovare
rent (n) (payment)	affitto	afēeto
rent /a villa/	affittare /una villa/	afēetare /ōōna vēela/
repair (vb)	aggiustare	ajōōstare
repairs	riparazioni (fpl)	rēeparatsyonēe
do r.	riparare	rēeparare
shoe r. (=shop)	r. scarpe	rēeparatsyonēe skarpe
watch r. (=shop)	r. orologi	rēeparatsyonēe
repay	*restituire	restēetwēere
r. me	mi r.	mēe restēetwēere
r. the money	r. il denaro	restēetwēere eel denaro
repeat	ripetere	rēepetere
insect r.	insetticida	ēensetēechēeda
replace	sostituire	sostēetwēere

163

REPLY

reply (n)	risposta	rēēsposta
r.-paid	r. pagata	rēēsposta pagata
report (n)	relazione (f)	relatsyone
report (vb)	riferire	rēēferēēre
r. a loss	r. una perdita	rēēferēēre ōōna perdēēta
represent	rappresentare	raprezentare
reproduction (=painting)	riproduzione (f)	rēēprodōōtsyone
request (n)	richiesta	rēēkyesta
make a r.	fare una r.	fare ōōna rēēkyesta
reservation (hotel, restaurant, theatre)	prenotazione (f)	prenotatsyone
make a r.	fare una p.	fare ōōna prenotatsyone
reserve (vb)	prenotare	prenotare
responsible	risponsabile (m & f)	rēēsponsabēēle
r. for / /	r. per / /	rēēsponsabēēle per / /
rest (n)	riposo	rēēpozo
have a r.	riposarmi	rēēpozarmēē
rest (vb)	riposarmi	rēēpozarmēē
restaurant	ristorante (m)	rēēstorante
self-service restaurant	r. self-service	rēēstorante self-servēēs
restrictions	restrizioni (fpl)	restrēētsyonēē
result	risultato	rēēzōōltato
retired (adj)	andato in pensione	andato ēēn pensyone
I'm r.	sono in p.	sono ēēn pensyone
return	ritorno	rēētorno
r. (ticket)	biglietto di andata e ritorno	bēēlyeto dēē andata e rēētorno
return (=give back)	dare in dietro	dare ēēn dyetro
r. /this sweater/	d. in d. /questa maglietta/	dare ēēn dyetro /kwesta malyeta/
return (= go back)	tornare	tornare
r. at 4.30	t. alle 4.30	tornare alle kwatro e medzo
r. in /July/	t. in /luglio/	tornare ēēn /lōōlyo/
r. on /Monday/	t. /lunedì/	tornare /lōōnedēē/

164

English	Italian	Pronunciation
reverse the charges	trasferire il pagamento a destinazione	tRasfeReere eel pagamento a desteenatsyone
I'd like to r. the c.	vorrei t. il p. a d.	voRey tRasfeReere eel pagamento a desteenatsyone
reward (n)	premio –mi	pRemyo pRemee
reward (vb)	premiare	pRemyaRe
rheumatism	reumatismo	Reoomateezmo
rib (part of body)	costola	kostola
ribbon	nastro	nastRo
a piece of r.	un pezzo di n.	oon petso dee nastRo
typewriter r.	n. da macchina	nastRo da makeena
rice	riso	Reezo
rich	ricco (m) richi (mpl) ricca (f) ricche (fpl)	Reeko Reekee Reeka Reeke
ride (vb)	cavalcare	kavalkaRe
r. a bicycle	andare in bicicletta	andaRe een beecheekleta
r. a horse	c.	kavalkaRe
go for a r. (in a car)	fare un giro in macchina	faRe oon jeeRo een makeena
riding (=horse r.)	equitazione (f)	ekweetatsyone
go r.	andare a cavalcare	andaRe a kavalkaRe
right (=correct)	giusto	joosto
right (=not left)	destro	destRo
right-handed	non mancino	non mancheeno
ring	anello	anelo
/diamond/ r.	a. di /diamante/	anelo dee /dyamante/
engagement r.	a. di fidanzamento	anelo dee feedantsamento
wedding r.	fede (f)	fede
ring (vb) at the door	suonare il campanello	swonaRe eel kampanelo
ring road	circonvallazione (f)	cheeRkonvalatsyone
rinse (n) (clothes)	sciampoo (m)	shampo
colour r.	s. colorante	shampo koloRante
rinse (vb)	sciacquare	shakwaRe
ripe	maturo	matooRo
river (large)	fiume (m)	fyoome
river (small)	fiume (m)	fyoome

	words ending in –o or marked (m)	words ending in –a or marked (f)
the	il/l'/lo	la/l'
the (plural)	i/gl'/gli	le/l'

road	strada	strada
main r.	s. principale	strada prēencheepale
ring r.	circonvallazione (f)	cheerkonvalatsyone
side r.	s. secondaria	strada sekondarya
roast (vb)	arrostire – arrosto	arosteere – arosto
r. beef	manzo arrosto	mandzo arosto
r. chicken	pollo arrosto	polo arosto
rock (n)	roccia –cce	rocha roche
rod (=fishing r.)	canna da pesca	kana da peska
roll (=bread r.)	panino	paneeno
a r. of /toilet paper/	un rotolo di /carta igienica/	oon rotolo dee /karta eejyeneeka/
roller skating	pattinaggio a rotelle	pateenajo a rotele
go r. s.	fare p. a r.	fare pateenajo a rotele
roof	tetto	teto
roof rack	portapacchi (m) –	portapakee
room	camera	kamera
double r.	c. doppia	kamera dopya
quiet r.	c. tranquilla	kamera trankweela
r. service	servizio in c.	serveetsyo een kamera
r. with a view	c. con vista	kamera kon veesta
single r.	c. singola	kamera seengola
twin-bedded r.	c. con due letti	kamera kon dooe letee
with /shower/	con /doccia/	kon /docha/
without /bath/	senza /bagno/	sentsa /banyo/
rope	corda	korda
tow r.	c. per traino	korda per trayno
rose	rosa	roza
a bunch of roses	un mazzo di rose	oon madzo dee roze
rotten	marcio –ci	marcho marchee
rough (=not calm)	mosso	moso
rough (=not smooth)	ruvido	rooveedo
roughly (=approximately)	approssimativamente	aproseemateevamente
round (adj)	rotondo	rotondo
roundabout (n)	rotonda	rotonda
route	percorso	perkorso
row (a boat)	remare	remare
row (of seats)	fila	feela
the /first/ r.	la /prima/ f.	la /preema/ feela
rowing boat	barca a remi	barka a remee
rub	strofinare	strofeenare

rubber (=eraser)	gomma da cancellare	goma da kanchelaʀe
rubber (substance)	gomma	goma
r. boots	stivali di g. (mpl)	steevalee dee goma
rubber band	elastico	elasteeko
rubbish (=litter)	rifiuti (mpl)	ʀeefyootee
rucksack	zaino	tsayno
rude	scortese (m & f)	skoʀteze
rug	tappetino	tapeteeno
rugby	rugby (m)	ʀagbee
a game of r.	una partita di r.	oona parteeta dee ʀagbee
rules	regole (fpl)	ʀegole
rum	rhum (m)	ʀoom
run (vb)	correre – corso	koʀeʀe – koʀso
run (vb) (colour)	macchiare	makyaʀe
does it r.?	macchia?	makya
run over / /	investire / /	eenvesteeʀe / /
run-resistant (tights etc)	anti smagliatura (m, f & pl)	antee zmalyatoora
rush hour	ora di punta	oʀa dee poonta

S

saccharine	saccarina	sakaʀeena
s. tablet	pastiglia di s.	pasteelya dee sakaʀeena
sad	triste (m & f)	tʀeeste
saddle	sella	sela
safe (adj)	sicuro	seekooʀo
safe (n)	sicuro	seekooʀo
safety belt	cintura di sicurezza	cheentoora dee seekooʀetsa
safety pin	spilla di sicurezza	speela dee seekooʀetsa
sail (n)	vela	vela
sail (vb)	veleggiare	velejaʀe
sailing	veleggiare	velejaʀe
go s.	andare in barca a vela	andaʀe een baʀka a vela
sailor	marinaio	maʀeenayo
saint	santo	santo
salad	insalata	eensalata
green s.	i. verde	eensalata veʀde
mixed s.	i. mista	eensalata meesta
s. dressing	condimento per i.	kondeemento peʀ eensalata

salary	stipendio –di	steependyo steependee
sale	vendita	vendeeta
sales manager	direttore (m) delle vendite	deeretore dele vendeete
salmon	salmone (m)	salmone
smoked s.	s. affumicato	salmone afoomikato afoomeekato
salt (n)	sale (m)	sale
salted	salato	salato
same	stesso	steso
the s. as / /	lo s. di / /	lo steso dee / /
sand	sabbia	sabya
sandals	sandali (mpl)	sandalee
a pair of s.	un paio di s.	oon payo dee sandalee
sandwich	panino imbottito	paneeno eemboteeto
a /cheese/ s.	un panino con /formaggio/	oon paneeno kon /formajo/
sandy	sabbioso	sabyozo
sanitary towels	assorbenti (mpl)	asorbentee
sardines	sardine (fpl)	sardeene
satin (adj)	di raso	dee razo
satin (n)	raso	razo
satisfactory	soddisfacente (m & f)	sodeesfachente
Saturday	sabato	sabato
on Saturday	s.	sabato
on Saturdays	di s.	dee sabato
sauce	salsa	salsa
saucepan	pentolino	pentoleeno
saucer	piattino	pyateeno
a cup and s.	una tazza e p.	oona tatsa e pyateeno
sauna	sauna	saoona
sausage	salsiccia –cce /salame (m)	salseecha salseeche/ salame
save (money)	risparmiare	reesparmyare
save (=rescue)	salvare	salvare
savoury (=not sweet)	salatino	salateeno
say (something)	dire – detto	deere – deto
scale (on a map)	scala	skala
large s.	s. grande	skala grande
small s.	s. piccola	skala peekola

	words ending in –o or marked (m)	words ending in –a or marked (f)
a	un/uno	una/un'
some	del/dell'/dello	della/dell'
some (plural)	dei/degl'/degli	delle

English	Italian	Pronunciation
scales (=weighing machine)	bilancia (s)	beelancha
scallops	conchiglie (fpl)	konkeelye
scar	cicatrice (f)	cheekatreeche
scarf	sciarpa	sharpa
/silk/ s.	s. di /seta/	sharpa dee /seta/
scenery	panorama (m)	panorama panoramee
schedule	programma (m) –i	programa programee
school	scuola	skwola
language s.	s. di lingue	skwola dee leengwe
schoolboy	studente (m)	stoodente
schoolgirl	studentessa	stoodentesa
science	scienza	shyentsa
scissors	forbici (fpl)	forbeechee
a pair of s.	un paio di f.	oon payo dee forbeechee
scooter (=child's s.)	scooter (m)	skooter
motor s.	scooter (m)	skooter
score /a goal/	segnare /un gol/	senyare /oon gol/
scratch (n)	graffio –i	grafyo grafee
scratch (vb)	graffiare	grafyare
scream (n)	grido	greedo
screen (=film s.)	schermo	skermo
screen (=movable partition)	paravento	paravento
screw	vite (f)	veete
screwdriver	cacciavite (f)	kachaveete
sculpture	scultura	skooltoora
sea	mare (m)	mare
by s.	per m.	per mare
seafood	frutti (mpl) di mare	frootee dee mare
search (n)	ricerca	reecherka
search (vb)	ricercare	reecherkare
seasick		
be s.	avere mal di mare	avere mal dee mare
I feel s.	ho m. di m.	o mal dee mare
season	stagione (f)	stajone
season ticket	abbonamento	abonamento
seasoning	condimento	kondeemento
seat	posto	posto
at a theatre	al teatro	al teatro
at the back	di dietro	dee dyetro
at the front	davanti	davantee

169

by the exit	vicino all'uscita	vēēchēēno aloōshēēta
by the window	vicino alla finestra	vēēchēēno ala fēēnestra
in a non-smoker (train)	scompartimento per non fumatori	skompartēēmento per non foōmatorēē
in a non-smoking section (aeroplane)	nella sezione per non fumatori	nela setsyone per non foōmatorēē
in a smoker (train)	scompartimento per fumatori	skompartēēmento per foōmatorēē
in the middle	in mezzo	ēēn medzo
in the smoking section (aeroplane)	nella sezione per fumatori	nela setsyone per foōmatorēē
on a coach	in pullman	ēēn poōlman
on a train	in treno	ēēn treno
second (of time)	secondo	sekondo
second-hand	di seconda hano	dēē sekonda mano
a s.-h. car	una macchina usata	ōōna makēēna oōzata
secret (adj)	segreto	segreto
secret (n)	segreto	segreto
secretary	segretaria	segretarya
security	sicurezza	sēēkoōretsa
s. check	controllo speciale di s.	kontrolo spechale dēē sēēkoōretsa
s. control	controllo di s.	kontrolo dēē sēēkoōretsa
sedative	calmante (m)	kalmante
see /the manager/	vedere /il direttore/	vedere /ēēl dēērettore/
s. /the menu/	v. /il menu/	vedere /ēēl menoō/
self-addressed envelope	busta indirizzata a se	boōsta ēēndēērēētsata a se
sell	vendere	vendere
Sellotape (tdmk)	nastroadesivo	nastroadezēēvo
send	spedire	spedēēre
s. /a message/	s. /un messaggio/	spedēēre /oōn mesajo/
s. / / to me	s. / / a me	spedēēre / / a me
separate (adj)	separato	separato
September	settembre (m)	setembre
septic	settico	setēēko

170

serve	servire	seʀVĒĒʀE
service (car)	controllare	kontʀoLAʀE
service (church)	funzione (f)	fōōntsyone
service (=extra charge)	servizio –zi	seʀVĒĒtsyo serVĒĒtsee
room s.	s. in camera	seʀVĒĒtsyo ēēn kameʀa
24-hour s.	s. continuo	seʀVĒĒtsyo kontēēnwo
serviette	tovagliolo	tovalyolo
set (n)	servizio –zi	seʀVĒĒtsyo serVĒĒtsee
dinner s.	s. da pranzo	seʀVĒĒtsyo da pʀantso
tea s.	s. da tè	seʀVĒĒtsyo da te
set (vb) (hair)	mettere in piega	meteʀe ēēn pyega
shampoo and s. (n)	messa in piega	mesa ēēn pyega
several	parecchi	paʀekēē
sew	cucire	kōōchēēʀe
sewing	cucire	kōōchēēʀe
do some s.	cucire un pò	kōōchēēʀe ōōn po
sex	sesso	seso
shade	ombra	ombʀa
in the s.	all'o.	alombʀa
shade (colour)	ombretto	ombʀeto
shake (vb)	scuotere – scosso	skwoteʀe – skoso
s. hands	dare la mano – dato la mano	daʀe la mano – dato la mano
shampoo (n)	shampoo (m)	shampo
a bottle of s.	una bottiglia di s.	ōōna botēēlya dēē shampo
a sachet of s.	un sachet di s.	ōōn sashe dēē shampo
s. and blow dry	s. e asciugar col fon	shampo e ashōōgaʀ kol fon
s. and set	messa in piega	mesa ēēn pyega
shampoo (vb)	fare lo shampoo – fatto lo shampoo	faʀe lo shampo – fato lo shampo
shape (n)	forma	foʀma
share (vb)	condividere – condiviso	kondēēvēēdeʀe – kondēēvēēzo
sharp (of things)	acuto	akōōto
sharpen	affilare	afēēlaʀe
shave (n)	rasatura	ʀazatōōʀa

	words ending in –o or marked (m)	words ending in –a or marked (f)
the	il/l'/lo	la/l'
the (plural)	i/gl'/gli	le/l'

171

shave (vb)	fare la barba – fatto la barba	faʀe la baʀba – fato la baʀba
shaving brush	pennello da barba	penelo da baʀba
shaving cream	crema da barba	kʀema da baʀba
a tube of s. c.	un tubetto di c. da b.	ōōn tōōbeto dee kʀema da baʀba
shaving soap	sapone (m) da barba	sapone da baʀba
a stick of s. s.	un bastoncino di s. da b.	ōōn bastoncheeno dee sapone da baʀba
shawl	scialle (m)	shyale
she	lei	leee
sheath (=Durex)	Durex (m)	dōōʀeks
a packet of sheaths	un pacchetto di D.	ōōn paketo dee dōōʀeks
sheep	pecora	pekora
sheepskin	pelle (f) di pecora	pele dee pekoʀa
s. /rug/	/coperta/ di p. di p.	/kopeʀta/ dee pele dee pekoʀa
sheet (bed linen)	lenzuolo (m) lenzuola (fpl)	lentswolo lentswola
sheet (of paper)	foglio di carta	folyo dee kaʀta
shelf	scaffale (m)	skafale
book s.	libreria	leebʀeʀeea
shell (sea-s.)	conchiglia	konkeelya
shellfish	crostacei (mpl)	kʀostachey
sheltered	riparato	ʀeepaʀato
sherry	sherry (m)	sheʀee
a bottle of s.	una bottiglia di s.	ōōna boteelya dee sheʀee
a s.	uno s.	ōōno sheʀee
shiny	lucido	lōōcheedo
ship (n)	nave (f)	nave
ship (vb)	spedire	spedeeʀe
shirt	camicia –ce	kameecha kameeche
casual s.	c. sportiva	kameecha spoʀteeva
/cotton/ s.	c. di /cotone/	kameecha dee /kotone/
formal s.	c. formale	kameecha foʀmale
short-sleeved s.	c. a maniche corte	kameecha a maneeke koʀte
shock (n)	scossa	skosa
electric s.	s. elettrica	skosa eletʀeeka
state of s.	stato di collasso	stato dee kolaso
shockproof (eg of watch)	resistente all'urto	ʀezeestente alōōʀto

172

shoebrush	spazzola per le scarpe	spatsola peR le skaRpe
shoelaces	lacci (mpl)	lachēē
a pair of s.	un paio di l.	ōōn payo dēē lachēē
shoepolish	lucido per le scarpe	lōōchēēdo peR le skaRpe
shoes	scarpe (fpl)	skaRpe
a pair of s.	un paio di s.	ōōn payo dēē skaRpe
boy's s.	s. da bambino	skaRpe da bambēēno
girl's s.	s. da bambina	skaRpe da bambēēna
flat-heeled s.	s. con tacchi bassi	skaRpe kon takēē basēē
high-heeled s.	s. con tacchi alti	skaRpe kon takēē altēē
ladies' s.	s. da donna	skaRpe da dona
men's s.	s. da uomo	skaRpe da womo
walking s.	s. da camminare	skaRpe da kamēēnare
shoeshop	negozio –zi di calzature	negotsyo dēē kaltsatōōre negotsēē dēē kaltsatōōre
shoot (vb) (sport)	sparare	sparare
shop	negozio –zi	negotsyo negotsēē
shop assistant	commesso (m) commessa (f)	komeso komesa
shopping	spesa	speza
go s.	fare la s. – fatto la	fare la speza – fato la speza
shopping bag	borsa per la spesa	boRsa peR la speza
shopping centre	centro di shopping	chentRo dēē shopēēng
shore	spiaggia –gge	spyaja spyaje
short (people)	basso	baso
short (things)	corto	koRto
short (time)	breve (m & f)	breve
short circuit	corto circuito	koRto chēēRkwēēto
shorten	abbreviare	abrevyare
shorts	pantaloncini (mpl)	pantalonchēēnēē
a pair of s.	un paio di p.	ōōn payo dēē pantalonchēēnēē
shot (n)	sparo	sparo
shoulder	spalla	spala
shout (n)	grido	grēēdo

shout (vb)	gridare	gʀeedaʀe
show	mostra	mostʀa
fashion s.	sfilata di moda	sfeelata dee moda
floor s.	cabaret (m)	kabaʀe
strip s.	spogliarello	spolyaʀelo
variety s.	spettacolo di varietà	spetakolo dee vaʀyeta
show (vb)	far vedere	far vedeʀe
s. /it/ to me	farme/lo/ vedere	faʀme/lo/vedeʀe
shower (=s. bath)	doccia –ce	docha doche
shrimps	gamberetti (mpl)	gambeʀetee
shutters	imposte (fpl)	eemposte
shy	timido	teemeedo
sick	nausea	naoozea
I feel s.	mi sento n.	mee sento naoozea
side (n) (in game)	squadra	skwadʀa
side (n) (of object)	lato	lato
sights (of a town)	luoghi interessanti	lwogee eenteʀesantee
sightseeing	visitare i luoghi interessanti	veezeetaʀe ee lwogee eenteʀesantee
go s.	andare a v. i l. i.	andaʀe a veezeetaʀe ee lwogee eenteʀesantee
sign /your name/	firmare /suo nome/	feeʀmaʀe /sooo nome/
s. here	firmi qui	feeʀmee qwee
sign (n)	indicazione (f)	eendeekatsyone
signal (n)	segnale (m)	senyale
signal (vb)	segnalare	senyalaʀe
signature	firma	feeʀma
signpost	palo indicatore	palo eendeekatoʀe
silence	silenzio	seelentsyo
silent	silenzioso	seelentsyozo
silk (adj)	di seta	dee seta
silk (n)	seta	seta
silver (adj)	d'argento	daʀjento
silver (n)	argento	aʀjento
similar	simile (m & f)	seemeele
simple	semplice (m & f)	sempleeche
sincere	sincero	seencheʀo

	words ending in –o or marked (m)	words ending in –a or marked (f)
a	un/uno	una/un'
some	del/dell'/dello	della/dell'
some (plural)	dei/degl'/degli	delle

sing	cantare	kantare
singer	cantante (m & f)	kantante
single (=not married)	non sposato	non spozato
s. bed	letto singolo	leto seengolo
s. ticket	biglietto semplice	beelyeto sempleeche
sink (n)	secchaio –ai	sekyayo sekyay
sink (vb)	affondare	afondare
sister	sorella	sorela
sister-in-law	cognata	konyata
sit (see seat)	sedere	sedere
please s. down	si accomodi, prego	see akomodee prego
site	luogo –ghi	lwogo lwogee
camping s.	campeggio	kampejo
caravan s.	campeggio per roulotte	kampejo per roolot
size	misura	meezoora
large s.	m. grande	meezoora grande
medium s.	m. media	meezoora medya
small s.	m. piccola	meezoora peekola
skating	pattinaggio	pateenajo
go s.	andare a pattinare	andare a pateenare
ice-s.	p. sul ghiaccio	pateenajo sool gyacho
roller-s.	pattinare	pateenare
sketch (n)	schizzo	skeetso
sketchpad	blocco –chi da disegno	bloko da deezenyo blokee da deezenyo
ski-boots	scarponi (mpl) da sci	skarponee da shee
a pair of s. b.	un paio di s. da s.	oon payo dee skarponee da shee
skid (n)	slittamento	zleetamento
skid (vb) (car)	slittare	zleetare
skiing	sciare	shyare
go s.	andare a s.	andare a shyare
water-s.	sci d'acqua	shee dakwa
ski lift	ski lift (m)	shee leeft
skin	pelle (f)	pele
skin diving	tuffarmi in apnea	toofarmee een apnea
go s. d.	andare a t.i.a.	andare a toofarmee een apnea
skirt	sottana	sotana
long s.	s. lunga	sotana loonga
short s.	s. corta	sotana korta

skis	sci (mpl)	shee
a pair of s.	un paio di s.	oon payo dee shee
water s.	s. d'acqua	shee dakwa
sky	cielo	chyelo
sleep (n)	sonno	sono
sleep (vb)	dormire	dormeere
sleeper (on a train)	vagone (m) letto	vagone leto
sleeping bag	sacco –chi a pelo	sako a pelo sakee a pelo
sleeping berth	cuccetta	koocheta
sleeping car	vagone (m) letto	vagone leto
sleeping pill	sonnifero	soneefero
sleepy	sonnolente (m & f)	sonolente
be s.	avere sonno	avere sono
I'm s.	ho sonno	o sono
sleeves	maniche (fpl)	maneeke
long s.	m. lunghe	maneeke loonge
short s.	m. corte	maneeke korte
sleeveless	senza m.	sentsa maneeke
slice (n)	fetta	feta
a s. of / /	une f. di / /	oona feta dee / /
slice (vb)	tagliare	talyare
slide viewer	macchina per diapositive	makeena per dyapozeeteeve
slides	diapositive (fpl)	dyapozeeteeve
colour s.	d. a colore	dyapozeeteeve a kolore
slippers	pantofole (fpl)	pantofole
a pair of s.	un paio di p.	oon payo dee pantofole
slippery	scivoloso	sheevolozo
slope	discesa	disheza
slot machine	distributore (m) a gettoni	deestreebootore a jetonee
slow	lento	lento
slower	più lento	pyoo lento
slowly	lentamente	lentamente
small (size)	piccolo	peekolo
smart (appearance)	elegante (m & f)	elegante
smell (n)	odore (m)	odore
smell (vb) (=have a certain smell)	avere l'odore di / / – avuto l'odore di / /	avere lodore dee / / – avooto lodore dee / /
smell (vb) (=perceive with nose)	sentire l'odore di / /	senteere lodore dee / /
smoke (n)	fumo	foomo
smoke /a cigarette/	fumare /una sigaretta/	foomare /oona seegareta/

176

smoked (of fish & meat etc)	affumicato	afoomeekato
s. /ham/	/prosciutto/ a.	/proshooto/ afoomeekato
smoker	fumatori (m, f & pl)	foomatoree
non-s.	non-f.	non-foomatoree
smooth	lisco –sci	leeshyo leeshee
snack	spuntino	spoonteeno
snack-bar	snack-bar (m)	snak-bar
snake	serpente (m)	serpente
snakebite	morso di s.	morso dee serpente
sneeze (vb)	*starnutire	starnooteere
snorkel (n)	snorkel (m)	snorkel
s. mask	mascera s.	maskera snorkel
s. tube	tubetta s.	toobeta snorkel
snorkel (vb)	fare snorkel – fatto snorkel	fare snorkel – fato snorkel
snow (n)	neve (f)	neve
snow (vb)	nevicare	neveekare
it's snowing	nevica	neveeka
soak	bagnare	banyare
soap	sapone (m)	sapone
a bar of s.	un pezzo di s.	oon petso dee sapone
s. flakes	s. in scaglie	sapone een skalye
shaving s.	s. da barba	sapone da barba
soapy	insaponato	eensaponato
sober	sobrio –ri	sobryo sobree
socket	presa	preza
electric razor s.	p. per rasoio	preza per razoyo
light s.	p. per la luce	preza per la looche
socks	calze (fpl)	kaltse
a pair of s.	un paio di c.	oon payo dee kaltse
long s.	c. lunge	kaltse loonge
short s.	calcini (mpl)	kaltzeenee
/woolen/ s.	c. /di lana/	kaltse /dee lana/
soda (water)	seltz	selts
a bottle of s. (w.)	una bottiglia di s.	oona boteelya dee selts
a glass of s. (w.)	un bicchiere di s.	oon beekyere dee selts
soft (=not hard)	morbido	morbeedo
	words ending in –o or marked (m)	words ending in –a or marked (f)
the	il/l'/lo	la/l'
the (plural)	i/gl'/gli	le/l'

177

sold	venduto	ven**doo**to
soldier	soldato	sol**da**to
sold out	esaurito	ezaoo**ree**to
sole (=fish)	sogliola	so**lyo**la
sole (of shoe)	suolo	**swo**lo
solid	solido	so**lee**do
some	di/un po' di	dee/oon po dee
s. /money/	dei /soldi/	dey /sol**dee**/
someone	qualcuno	kwal**koo**no
something	qualcosa	kwal**ko**za
somewhere	da qualche parte	da **kwal**ke **pa**rte
son	figlio –gli	**fee**lyo **fee**ly
song	canzone (f)	kan**tso**ne
folk s.	c. folk	kan**tso**ne folk
pop s.	c. pop	kan**tso**ne pop
son-in-law	genero	**ge**nero
soon	presto	**pre**sto
sore (adj)	irritato	eeree**ta**to
sore throat	mal (m) di gola	mal dee **go**la
sound (n)	suono	**swo**no
soup (clear)	minestra	mee**nes**tra
s. (thick)	brodo	**bro**do
/chicken/ s.	b. di /pollo/	**bro**do dee /**po**lo/
sour	aspro	**a**spro
south	sud (m)	sood
s.east	sudest (m)	soo**dest**
s.west	sudovest (m)	soo**do**vest
souvenir	ricordo	ree**kor**do
souvenir shop	negozio –zi di ricordi	ne**got**syo dee ree**kor**dee nego**tsee** dee ree**kor**dee
space (room)	spazio –zi	**spa**tsyo **spa**tsee
spade	badile (m)	ba**dee**le
spanner	chiave (f) inglese	**kya**ve een**gle**ze
adjustable s.	c. i. regolabile	**kya**ve een**gle**ze rego**la**beele
spare (adj)	di riserva	dee ree**zer**va
s. parts	ricambi (mpl)	ree**kam**bee
spare time	tempo libero	**tem**po **lee**bero
speak /English/	parlare /inglese/	par**la**re /een**gle**ze/
speak /to the manager/	parlare /col direttore/	par**la**re /kol deere**to**re/
special	speciale	spe**cha**le
speed	velocità	velo**chee**ta
speedboat	motoscafo	moto**ska**fo

178

spell	dire lettera per lettera – detto lettera per lettera	dēēre letera per letera – deto letera per letera
spend (money)	spendere – speso	spendere – spezo
spend (time)	passare	pasare
spice	spezia	spetsya
spicy	saporito	saporēēto
spider	ragno	ranyo
spilt	rovesciato	roveshato
spinach	spinaci (mpl)	spēēnachee
spine (part of body)	spina	spēēna
spirits (=alcohol)	liquori (mpl)	lēēkworēē
spit (vb)	sputare	spōōtare
splendid	meraviglioso	meravēēlyozo
spoil (vb)	rovinare	rovēēnare
sponge (bath s.)	spugna	spōōnya
spoon	cucchiaio –ai	kōōkyayo kōōkyay
spoonful	cucchiaio –ai	kōōkyayo kōōkyay
a s. of / /	un c. di / /	ōōn kōōkyayo dēē / /
sport	sport (m)	sport
sports car	macchina sportiva	makēēna sportēēva
spot (=blemish)	macchiolina	makyolēēna
spot (=dot)	punto	pōōnto
sprain (n)	storta	storta
sprained	storto	storto
spring (=season)	primavera	prēēmavera
in s.	in p.	ēēn prēēmavera
spring (=wire coil)	molla	mola
spring onion	cipollina	chēēpolēēna
sprouts (=Brussels s.)	cavolini (mpl) di Bruxelles	kavolēēnēē dēē brōōksel
square (place)	piazza	pyatsa
main s.	p. principale	pyatsa prēēnchēēpale
square (=scarf)	fazzoletto di testa	fatsoleto dēē testa
a /silk/ s.	un f. di /seta/	ōōn fatsoleto dēē /seta/
square (shape)	quadrato	kwadrato
squash	squash (m)	skwosh
a game of s.	una partita a s.	ōōna partēēta a skwosh
squeeze (vb)	spremere	spremere
stable (for horses)	stalla	stala
stadium	stadio	stadyo
staff (=employees)	personale (m)	personale
stage (in a theatre)	palcoscenico –chi	palkoshenēēko palkoshenēēkee

179

stain	macchia	makya
s. remover	smacchiatore (m)	smakyatoRe
stained	macchiato	makyato
stainless steel	acciaio inossidabile	achyayo eenoseedabeele
s. s. /cutlery/	/posateria/ di a. i.	/pozatereea/ dee achyayo eenoseedabeele
staircase	scala	skala
stairs	scale (fpl)	skale
stale	vecchio –chi	vekyo vekee
stale (bread)	vecchio –chi	vekyo vekee
stamp (n)	francobollo	fRankobolo
a /200/ lire s.	un f. da /200/ lire	oon fRankobolo da /dooechento/ leeRe
stand (vb)	stare	staRe
standard (adj)	standard	standaRd
star	diva	deeva
film s.	d. del cinema	deeva del cheenema
starch (n)	amido	ameedo
starch (vb)	inamidare	eenameedaRe
start (n)	partenza	paRtentsa
start (vb)	incominciare	eenkomeenchaRe
s. /the journey/	i. /il viaggio/	eenkomeenchaRe /eel vyajo/
starter (=hors d'oeuvre)	antipasto	anteepasto
state (n)	stato	stato
station (=railway s.)	stazione (f) ferroviaria	statsyone feRovyaRya
bus s.	s. di autobus	statsyone dee aootoboos
coach s.	s. di pullman	statsyone dee poolman
stationery	cartoleria	kaRtoleReea
statue	statua	statwa
stay at / /	stare a / /	staRe a / /
for a night	per una notte	peR oona note
for /two/ nights	per /due/ notti	peR /dooe/ notee
for a week	per una settimana	peR oona seteemana

	words ending in –o or marked (m)	words ending in –a or marked (f)
a	un/uno	una/un'
some	del/dell'/dello	della/dell'
some (plural)	dei/degl'/degli	delle

for /two/ weeks	per /due/ settimane	peʀ /dōōe/ seteēmane
till / /	fino a / /	feēno a / /
from / / till / /	da / / a / /	da / / a / /
steak	bistecca –che	beēsteka beēsteke
medium	non troppo cotta	non tropo kota
rare	al sangue	al sangwe
well-done	cotto bene	koto bene
steal	rubare	rōōbare
steam (vb)	cuocere a bagno maria – cotto a bagno maria	kwocheʀe a banyo mareēa – koto a banyo mareēa
steel	acciaio	achyayo
stainless s.	a. inossidabile	achyayo eēnoseēdabeēle
steep	ripido	ʀeēpeēdo
steer (vb) (boat)	virare	veēʀaʀe
steer (vb) (car)	guidare	gweēdaʀe
step (n) (movement)	passo	paso
step (n) (part of staircase)	gradino	gʀadeēno
stereo (adj)	stereo	steʀeo
s. equipment	equippaggiamento s.	ekweēpajamento steʀeo
stereo (n)	stereo	steʀeo
stern (of boat)	poppa	popa
steward (plane or boat)	steward (m)	styōōard
stewardess (plane or boat)	hostess (f) –	ostes
stick (n)	bastone (m)	bastone
sticking plaster	cerotto	cheʀoto
sticky	appiccicaticcio –cci	apeēcheēkateēcho apeēcheēkateēchee
sticky tape (eg Sellotape (tdmk))	nastro adhesivo	nastʀo adezeēvo
stiff	rigido	ʀeējeēdo
sting (n)	puntura	pōōntōōʀa
/bee/ s.	p. /d'ape/	pōōntōōʀa /dape/
sting (vb)	pungere – punto	pōōnjeʀe – pōōnto
stir (vb)	mescolare	meskolaʀe
stock (of things)	rifornimento	ʀeēforneēmento
stockings	calze (fpl)	kaltse
15/30 denier	quindici/trenta denier	kweēndeēchee/tʀenta denya
a pair of s.	un paio di c.	ōōn payo deē kaltse
/nylon/ s.	c. di /nailon/	kaltse deē naylon

181

stolen	rubato	Rōobato
stomach	stomaco –chi	stomako stomakēē
I've got a s. ache	ho mal di s.	o mal dēē stomako
I've got a s. upset	ho lo s. disturbato	o lo stomako dēēstōōrbato
stone (of fruit)	nocciolo	nochyolo
stone (substance)	pietra	pyetra
precious s.	p. preziosa	pyetra pretsyoza
stool	sgabello	zgabelo
stop (n)	fermata	fermata
bus s.	f. dell'autobus	fermata delaōōtobōōs
tram s.	f. del tram	fermata del tram
stop (vb)	fermare	fermare
stop at / /	fermarmi a / /	fermarmēē a / /
store (=department s.)	magazzino	magadzēēno
storm	temporale (m)	temporale
stormy	tempestoso	tempestoso
story	racconto	rakonto
straight	dritto	drēēto
stranger (n)	sconosciuto	skonoshōōto
strap	cinturino	chēēntōōrēēno
watch-s.	c. dell'orologio	chēēntōōrēēno delorolojo
strapless	senza cinturino	sentsa chēēntōōrēēno
straw (=drinking s.)	cannuccia –ce	kanōōcha kanōōche
strawberry	fragola	fragola
a punnet of strawberries	un cestino di fragole	ōōn chestēēno dēē fragole
streak (n) (of hair)	mèche (f)	mesh
i'd like my hair streaked	vorrei farmi le mèches	vorey farmēē le mesh
stream (n)	ruscello	rōōshelo
street	strada	strada
main s.	s. principale	strada prēēnchēēpale
stretcher	barella	barela
strike (n)	sciopero	shyopero
be on s.	essere in s.	esere ēēn shyopero
strike (vb) (of clock)	suonare	swonare
string	spago –ghe	spago spage
a ball of s.	un rotolo di s.	ōōn rotolo dēē spago
a piece of s.	un pezzo di s.	ōōn petso dēē spago
strip show	spogliarello	spolyarelo

striped	a righe	a $\overline{\text{ree}}$ge
strong (physically)	forte (m & f)	fo$\overline{\text{r}}$te
s. /coffee/	/caffè/ f.	/kafe/ fo$\overline{\text{r}}$te
stuck (eg a window)	bloccato	blokato
student	studente (m)	st$\overline{\text{oo}}$dente st$\overline{\text{oo}}$dentesa
	studentessa (f)	
studio	studio	st$\overline{\text{oo}}$dyo
study	studiare	st$\overline{\text{oo}}$dyare
s. at / /	s. a / /	st$\overline{\text{oo}}$dyare a / /
study /Italian/	studiare /italiano/	st$\overline{\text{oo}}$dyare /$\overline{\text{ee}}$talyano/
stuffing (food)	ripieno	r$\overline{\text{ee}}$pyeno
stuffing (material)	imbottitura	$\overline{\text{ee}}$mbot$\overline{\text{eetoo}}$ra
stupid	stupido	st$\overline{\text{oo}}$p$\overline{\text{ee}}$do
style	stile (m)	st$\overline{\text{ee}}$le
stylus	stilo	st$\overline{\text{ee}}$lo
ceramic	di ceramica	d$\overline{\text{ee}}$ cheram$\overline{\text{ee}}$ka
diamond	di diamante	d$\overline{\text{ee}}$ dyamante
sapphire	di zaffiro	d$\overline{\text{ee}}$ tsaf$\overline{\text{ee}}$ro
subscribe to / /	abbonarmi a / /	abona$\overline{\text{r}}$m$\overline{\text{ee}}$ a / /
subscription	abbonamento	abonamento
substance	sostanza	sostantsa
suburb	periferia	per$\overline{\text{ee}}$fer$\overline{\text{ee}}$a
subway	sottopassaggio –ggi	sotopasajo
		sotopasaj$\overline{\text{ee}}$
suede (n)	pelle (f) scamosciata	pele skamoshata
s. /jacket/	/giacca/ di p. s.	/jaka/ d$\overline{\text{ee}}$ pele
		skamoshata
suffer	soffrire – sofferto	sof$\overline{\text{ree}}$re – sofe$\overline{\text{r}}$to
s. from	s. di /mal di testa/	sof$\overline{\text{ree}}$re d$\overline{\text{ee}}$ /mal
/headaches/		d$\overline{\text{ee}}$ testa/
sugar	zucchero	ts$\overline{\text{oo}}$kero
a spoonful of s.	un cucchiaio di z.	$\overline{\text{oo}}$n k$\overline{\text{oo}}$kyayo d$\overline{\text{ee}}$
		ts$\overline{\text{oo}}$kero
sugar lump	zolletta di zucchero	tsoleta d$\overline{\text{ee}}$ ts$\overline{\text{oo}}$kero
suggest	*suggerire	s$\overline{\text{oo}}$jer$\overline{\text{ee}}$re
suit (n)	vestito	vest$\overline{\text{ee}}$to
suit (vb)	andare bene	anda$\overline{\text{r}}$e bene
suitable	adatto	adato
suitcase	valigia	val$\overline{\text{ee}}$ja
suite (= hotel s.)	appartamento	apartamento
summer	estate (f)	estate
in s.	d'estate	destate

	words ending in –o or marked (m)	words ending in –a or marked (f)
the	il/l'/lo	la/l'
the (plural)	i/gl'/gli	le/l'

sun	sole (m)	sole
in the s.	al s.	al sole
sunbathe	prendere il sole – preso il sole	prendere eel sole – prezo eel sole
sunbathing	bagni (mpl) di sole	banyee dee sole
sunburn	abbronzatura	abrondzatoora
sunburnt	abbronzato	abrondzato
Sunday	domenica	domeneeka
on Sunday	d.	domeneeka
on Sundays	di d.	dee domeneeka
sunglasses	occhiali (mpl) da sole	okyalee da sole
a pair of s.	un paio di o. da s.	oon payo dee okyalee da sole
polaroid s.	o. polaroid	okyalee polaroyd
sunny	soleggiato	solejato
sunrise	alba	alba
sunset	tramonto	tramonto
sunshade	parasole (m)	parasole
sunstroke	insolazione (f)	eensolatsyone
suntan (n)	abbronzatura	abrondzatoora
s. oil	lozione (f) solare	lotsyone solare
suntanned	abbronzato	abrondzato
supermarket	supermercato	soopermekato
supper	cena	chena
have s.	cenare	chenare
supply (n)	rifornimento	reeforneemento
supply (vb)	*rifornire	reeforneere
suppository	supposta	sooposta
sure	sicuro	seekooro
he's s.	è s.	e seekooro
surface (n)	superficie (f) –ci	sooperfeecho sooperfeechee
s. mail	posta via terra	posta veea tera
surfboard	asse (f) per acquaplano	ase per akwaplano
surfing	acquaplano	akwaplano
go s.	fare a. – fatto a.	fare akwaplano – fato akwaplano
surgery (=place)	ambulatorio –i	amboolatoryo amboolatoree
doctor's s.	a. del medico	amboolatoryo del medeeko
surname	cognome (m)	konyome
surplus	avanzo	avantso
surprise (n)	sorpresa	sorpreza

184

surprised	sorpreso	soRpRezo
s. /at the result/	s. /del risultado/	soRpRezo/del reezōōltato/
surveyor	agrimensore (m)	agreemensoRe
survive	sopravvivere – sopravvissuto	sopraveevere – sopraveesōōto
suspect (vb)	sospettare	sospetaRe
suspender belt	reggicalze (m)	Rejeekaltse
swallow (vb)	*inghiottire	eengyoteere
sweat (n)	sudore (m)	sōōdoRe
sweat (vb)	sudare	sōōdaRe
sweater	maglione (m)	malyone
/cashmere/ s.	m. /di cashmere/	malyone /dee kashmeeR/
long-sleeved s.	m. con maniche lunghe	malyone kon maneeke lōōnge
short-sleeved s.	m. con maniche corte	malyone kon maneeke koRte
sleeveless s.	m. senza maniche	malyone sentsa maneeke
sweep (vb)	spazzare	spatsaRe
sweet (=dessert)	dolce (m)	dolche
sweet (n) (=confectionery)	caramella	kaRamela
sweet (=not savoury)	dolce	dolche
swelling	gonfiore (m)	gonfyoRe
swim (n)	nuoto	nwoto
have a s.	fare il bagno – fatto il bagno	faRe eel banyo – fato eel banyo
swim (vb)	nuotare	nwotaRe
swimming	nuoto	nwoto
go s.	andare a fare il bagno	andaRe a faRe eel banyo
s. trunks (for women)	costume (m) da bagno	kostōōme da banyo
s. trunks (for men)	pantaloncini da bagno	pantaloncheenee da banyo
swimming pool	piscina	peesheena
heated s. p.	p. riscaldata	peesheena reeskaldata
indoor s. p.	p. interna	peesheena eenteRna
open air s. p.	p. all'aperto	peesheena alapeRto
public s. p.	p. pubblica	peesheena pōōbleeka
swing (n) (children's s.)	altalena	altalena
switch (=light s.)	interruttore (m)	eenteRōōtoRe

185

swollen	gonfiato	gonfyato
symptom	sintomo	sēentomo
synagogue	sinagoga	sēenagoga
synthetic	sintetico	sēenteteēko

T

table	tavola	tavola
table tennis	tennis (m) da tavolo	tenēēs da tavolo
a game of t. t.	una partita a t. da t.	ōona partēēta a tenēēs da tavolo
tablecloth	tovaglia	tovalya
tablemat	sottopiatto	sotopyato
tablespoonful of / /	cucchiaio –ai da tavola di / /	kōokyayo da tavola dēē / / kōokyay da tavola dēē / /
tailor	sarto	sarto
take	prendere – preso	prendere – prezo
take (time)	prendere – preso	prendere – prezo
take away (vb)	portare via	portare veēa
take-away meal	pasto da portar via	pasta da portar veēa
take off /a coat/	tolgiere /un cappotto/ – tolto /un cappotto/	tolyere /ōon kapoto/ – tolto /ōon kapoto/
take out (tooth)	fare levare – fatto levare	fare levare – fato levare
talcum powder	talco	talko
talk (n) (discussion, chat)	discussione (f)	dēēskōosyone
talk (vb)	parlare	parlare
t. to me about / /	parlarmi di / /	parlarmeē dēē / /
tall	alto	alto
tame (adj)	addomesticato	adomestēēkato
tampons	tamponi assorbenti (mpl)	tamponēē asorbentēē
a box of t. (eg Tampax (tdmk))	un pacchetto di t. a.	ōon paketo dēē tamponēē asorbentēē
tank	serbatoio	serbatoyo
water t.	s. d'acqua	serbatoyo dakwa

	words ending in –o or marked (m)	words ending in –a or marked (f)
a	un/uno	una/un'
some	del/dell'/dello	della/dell'
some (plural)	dei/degl'/degli	delle

tap	rubinetto	ʀoobeeneto
cold t.	r. di acqua fredda	ʀoobeeneto dee akwa fʀeda
hot t.	r. di acqua calda	ʀoobeeneto dee akwa kalda
tape	nastro	nastʀo
cassette	cassetta	kaseta
tape measure	metro a nastro	metʀo a nastʀo
tape recorder	registratore (m)	ʀejeestʀatoʀe
cassette recorder	r. a cassette	ʀejeestʀatoʀe a kasete
open reel recorder	r. a nastri	ʀejeestʀatoʀe a nastʀee
tartan	disegno scozzese	deezenyo skotseze
a t. skirt	una sottana scozzese	oona sotana skotseze
taste (n)	gusto	goosto
taste (vb) (=have a certain taste)	sapere di	sapeʀe dee
taste (vb) (perceive with tongue)	assagiare	asajaʀe
tasty	gustoso	goostozo
tax	tassa	tasa
airport t.	t. dell'aeroporto	tasa delaeʀopoʀto
tax free	esente da tasse	ezente da tase
taxi	taxi (m)	taksee
by t.	per t.	peʀ taksee
t. rank	stazione (f) di t.	statsyone dee taksee
taxi driver	autista (m & f) –i (mpl) –e (fpl) di taxi	aooteesta dee taksee aooteestee dee takee aooteeste dee taksee
tea	tè (m)	te
a cup of t.	una tazza di t.	oona tatsa dee te
a pot of t.	una teiera di t.	oona teyeʀa dee te
China t.	t. cinese	te cheeneze
Indian t.	t. indiano	te eendyano
tea towel	asciugapiatti (m) –	ashoogapyatee
tea (meal)	tè (m)	te
have t.	prendere il t. – preso il t.	pʀendeʀe eel te – pʀezo eel te
teabag	bustina di tè	boosteena dee te
teach	insegnare	eensenyaʀe
t. (me) /Italian/	(mi) insegnare /italiano/	(mee) eensenyaʀe /eetalyano/
teacher	insegnante (m & f)	eensenyante
team	squadra	skwadʀa

teapot	teiera	teyeʀa
tear (n) (= hole in material)	strappo	stʀapo
tear (vb) (material)	stracciare	stʀachaʀe
teaspoon	cucchiaino	kōōkyayno
a teaspoonful of / /	un c. di / /	ōōn kōōkyayno dēē / /
teat	tettarella	tetaʀela
teenager	adolescente (m & f)	adoleshente
teetotal	astemio –mi	astemyo astemēē
telegram	telegramma (m) –mi	telegʀama telegʀamēē
t. form	modulo di t.	modōōlo dēē telegʀama
send a t.	mandare un t.	mandaʀe ōōn telegʀama
telephone /phone (n)	telefono	telefono
call box	cabina telefonica	kabēēna telefonēēka
t. call	telefonata	telefonata
t. directory	elenco telefonico	elenko telefonēēko
on the phone	al t.	al telefono
telephone (vb)	telefonare	telefonaʀe
t. Reception	t. all'ufficio recevimento	telefonaʀe al ōōfēēcho ʀēēchevēēmento
t. the exchange	t. al centralino	telefonaʀe al chentʀalēēno
t. the operator	t. al centralino	telefonaʀe al chentʀalēēno
t. this number	t. questo numero	telefonaʀe kwesto nōōmeʀo
television/TV (infml)	televisione (f)	televēēzyone
portable t.	t. portatile	televēēzyone poʀtatēēle
t. aerial	antenna della t.	antena dela televēēzyone
t. channel	canale	kanale
t. programme	programma televisiva	pʀogʀama televēēzēēva
t. set	apparecchio televisivo	apaʀekyo televēēzēēvo
on t./on TV	alla t.	ala televēēzyone
telex (vb)	mandare per telex	mandaʀe peʀ teleks
tell me (something) about / /	raccontarmi di / /	ʀakontaʀmēē dēē / /
he told /me/ about it	/me/ ne ha parlato	/me/ ne a paʀlato

188

temperature (atmosphere, body)	temperatura	temperatōōra
temple	tempio	tempyo
temporary	provvisorio –ri	provēēzoryo provēēzorēē
tender (eg of meat)	tenero	tenero
tennis	tennis (m)	tenēēs
a game of t.	una partita a t.	ōōna partēēta a tenēēs
tent	tenda	tenda
term (=expression)	termine (m)	termēēne
term (=period of time)	trimestre (m)	trēēmestre
terminal	terminale (m)	termēēnale
air t.	t. (m) aereo	termēēnale aereo
terminus	capolinea	kapolēēnea
bus t.	c. dell'autobus	kapolēēnea del aōōtobōōs
railway t.	stazione (f) di testa	statsyone dēē testa
tram t.	c. del tram	kapolēēnea del tram
terms	condizioni (fpl)	kondēētsyonēē
terrace	terrazzo	teratso
terrible	terribile	terēēbeele
test (n)	prova	prova
test (vb)	provare	provare
textbook	libro di testo	lēēbro dēē testo
thank you for / / (vb)	ringraziarla per / /	rēēngratsyarla per / /
t. y. f. your hospitality	la ringrazio della sua ospitalità	la rēēngratsyo dela sōōa ospēētalēēta
theatre	teatro	teatro
t. programme	programma (m) –mi	programa programēē
theft	furto	fōōrto
then	poi	poy
there	là	la
thermometer	termometro	termometro
Centigrade t.	t. in centigradi	termometro ēēn chentēēgradēē
Fahrenheit t.	t. in fahrenheit	termometro ēēn farenhayt
clinical t.	t. clinico	termometro klēēnēēko

	words ending in –o or marked (m)	words ending in –a or marked (f)
the	il/l'/lo	la/l'
the (plural)	i/gl'/gli	le/l'

they	loro	loʀo
thick	spesso	speso
thigh	coscia –sce	kocha koshe
thin (coat etc)	leggero	lejeʀo
thin (of person)	magro	magʀo
thing	cosa	koza
things	roba	ʀoba
(=belongings)		
think about	pensare a /qualcosa/	pensaʀe a
/something/		/kwalkoza/
thirsty		
be t.	avere sete – avuto sete	aveʀe sete – avōoto sete
I'm t.	ho s.	o sete
thousand	mille	mēele
thousands of / /	migliaia di / /	mēelyaya dēe / /
thread	filo	fēelo
a reel of t.	un rocchetto di f.	ōon ʀoketo dēe fēelo
throat	gola	gola
sore throat	mal (m) di g.	mal dēe gola
t. pastilles	pastiglie (fpl) per la g.	pastēelye peʀ la gola
thumb	pollice (m)	polēeche
thunderstorm	temporale (m)	tempoʀale
Thursday	giovedì (m)	jovedēe
on Thursday	g.	jovedēe
on Thursdays	di g.	dēe jovedēe
ticket	biglietto	beelyeto
child's t.	b. ridotto per ragazzo	beelyeto ʀēedoto peʀ ʀagatso
first class t.	b. di prima classe	beelyeto dēe prēema klase
group t.	b. collettivo	beelyeto koletēevo
return t.	b. di andata e ritorno	beelyeto dēe andata e ʀēetorno
season t.	abbonamento	abonamento
second class t.	b. di seconda classe	beelyeto dēe sekonda klase
single	b. semplice	beelyeto semplēeche
ticket office	biglietteria	beelyeteʀēea
tide	marea	maʀea
high t.	alta m.	alta maʀea
low t.	bassa m.	basa maʀea
tidy (of people)	ordinato	oʀdēenato
tidy (things)	ordinato	oʀdēenato

tidy (vb)	mettere in ordine – messo in ordine	metere ēēn oRdēēne – meso ēēn oRdēēne
tie (n)	cravatta	kRavata
tie (vb)	legare	legaRe
tiepin	ferma cravatta	ferma kRavata
tight	stretto	stReto
tights	calza maglia	kaltsa malya
a pair of t.	una c. m.	ōōna kaltsa malya
till (=until)	fino a	fēēno a
time	tempo	tempo
the t. (clock)	l'ora	loRa
/6/ times	/sei/ volte	/sey/ volte
have a good t.	divertirmi	dēēveRtēēRmēē
timetable	orario	oRaRyo
bus t.	o. dell'autobus	oRaRyo delaōōtoboōs
coach t.	o. dei pullman	oRaRyo dey pōōlman
train t.	o. dei treni	oRaRyo dey trenēē
tin	barattolo	baRatolo
a t. of / /	un b. di / /	ōōn baRatolo dēē / /
tin opener	apriscatole (m) –	apRēēskatole
tint (n) (=hair t.)	tintura	tēēntōōRa
tint (vb)	tingere – tinto	tēēnjere – tēēnto
tip (n) (money)	mancia –ce	mancha manche
tip (vb) (money)	dare la mancia – dato la mancia	daRe la mancha – dato la mancha
t. /the waiter/	dare la mancia /al cameriere/	daRe la mancha /al kamaRyeRe/
tired	stanco (m) –chi (mpl) stanca (f) – che (fpl)	stanko stankēē stanka stanke
tiring	faticoso	fatēēkozo
tissues/Kleenex (tdmk)	fazzoletti di carta	fatsoletēē dēē kaRta
a box of t.	una scatola di f.	ōōna skatola dēē fatsoletēē
title	titolo	tēētolo
to	a	a
toast (n)	tost	tost
a slice of t.	una fetta di t.	ōōn feta dēē tost
toast (vb)	tostare	tostaRe
tobacco	tabacco	tabako
tobacconist's	tabacchi	tabakēē
today	oggi	ojēē

191

TOE

toe	dito del piede –a del piede	dēeto del pyede dēeta del pyede
toenail	unghia del d. del p.	ōongya del dēeto del pyede
together	insieme	ēensyeme
toilet	toilette (f)	twalet
toilet paper	carta igienica	karta ēejyenēeka
a roll of t. p.	un rotolo di c. i.	ōon rotolo dēe karta ēejyenēeka
toilet water	acqua di colognia	akwa dēe kolonya
tomato	pomodoro	pomodoro
t. sauce	conserva di p.	konserva dēe pomodoro
tomato juice	succo –chi di pomodoro	sōoko dēe pomodoro sōokēe dēe pomodoro
a bottle of t.j.	una bottiglia di s. di p.	ōona botēelya dēe sōoko dēe pomodoro
a can of t. j.	un barattolo di s. di p.	ōon baratolo dēe sōoko dēe pomodoro
a glass of t. j.	un bicchiere di s. di p.	ōon bēekyere dēe sōoko dēe pomodoro
tomorrow	domani	domanēe
ton	tonnellata	tonelata
tongue (food)	lingua	leengwa
tongue (organ of mouth)	lingua	lēengwa
tonic (water)	tonico –chi	tonēeko tonēekēe
tonight	stanotte	stanote
tonsillitis	tonsillite (f)	tonsēelēete
too (=more than can be endured)	troppo	tropo
t. /big/	t. /grande/	tropo /grande/
tool	arnese (m)	arneze
tooth	dente (m)	dente
wisdom t.	d. de giudizio	dente del jōodēetsyo
toothache	mal di denti	mal dēe dentēe
toothbrush	spazzolino da denti	spatsolēeno da dentēe

	words ending in –o or marked (m)	words ending in –a or marked (f)
a	un/uno	una/un'
some	del/dell'/dello	della/dell'
some (plural)	dei/degl'/degli	delle

192

English	Italian	Pronunciation
toothpaste	dentifricio	dentēēfrēēcho
a tube of t.	un tubo di d.	ōōn tōōbo dēē dentēēfrēēcho
toothpick	stuzzicadenti (m) –	stōōtsēēkadentēē
top	parte (f) superiore	parte sōōperyore
the t. of / /	la p. s. di / /	la parte sōōperyore dēē / /
torch	pila	pēēla
tortoiseshell (adj)	di tartaruga	dēē tartarōōga
total (adj)	totale	totale
total (n)	totale (m)	totale
touch (vb)	toccare	tokare
tough (food)	duro	dōōro
tour	visita	vēēzeeta
conducted t.	v. guidata	vēēzeeta gwēēdata
tourist	turista (m & f) –i (mpl) –e (fpl)	tōōrēēsta tōōrēēstee tōōrēēste
t. class	classe (f) turistica	klase tōōrēēsteeka
t. office	ufficio turistico	ōōfeecho tōōrēēsteeko
tow rope	corda per traino	korda per trayno
tow (vb)	trainare	traynare
towel (=bath t.)	asciugamano	ashōōgamano
towelling (material)	tela per asciugamani	tela per ashōōgamanēē
tower	torre (f)	tore
town	città –	chēēta
t. centre	centrocittà	chentrochēēta
t. hall	municipio	mōōnēēchēēpyo
toxic	tossico	tosēēk0
toy	giocattolo	jokatolo
t. shop	negozio –zi di giocattoli	negotsyo dēē jokatolee negotsēē dēē jokatolee
track (of animal)	traccia –ce	trachya trache
track (of tape)	pista	pēēsta
track (=race t.)	pista	pēēsta
traditional	tradizionale	tradēētsyonale
traffic	traffico	trafeeko
traffic jam	ingorgo stradale	ēēngorgo stradale
traffic lights	semaforo (m)	semaforo
trailer	rimorchio –chi	rēēmorkyo rēēmorkee
train	treno	treno
boat t.	t. per nave	treno per nave
express t.	rapido	rapēēdo

fast t.	espresso	espreso
slow t.	t. locale	treno lokale
train driver	macchinista (m) –i	makeeneesta
		makeeneestee
tram	tram (m)	tram
t. stop	fermata del t.	fermata del tram
t. terminus	capolinea del t.	kapoleenea del
		tram
the t. for / /	il t. per / /	eel tram per / /
by t.	in t.	een tram
tranquiliser	tranquillante (m)	trankweelante
transfer (vb)	*trasferire	trasfereere
transformer	trasformatore (m)	trasformatore
transistor (also t.	transistore (m)	tranzeestore
radio)		
transit passenger	viaggiatore (m & f)	vyajatore een
	in transito	tranzeeto
in transit	in transito	een tranzeeto
translate	tradurre – tradotto	tradoore – tradoto
translation	traduzione (f)	tradootsyone
transparent	trasparente (m & f)	trasparente
transport (n)	trasporto	trasporto
public t.	t. pubblico	trasporto
		poobleeko
trap (n)	trappola	trapola
trap (vb)	prendere in trappola	prendere een
	– preso in trappola	trapola – prezo
		een trapola
travel (vb)	viaggiare	vyajare
by air	in aereo	een aereo
by boat, by bus	in barca, in	een barka een
	autobus	aootoboos
by coach, by car	in pullman, in	een poolman een
	macchina	makeena
by hovercraft	in hovercraft	een overkraft
by sea	per mare	per mare
by train, by tram,	in treno, in tram,	een treno een
by underground	in metropolitana	tram een
		metropoleeetana
on foot	a piedi	a pyedee
on the ferry	in traghetto	een trageto
overland	per terra	per terra
to / /	a / /	a / /
travel agent's	agenzia di viaggio	ajentsya dee vyajo
traveller's cheque	traveller's cheque	travelers chek
	(m)	
tray	vassoio	vasoyo
treat (medically)	curare	koorare

treatment	cura	kōora
tree	albero	albero
triangular	triangolare	tryangolare
trim (haircut)	taglio di capelli	talyo dēē kapeli
trim (vb)	tagliare	talyo dēē kapelēē
trip (n)	gita	jēēta
coach t.	g. in pullman	jēēta ēēn pōolman
tripod	treppiede (m)	trepyede
trolley (=luggage t.)	carrello	karelo
tropical	tropicale (m & f)	tropēēkale
trot (vb)	trottare	trotare
trouble	guai (mpl)	gway
I'm in t.	sono nei g.	sono ney gway
trousers	pantaloni (mpl)	pantalonēē
a pair of t.	un paio di p.	ōōn payo dēē pantalonēē
trout	trota	trota
true	vero	vero
trunk (for luggage)	baule (m)	baōole
trunk (of tree)	tronco –chi	tronko tronkēē
trust (vb)	fidarmi	fēēdarmēē
I t. /her/	me /le/ fido	me /le/ fēēdo
truth	verità	verēēta
tell the t.	dire la v. – detto la v.	dēēre la verēēta – deto la verēēta
try on /this sweater/	provare /questa maglione/	provare /kwesta malyone/
try /this ice-cream/	provare /questo gelato/	provare /kwesto jelato/
T-shirt	maglietta	malyeta
tube	tubo	tōobo
a t. of / /	un t. di / /	ōōn tōobo dēē / /
tube (for a tyre)	camera d'aria	kamera darya
Tuesday	martedì (m)	martedēē
on Tuesday	m.	martedēē
on Tuesdays	di m.	dēē martedēē
tulip	tulipano (m)	tōolēēpano
a bunch of tulips	un mazzo di tulipani	ōōn madzo dēē tōolēēpanēē
tunnel (n)	galleria	galerēēa
turkey	tacchino	takēēno
turn off (switch)	spegnere – spento	spenyere – spento
turn on (switch)	accendere – acceso	achendere – achezo

	words ending in –o or marked (m)	words ending in –a or marked (f)
the	il/l'/lo	la/l'
the (plural)	i/gl'/gli	le/l'

turnip	rapa	ʀapa
turntable (on record player)	piatto	pyato
turpentine	trementina	tʀementēēna
tweed	tweed (m)	twēēd
tweezers	pinzette (fpl)	pēēntsete
a pair of t.	un paio di p.	ōōn payo dēē pēēntsete
twice	due volte	dōōe volte
twin	gemello	jemelo
t. beds	due letti uguali	dōōe letēē ōōgwalēē
type (vb)	battere a macchina	batere a makēēna
typewriter	macchina da scrivere	makēēna da skʀēēveʀe
typhoid	tifoide (m)	tēēfoyde
typical	tipico	tēēpēēko
typist	dattilografa	datēēlogʀafa
tyre	gomma	goma

U

ugly	brutto	bʀōōto
ulcer	ulcera	ōōlcheʀa
umbrella	ombrello	ombʀelo
beach u.	ombrellone (m)	ombʀelone
umpire	arbitro	aʀbēētʀo
uncle	zio	dzēēo
uncomfortable	scomodo	skomodo
unconscious	senza conoscenza	sentsa konoshentsa
under	sotto	soto
undercooked	non cotto abbastanza	non koto abastantsa
underground (u. railway train)	metropolitana	metʀopolēētana
by u.	in m.	ēēn metʀopolēētana
underpants (for men)	mutande (fpl)	mōōtande
a pair of u.	un paio di m.	ōōn payo dēē mōōtande
understand	*capire	kapēēʀe
I don't u.	non capisco	non kapēēsko
underwear	biancheria intima	byankeʀēēa ēēntēēma
children's u.	b. i. per bambini	byankeʀēēa ēēntēēma peʀ bambēēnēē

196

men's u.	b. i. per uomini	byankeʀēēa ēēntēēma peʀ womēēnēē
women's u.	b. i. per donne	byankeʀēēa ēēntēēma peʀ done
unfashionable	fuori moda	fwoʀēē moda
unfasten	slacciare	zlachaʀe
unfortunately	sfortunatamente	sfoʀtōōnatamente
unfriendly	freddo	fʀedo
uniform (n)	divisa	dēevēēza
in u.	in d.	ēēn dēevēēza
unique	unico	ōōnēēko
university	università –	ōōnēēveʀsēēta
unlocked	aperto	apeʀto
unlucky		
be u.	essere sfortunato – stato sfortunato	esere sfoʀtōōnato – stato sfoʀtōōnato
he's u.	è sfortunato	e sfoʀtōōnato
unpack	disfare le valigie – disfatto le valigie	dēesfaʀe le valēēje – dēesfato le valēēje
unpleasant	sgradevole (m & f)	zgʀadevole
unripe	acerbo	acheʀbo
untie	slegare	zlegaʀe
until	fino a	fēēno a
unusual	insolito	ēēnsolēēto
up	su	sōō
are you going u.?	va in s.?	va in sōō
be u. (=out of bed)	essere alzato – stato alzato	esere altsato – stato altsato
upset (adj)	disturbato	dēestōōʀbato
I've got a stomach u.	ho lo stomaco d.	o lo stomako dēestōōʀbato
upside-down	rovesciato	ʀoveshato
upstairs	di sopra	dēē sopra
urgent	urgente (m & f)	ōōʀjente
urinate	orinare	oʀēēnaʀe
urine	orina	oʀēēna
us	noi	noy
useful	utile (m & f)	ōōtēēle
use /your phone/	usare /il suo telefono/	ōōzaʀe /ēel sōō telefono/
usually	di solito	dēē solēēto
utensil	utensile (m)	ōōtensēēle

197

V -necked sweater	maglione (m) con collo a V	/malyone/ kon kolo a vee
vacancy (job)	posto vacante	posto vakante
vacancy (room)	camera libera	kamera leebera
vacant	libero	leebero
vaccinate	vaccinare	vacheenare
vaccination (f)	vaccinazione (f)	vacheenatsyone
vaccine	vaccino	vacheeno
vacuum cleaner	aspirapolvere (m)	aspeerapolvere
vacuum flask	termos (m)	termos
valid /passport/	/passaporto/ valido	/pasaporto /valeedo
valley	valle (f)	vale
valuable	prezioso	pretsyozo
valuables (pl)	oggetti preziosi (mpl)	ojetee pretsyozee
value (n)	valore (m)	valore
value (vb)	valutare	valootare
van	furgone (m)	foorgone
luggage v.	bagagliaio	bagalyayo
vanilla	vaniglia	vaneelya
variety	varietà –	varyeta
various	vario –ri	varyo varee
varnish (n)	vernice (f)	verneeche
nail v.	smalto per le unghie	zmalto per le oongye
varnish (vb) (eg boat)	verniciare	verneechare
vase (=flower v.)	vaso	vazo
vaseline	vasellina	vazeleena
a tube of v.	un tubo di v.	oon toobo dee vazeleena
V.A.T.	I.V.A. (f)	eeva
veal	vitello	veetelo
vegetables	verdura (fs)	verdoora
fresh v.	v. fresca	verdoora freska
mixed v.	v. mista	verdoora meesta
vegetarian	vegetariano	vejetaryano
vehicle	veicolo	veeekolo
vein	vena	vena
velvet	velluto	velooto
venereal disease (VD)	malattia venerea	malateea venerea
venison	carne (f) di cervo	karne dee chervo
ventilator	ventilatore (m)	venteelatore

	words ending in –o or marked (m)	words ending in –a or marked (f)
a	un/uno	una/un'
some	del/dell'/dello	della/dell'
some (plural)	dei/degl'/degli	delle

very	molto	molto
vest	maglia	malya
cotton v.	m. di cotone	malya dēē kotone
woollen v.	m. di lana	malya dēē lana
via	via	vēēa
travel v. /Rome/	viaggiare v. /Roma/	vjajare vēēa /ʀoma/
vicar	parroco –chi	paʀoko paʀokēē
view (n)	panorama (m) –mi	panoʀama panoʀamēē
viewfinder	mirino	mēēʀēēno
villa (=holiday v.)	villa	vēēla
village	paese (m)	paeze
vinegar	aceto	acheto
a bottle of v.	una bottiglia di a.	ōōna botēēlya dēē acheto
oil and v.	olio e a.	olyo e acheto
violin	violino	vyolēēno
visa	visto	vēēsto
visibility	visibilità	vēēzēēbēēlēēta
visit /a museum/	visitare /un museo/	vēēzēētaʀe /ōōn mōōzeo/
vitamin pills	pillole (fpl) di vitamina	pēēlole dēē vēētamēēna
a bottle of v. p.	una bottiglia di p. di v.	ōōna botēēlya dēē pēēlole dēē vēētamēēna
vodka	vodka	vodka
a bottle of v.	una bottiglia di v.	ōōna botēēlya dēē vodka
a v.	una v.	ōōna vodka
voice	voce (f)	voche
volt	volt (m)	volt
/110/ volts	/110/ v.	/chentodyechēē/ volt
voltage	voltaggio	voltajo
high v.	v. alto	voltajo alto
low v.	v. basso	voltajo baso
volume (content)	volume (m)	volōōme
volume (noise)	volume (m)	volōōme
vomit (n)	vomito	vomēēto
vomit (vb)	vomitare	vomēētaʀe
voucher	buono	bwono
hotel v.	b. di albergo	bwono dēē albeʀgo
voyage (n)	viaggio –ggi	vjajo vyajēē

199

waist	vita	vēēta
waistcoat	panciotto	panchyoto
wait /for me/	aspettar/mi/	aspetaℝ/mēē/
please wait /for me/	prego /mi/ aspetti	pℝego /mēē/ aspetēē
waiter	cameriere (m)	kameℝyeℝe
waiting room	sala d'aspetto	sala daspeto
waitress	cameriera	kameℝyeℝa
wake /me/ up	svegliar/mi/	zvelyaℝ/mēē/
walk (n)	passeggiata	pasejata
go for a w.	fare una p.	faℝe ōōna pasejata
walk (vb)	camminare	kamēēnaℝe
walking	passeggiare	pasejaℝe
do some w.	fare una p.	faℝe ōōna pasejaℝe
walking stick	bastone (m) da passeggio	bastone da pasejo
wall (=inside w.)	muro	mōōℝo
wallet	portafoglio (m) –	poℝtafolyo
walnut (nut)	noce (m)	noche
walnut (wood)	di noce	dēē noche
want	volere	voleℝe
w. /a room/	volere /una camera/	voleℝe /ōōna kameℝa/
w. to /buy/ it	v. /comprar/lo	voleℝe /kompℝaℝ/lo
war	guerra	gweℝa
ward (in hospital)	corsia	koℝsēēa
wardrobe	guardaroba	gwaℝdaℝoba
warm (adj)	caldo	kaldo
warm (vb)	riscaldare	ℝēēskaldaℝe
warn	avvertire	aveℝtēēℝe
warning	avvertimento	aveℝtēēmento
wash (n)	lavata	lavata
have a w.	lavarmi	lavaℝmēē
wash (vb)	lavare	lavaℝe
washbasin	lavandino	lavandēēno
washing machine	lavatrice (f)	lavatℝēēche
washing powder	detersivo	deteℝsēēvo
wash up	lavare i piatti	lavaℝe ēē pyatēē
wasp	vespa	vespa
w. sting	puntura di v.	pōōntōōℝa dēē vespa
waste (vb)	sprecare	spℝekaℝe
wastepaper basket	cestino per i rifiuti	chestēēno peℝ ēē ℝēēfyōōtēē

watch /TV/	guardare /la televisione/	gwaRdaRe /la televeeezyone/
watch (n)	orologio –gi	oRolojo oRolojee
w. strap	cinturino d'o.	cheentooReeno doRolojo
face (of w.)	quadrante (m)	kwadRante
hand (of w.)	lancetta	lancheta
watchmaker's	orologiaio	oRolojyayo
water	acqua	akwa
cold w.	a. fredda	akwa fReda
drinking w.	a. potabile	akwa potabeele
hot w.	a. calda	akwa kalda
running w.	a. corrente	akwa koRente
watercolour (=painting)	acquarello	akwaRelo
waterproof (adj)	impermeabile (m & f)	eempeRmeabeele
water skiing	sci acquatico	shee akwateeko
go w. s.	fare lo s. a.	faRe lo shee akwateeko
watt	watt (m)	vat
/100/ watts	/100/ w.	/chento/ vat
wave (radio)	onda	onda
medium w.	o. media	onda medya
long w.	o. lunga	onda loonga
short w.	o. corta	onda koRta
VHF	alta frequenza	alta fRekwentsa
wave (sea)	onda	onda
wax	cera	cheRa
we	noi	noy
weak (physically)	debole (m & f)	debole
wear (vb) (clothes)	indossare	eendosaRe
weather	tempo	tempo
w. conditions	condizioni (fpl) atmosferiche	kondeetsyonee atmosfeReeke
w. forecast	previsioni (fpl) del t.	preveeezyonee del tempo
wedding	matrimonio	matReemonyo
Wednesday	mercoledì	meRkoledee
on Wednesday	m.	meRkoledee
on Wednesdays	di m.	dee meRkoledee
week	settimana	seteeemana
this w.	questa s.	kwesta seteeemana

	words ending in –o or marked (m)	words ending in –a or marked (f)
the	il/l'/lo	la/l'
the (plural)	i/gl'/gli	le/l'

last w.	la s. scorsa	la set<u>ee</u>mana skoRsa
next w.	la s. prossima	la set<u>ee</u>mana pros<u>ee</u>ma
weekend	fine (f) settimana	f<u>ee</u>ne set<u>ee</u>mana
weekly (adj)	settimanale	set<u>ee</u>manale
twice w.	due volte alla settimana	d<u>oo</u>e volte ala set<u>ee</u>mana
weigh	pesare	pezaRe
weight	peso	pezo
w. limit	limite (m) di p.	l<u>ee</u>m<u>ee</u>te d<u>ee</u> pezo
welcome (vb)	dare il benvenuto – dato il benvenuto	daRe <u>ee</u>l benven<u>oo</u>to – dato <u>ee</u>l benven<u>oo</u>to
w. to / /	benvenuto a / /	benven<u>oo</u>to a / /
well (=all right)	bene	bene
well-done (eg of steak)	cotto bene	koto bene
Wellingtons	stivali (mpl) di gomma	st<u>ee</u>vale d<u>ee</u> goma
west	ovest (m)	ovest
Western (=film)	western (m)	westeRn
wet	bagnato	banyato
I'm w.	sono b.	sono banyato
it's w.	c'è tempo piovoso	che tempo pyovozo
/this towel/ is w.	/quest'asciugamano/ è b.	/kwestash<u>oo</u>gamano/ e banyato
what?	cosa?	koza
at w. time?	a che ora?	a ke oRa
wheel	ruota	Rwota
wheelchair	sedia a rotelle	sedya a Rotele
when?	quando?	kwando
where?	dove?	dove
which?	quale?	kwale
w. /plane/?	q. /aeroplano/?	kwale /aeRoplano/
whisky	whisky (m)	w<u>ee</u>sk<u>ee</u>
a bottle of w.	una bottiglia di w.	<u>oo</u>na bot<u>ee</u>lya d<u>ee</u> w<u>ee</u>sk<u>ee</u>
a w.	un w.	<u>oo</u>n w<u>ee</u>sk<u>ee</u>
whistle (n)	fischio –chi (pl)	f<u>ee</u>skyo f<u>ee</u>sk<u>ee</u>
white	bianco (m) –chi (mpl) bianca (f) –che (fpl)	byanko byank<u>ee</u> byanka byank<u>ee</u>
w. coffee	cappuccino	kap<u>oo</u>ch<u>ee</u>no
who?	chi?	k<u>ee</u>
whole	intero	<u>ee</u>enteRo
a w. /month/	/un mese/ intero	/<u>oo</u>n meze/ <u>ee</u>enteRo

the w. /month/	tutto /il mese/	tōōto /eel meze/
whose?	di chi?	dee kee
why?	perchè	peRke
wick (lamp, lighter)	lucignolo	loocheenyolo
wide	largo	laRgo
widow	vedova	vedova
widower	vedovo	vedovo
width	larghezza	laRgetsa
wife	moglie –gli (pl)	molye moly
wig	parucca –cche (pl)	paRooka paRooke
wild (=not tame)	selvaggio	selvajyo
w. animal	animale (m) selvatico	aneemale selvateeko
win (vb)	vincere – vinto	veenchere – veento
wind (n)	vento	vento
wind (vb) (clock)	caricare	kaReekare
window	finestra	feenestra
french w.	porta-f.	porta-feenestra
shop w.	vetrina	vetreena
windy	ventoso	ventozo
it's w.	è v.	e ventozo
wine	vino	veeno
a bottle of w.	una bottigiia de v.	oona boteelya dee veeno
a carafe of w.	una caraffa di v.	oona kaRafa dee veeno
a glass of w.	un bicchiere di v.	oon beekyere dee veeno
a half bottle of w.	una mezza bottiglia di v.	oona medza boteelya dee veeno
dry w.	v. secco	veeno seko
red w.	v. rosso	veeno Roso
rosé	v. rosé	veeno Roze
sparkling w.	v. frizzante	veeno fReetsante
sweet w.	v. dolce	veeno dolche
white w.	v. bianco	veeno byanko
wine glass	bicchiere (m) da vino	beekyere da veeno
wine list	lista di vini	leesta dee veenee
wine merchant's	negozio –zi (pl) di vini	negotsyo dee veenee negotsee dee veenee
wing (bird or plane)	ala	ala
winter	inverno	eenverno
in w.	d'i.	deenverno
wipe (vb)	asciugare	ashoogare
wire	filo	feelo
a piece of w.	un pezzo di f.	oon petso dee feelo

with	con	kon
without	senza	sentsa
witness (n)	testimonio –ni	testeemonyo testeemonee
woman	donna	dona
wonderful	meraviglioso	meraveelyozo
wood (of trees)	bosco	bosko
wood (substance)	legno	lenyo
wooden	di legno	dee lenyo
wool	lana	lana
woollen	di lana	dee lana
word	parola	parola
work (n)	lavoro	lavoro
do some w.	fare un po' di l. – fatto un po' di l.	fare oon po dee lavoro – fato oon po dee lavoro
work (vb) (of machines)	funzionare	foontsyonare
work (vb) (of people)	lavorare	lavorare
world (the w.)	mondo	mondo
worn-out	consunto	konsoonto
worried	preoccupato	preokoopato
worse (in health)	peggio	pejo
he's w.	sta p.	sta pejo
worse (things)	peggio	pejo
w. than / /	p. di / /	pejo dee / /
it's w.	è p.	e pejo
worst	il peggiore	eel pejore
the w. /hotel/	/l'albergo/ p.	/lalbergo/ pejore
the w. /room/	/la camera/ p.	/la kamera/ pejore
worth		
be w.	valere	valere
it's w. /100,000/ lire	vale /un millione/ di lire	vale /oon meelyone/ dee leere
wound (=injury)	ferita	fereeta
wrap (vb)	incartare	eenkartare
gift-wrap (vb)	confezionare per regalo	konfetsyonare per regalo
wreath (funeral w.)	corona	korona
wreck (n)	naufragio –gi	naoofrajo naoofrajee
wrist	polso	polso
write	scrivere – scrito	skreevere – skreeto

	words ending in –o or marked (m)	words ending in –a or marked (f)
a	un/uno	una/un'
some	del/dell'/dello	della/dell'
some (plural)	dei/degl'/degli	delle

writing paper	carta da scrivere	kaʀta da skʀēēveʀe
wrong	sbagliato	zbalyato
be w.	avere torto – avuto torto	aveʀe toʀto – avōōto toʀto
I'm w.	ho t.	o toʀto
w. number	numero s.	nōōmeʀo zbalyato

X

| x-ray | raggio x | ʀajo ēēks |

Y

yacht	panfilo	panfēēlo
year	anno	ano
last y.	l'a. scorso	lano skoʀso
next y.	l'a. prossimo	lano pʀosēēmo
this y.	quest'a.	kwestano
yearly	annuale (m & f)	anōōale
yellow	giallo	jalo
yesterday	ieri	yeʀēē
yoghurt	yogurt (m)	yogōōʀt
a carton of y.	un vasetto di y.	ōōn vazeto dēē yogōōʀt
plain y.	y. semplice	yogōōʀt semplēēche
fruit y.	y. con sapore di frutta	yogōōʀt kon sapoʀe dēē fʀōōta
young	giovane (m & f)	jovane
young man	giovanotto	jovanoto
young woman	donna giovane	dona jovane
youth hostel	ostello per la gioventù	ostelo peʀ la joventōō

Z

zero (=nought)	zero	dzeʀo
zero (nought degrees)	zero	dzeʀo
above z.	sopra z.	sopʀa dzeʀo
below z.	sotto z.	soto dzeʀo
zip (n)	chiusura lampo (f) chiusure lampo (pl)	kyōōzōōʀa lampo kyōōzōōʀe lampo
zoo	zoo (m)	tsōō
zoom lens	lente (f) zoom	lente tsōōm

205

eating out

It is impossible to give an exhaustive list of all the good things in *la cucina italiana* (Italian cooking). Every restaurant and family have their own specialities and varieties. Here, however, are all the main foods in groups: *antipasti* (hors d'oeuvres) *pasta asciutta* (pasta in various forms); rice dishes; soups; fish; meat; poultry and game; vegetables; fruit; sweets; ice creams; cheeses; pizza. At the end of this section there is a selection of regional specialities including some of the principal wines.

Remember:
I'd like / / please — Vorrei / / per favore
Have you got / / please? — Ha / / per favore?
At the start of a meal, Italians often wish each other — Buon appetito!
The reply is 'Thank you – the same to you' — Grazie, altrettanto

Be careful when ordering coffee:
Un caffè per favore — A black coffee please
Un cappuccino per favore — A white coffee please (coffee ready made with whipped milk)
Caffè e latte per favore — A pot of coffee (coffee and milk separately)

Antipasti (hors d'oeuvres)

antipasto misto (antēēpasto mēēsto)	mixture of salame, ham and other salt meats
bresaola (bResaola)	dried salt beef
carciofi (kaRchofēē)	artichokes (often the hearts served with oil)
crostini (kRosfēēnēē)	fried or baked bread with cheese, anchovies etc.
culatello di zibello (kōōlatelo dēē dsēēbelo)	specially cured rump of pork
fagioli con tonno (fajolēē kon tono)	Tuscan beans with tunny fish
fagiolini (fajolēēnēē)	French beans
fonduta (fondōōta)	melted cheese
frittelle (fRēētele)	fritters
frutti di mare (fRōōtēē dēē maRe)	shellfish
mortadella (moRtadela)	Bologna sausage
olive (olēēve)	olives
paté di tonno (pate dēē tono)	tunny fish paté
peperoni ripieni (pepeRonēē Rēēpyenēē)	stuffed peppers
pomodori (pomodoRēē)	tomatoes
prosciutto cotto (pRoshōōto coto)	cooked ham
prosciutto crudo (pRoshōōto cRōōdo)	raw ham or Parma ham (a great delicacy)

Pasta asciutta

bucatini (bookafēēnēē)	spaghetti with a tiny hole down the middle
b. ai quattro formaggi (bookafēēnēē aēē kwatRo foRmajēē)	b. with four cheeses (may vary)
b. alla Napoletana (bookafēēnēē ala napoletana)	b. with tomatoes, peppers and garlic
b. con salsiccie (bookafēēnēē kon salsēēchye)	b. with sausage meat
b. in salsa verde (bookafēēnēē ēēn salsa veRde)	b. with spinach

cannelloni (kanelonee)
rolls of pasta stuffed with meat sauce, served with melted cheese

cappelletti (kapeletee)
(see also tortellini)
'little hats' of stuffed pasta

c. in brodo (kapeletee een brodo)
c. in clear soup

c. asciutti (kapeletee ashootee)
c. served with sauce and cheese

farfalle (farfale)
pasta cut in butterfly shapes

fettucine (fetoocheene)
pasta cut in 'ribbons'

f. con mozzarella (fetoocheene kon motsarela)
f. with soft Neapolitan cheese

f. ai funghi (fetoocheene aee foongee)
f. with mushrooms

f. con ragù di pollo (fetoocheene kon ragoo dee polo)
f. with chicken sauce

gnocchi (nyokee)
little dumplings of flour or potato-flour

lasagne al forno (lasanye al forno)
broad strips of pasta with ragoût and béchamel sauce in alternating layers.

l. verde (lasanye verde)
green l. (made with spinach)

linguine (leengweene)
flattened spaghetti

l. ai piselli (leengweene aee peeselee)
l. with peas

l. al prosciutto (leengweene al proshooto)
l. with ham

maccheroncini (makeroncheenee)
small macaroni

maccheroni (makeronee)
macaroni

penne (pene)
small tubes of pasta, served with ragoût and béchamel sauce

ravioli (ravyolee)
pasta squares with meat inside

rigatoni (reegatonee)
pasta like 'penne' but ribbed

spaghetti (spagetee)
spaghetti

s. all'amatriciana (spagetee alamatreechana)
s. with pork, onion and tomato sauce served with cheese made from sheep's milk

s. alla carbonara (spagetee ala karbonara)
s. with bacon and egg sauce

209

s. alla marinara   (spa**ge**tēē ala ma**rēē**na**r**a) — s. with peppers

s. con ragù   (spa**ge**tēē kon **r**a**gōō**) — s. with meat sauce

s. con tonno   (spa**ge**tēē kon **to**no) — s. with tunny fish

s. con vongole   (spa**ge**tēē kon **von**gole) — s. with mussels

tagliatelli   (talya**te**le) — pasta cut in 'ribbons'

t. alla Bolognese   (talya**te**le ala bolo**nye**se) — t. with beef and pork sauce

tortellini   (**t**o**r**te**lēē**nēē) — stuffed pasta from Bologna

(see also cappelletti)

Rice dishes

riso in bianco   (**rēē**so **ēē**n **bēē**anko) — boiled rice with Parmesan cheese

riso quattro formaggi   (**rēē**so **kwa**t**r**o fo**r**ma**jēē**) — boiled rice with four cheeses

risotto con pesce   (**rēē**soto kon **pe**she) — freshwater fish risotto

risotto con scampi   (**rēē**soto kon **skam**pēē) — scampi risotto

risotto frutti di mare   (**rēē**soto f**rōō**tēē dēē ma**r**e) — shellfish risotto

Soups

brodo lungo   (b**r**odo **lōōn**go) — thin broth

minestra   (**mēē**nest**r**a) — soup (usually thick)

minestrina   (**mēē**nest**rēē**na) — thin or clear soup

minestrone   (**mēē**nest**r**one) — thick soup (often with rice or vegetables)

zuppa di cozze   (**tsōō**pa dēē **cot**se) — mussel soup

zuppa di gamberi   (**tsōō**pa dēē **gam**be**rēē**) — prawn soup

zuppa di pesce   (**tsōō**pa dēē **pe**she) — mixed fish soup (varies in each seaside town)

210

Fish

acciughe/alici (ach$\overline{oo}$ge/ al$\overline{ee}$ch$\overline{ee}$)	anchovies
anguilla (angw$\overline{ee}$la)	eel
aragosta (aʀagosta)	lobster
baccalà (bacala)	salt cod
calamari/calamaretti (kalamaʀ$\overline{ee}$/kalamaʀet$\overline{ee}$)	squid
cozze (kotse)	mussels
fritto misto (fʀ$\overline{ee}$eto m$\overline{ee}$sto)	mixed fish fry-up
gamberetti (gambeʀet$\overline{ee}$)	prawns
merluzzo (meʀl$\overline{oo}$tso)	cod
palombo (palombo)	dog-fish
polipi (pol$\overline{ee}$ep$\overline{ee}$)	baby octopus
sarde (saʀde)	sardines
seppie (sepye)	cuttle fish
sgombri (sgombʀ$\overline{ee}$)	mackerel
sogliola (solyeeola)	sole
tonno (tono)	tunny fish
triglie (tʀ$\overline{ee}$lye)	red mullet

Meat, poultry and game

abbacchio (abakyo)	suckling lamb
agnello (anyelo)	lamb
anitra (an$\overline{ee}$tʀa)	duck
a. in agrodolce (an$\overline{ee}$tʀa $\overline{ee}$n agʀodolche)	d. in sweet-sour sauce
bistecca (b$\overline{ee}$steka)	steak
bollito (bol$\overline{ee}$to)	mixed boiled meats
braciola (bʀachyola)	cutlet, chop
capretto ((kapʀeto)	kid
cervella (cheʀvela)	brain
cervo (cheʀvo)	venison
cinghiale (ch$\overline{ee}$ngyale)	boar
coniglio (kon$\overline{ee}$elyo)	rabbit
costolette/cotolette (kostolete/ kotolete)	cutlets
cotechino (kotek$\overline{ee}$no)	spiced sausage
cuore (kwoʀe)	heart
fagiano (fajano)	pheasant

211

faraona (faʀaona)	guinea-fowl
fegato (fegato)	liver
fritto misto (frēēto mēēsto)	mixed fry-up
lepre (lepʀe)	hare
l. in casseruola (lepʀe ēēn caseʀōōola)	stewed h.
lesso (leso)	boiled meat
maiale (mayale)	pork
manzo (mandso)	beef
montone (montone)	mutton
ossobuco (osobōōko)	shin of veal
pernice (peʀnēēche)	partridge
piccate (pēēkate)	escalopes
piccioni (pēēchyonēē)	pigeons
pollo (polo)	chicken
p. alla cacciatora (polo ala cachatoʀa)	c. stew
p. al diavolo (polo al dyavolo)	grilled c.
polpette (polpete)	meat balls
polpettone (polpetone)	meat roll
prosciutto (pʀoshōōto)	ham
rognone (ʀonyone)	kidney
salame (salame)	pork sausage (varies in each region)
salsicce (salsēēche)	sausages
saltimbocca (saltēēmboka)	dish of veal, ham, sage and marsala
scaloppine (skalopēēne)	escalopes
spezzatino (spetsafēēno)	stew
spiedino (spyedēēno)	meats roasted on a spit
stufato (stōōfato)	stew
tacchino (takēēno)	turkey
trippa (trēēpa)	tripe
uccelli (ōōchelēē)	birds
vitello (vēētelo)	veal
zampone (tsampone)	spiced sausage like 'cotechino', stuffed in pig's trotters

Vegetables

aglio (alyo)	garlic
asparagi (aspaʀagēē)	asparagus

212

carciofi (kaRchofee)	artichokes
c. ripieni (kaRchofee Reepyenee)	stuffed a.
carote (kaRote)	carrots
cavolfiore (kavolfyoRe)	cauliflower
cavolini di bruxelles (kavoleenee dee brooksel)	brussels sprouts
cavolo (kavolo)	cabbage
cipolle (cheepole)	onions
fagioli (fajolee)	Tuscan beans
fagiolini (fajoleenee)	French beans
funghi (foongee)	mushrooms
insalata (eensalata)	salad
mamme romane (mame Romane)	large Roman artichokes
melanzane (melantsane)	aubergines
patate (patate)	potatoes
p. al forno (patate al foRno)	oven-cooked p.
p. arrosto (patate aRosto)	roast p.
p. fritte (patate fReete)	chips
patatine (patafeene)	crisps
purè di p. (pooRe dee patate)	mashed p.
peperoni (pepeRonee)	peppers
peperonata (pepeRonata)	pepper and tomato stew
piselli (peeselee)	peas
pomodoro (pomodoRo)	tomato
radicchio (Radeechyo)	chicory
radicchio rosso (Radeechyo Roso)	crispy dark red lettuce
ravanello (Ravanelo)	radish
spinaci (speenachee)	spinach
verze (veRdse)	cabbage
zucchine (tsoocheene)	courgettes

Fruit

Fruit is an indispensable part of any Italian main meal and is often the only sweet eaten.

albicocca (albeekoka)	apricot
ananas (ananas)	pineapple
arancia (aRancha)	orange

213

ciliegia (chēēlyeja)	cherry
cocomero (koko**me**Ro)	water melon
fico (**fēē**ko)	fig
fragola (**fr**agola)	strawberry
lampone (lam**po**ne)	raspberry
limone (lēē**mo**ne)	lemon
mela (**me**la)	apple
melone (me**lo**ne)	melon
mora (**mo**Ra)	blackberry
noce di cocco (**no**che dēē **ko**ko)	coconut
pera (**pe**Ra)	pear
pesca (**pe**ska)	peach
pompelmo (pom**pel**mo)	grapefruit
prugna (**pr**ōō**nya**)	plum
susina (sōō**sēē**na)	plum
uva (**ōō**va)	grapes
u. bianche (**ōō**va **byan**ke)	white g.
u. nere (**ōō**va **ne**Re)	black g.

Sweets

Puddings are not a great Italian speciality but you can usually find:

budino (bōō**dēē**no)	pudding
b. di cioccolata (bōō**dēē**no dēē choko**la**ta)	chocolate p.
b. di riso (bōō**dēē**no dēē **rēē**so)	rice p.
creme caramel (**kr**eme ka**ra**mel)	caramel
crostata di frutta (k**ro**sta**ta** dēē **fr**ōōta)	fruit tart (various fruits)
macedonia di frutta (mache**do**nya dēē **fr**ōōta)	fruit salad
torta (**tor**ta)	cake
t. di frutta (**tor**ta dēē **fr**ōōta)	fruit c.
t. di mandorle (**tor**ta dēē man**dor**le)	almond c.

214

Ice creams

gelati (jela$\overline{\text{tee}}$)	ice creams
gelato di banana (jelato d$\overline{\text{ee}}$ banana)	banana
di caffè (d$\overline{\text{ee}}$ kafe)	coffee
di cioccolata (d$\overline{\text{ee}}$ chokolata)	chocolate
di fragola (d$\overline{\text{ee}}$ **fra**gola)	strawberry
di limone (d$\overline{\text{ee}}$ l$\overline{\text{ee}}$mone)	lemon
di malaga (d$\overline{\text{ee}}$ **ma**laga)	wine-flavoured
di noce (d$\overline{\text{ee}}$ **no**che)	walnut
di nocciola (d$\overline{\text{ee}}$ no**cho**la)	hazelnut
di torrone (d$\overline{\text{ee}}$ to**ro**ne)	nougat
gelato in cono (jelato $\overline{\text{ee}}$n **ko**no)	ice cream in cone
gelato in coppa (jelato $\overline{\text{ee}}$n **ko**pa)	ice cream in a tub
ghiacciolo (gya**cho**lo)	iced lolly
mattonella (mato**ne**la)	wafer sandwich
panna montata (**pa**na mon**ta**ta)	whipped cream
pinguino (p$\overline{\text{ee}}$ng**gwee**no)	ice cream on stick (literally 'penguin')
semifreddo (sem$\overline{\text{ee}}$**fre**do)	not quite iced cream
sfusa (**sfoo**sa)	mixed flavours
sorbetto (so**rbe**to)	soft ice cream

Cheeses

There is a large variety of Italian cheeses. Here is a list of the ones you are most likely to come across.

asiago (a**sya**go)	mild mountain cheese from the Veneto
bel paese (bel pa**e**se)	another mild, soft cheese
cacciotto (ca**cho**to)	made of cow's and sheep's milk, from the Marches
fontina (fon**fee**na)	fat, creamy cheese from Piemonte
gorgonzola (go**rgo**n**dso**la)	the most famous Italian cheese
g. dolce (go**rgo**n**dso**la **dol**che)	mild g.
g. piccante (go**rgo**n**dso**la p$\overline{\text{ee}}$**kan**te)	strong g.

215

grana (**gr**ana)	another name for Parmesan
mascarpone (mas**ka**r**pone**)	double cream cheese wrapped in muslin
mozzarella (motsa**r**ela)	Neapolitan buffalo's milk cheese used in most pizzas (can also be eaten raw with oil and pepper)
parmigiano (par**mee**jano)	Parmesan, often grated for sprinkling on pasta, soup etc. (Can also be eaten by itself)
pecorino (peko**ree**no)	sheep's milk cheese, particularly from Sardinia
provola (**pr**ovola)	buffalo cheese
ricotta (r**ee**kota)	soft sheep's milk cheese
stracchino (stra**kee**no)	soft, fatty cheese from Lombardy
taleggio (ta**le**jo)	soft, fatty cow's milk cheese

Pizza

Pizza is increasingly popular, particularly among young people. It's cheap, simple and delicious. Every pizzeria has its own varieties. These are the most common 'pizze':

calzone (kal**tsone**)	the dough base is folded over like a pancake and contains ricotta and mozzarella cheeses, ham and tomatoes
capricciosa (kap**ree**chosa)	tomatoes, mozzarella, artichokes, mushrooms, anchovies, olives
carciofini (karcho**fee**nee)	tomatoes, mozzarella, artichokes
frutti di mare (**fr**oo**tee** d**ee** **ma**re)	seafood
funghi (**foon**gee)	tomatoes, mozzarella and mushrooms
margherita (marge**ree**ta)	tomatoes and mozzarella (the classic pizza)
marinara (ma**ree**na**r**a)	tomatoes and anchovies
prosciutto (pro**shoo**to)	tomatoes, mozzarella and ham
provenzale (**pr**oven**tsale**)	tomatoes, olives, anchovies and marjoram
quattro stagioni (**kwa**tro sta**jo**nee)	the base is divided into four areas, one romana, one mushroom, one artichoke, one ham

| romana (ROmana) | tomatoes, mozzarella and anchovies |
| salsiccia (salsēecha) | tomatoes, mozzarella and sausage |

REGIONAL SPECIALITIES AND WINES

Italian wines are numerous. The most well-known are given below, listed according to the regions where they are mainly produced.

Abruzzo

Food: arrosto di castrato
    (aROsto dēe kasTRato) — roast mutton

bigoli alla chitarra
    (bēegolēe ala kēetaRa) — flattened macaroni

brodetto di pesce
    (bROdeto dēe peshe) — fish soup

Wine: cerasuolo d'Abruzzo
    (cheRaswolo dabRutso) — red

montepulciano rosso
    (montepōolchano ROso) — red

Basilicata

Food: pesce spada arrosto
    (peshe spada aROsto) — roast sword fish

pollo con polenta (polo kon polenta) — chicken with maize–flour pudding

spaghetti alla ricotta
    (spagetēe ala Rēekota) — spaghetti with cottage cheese

Wine: malvasia (malvasēea) — sweet dessert wine found throughout southern Italy

moscato (moskato) — white, found throughout southern Italy

Calabria

Food: carciofi in tortiera
    (kaRchofēe ēen toRtyeRa) — artichoke pie

lucanica (lōokanēeka) — sausage

pecorino (pekoREeno) — sheep's milk cheese

soffrito (sofREeto) — onion sauce

217

Wine : ciro   (chēēRO)   white and red – the most well-
                                     known Calabrian wine
        malvasia   see above
        moscato   see above

Campania

Food : agnello e capretto al   roast lamb and kid
       forno   (anyelo e
       kaPREto al foRno)
       maccheroni   macaroni
       (makeRonēē)
       fusilli alla ricotta   type of pasta with cottage cheese
       (fōōsēēlēē ala Rēēkota)
       mozzarrella in carrozza   mozzarella cheese and bread fried
       (motsaRela ēēn caRotsa)   together
Wine : capri   (kaPRēē)   white
       falerno   (faleRno)   white and red
       lacrima Christi   sweet white
       (lakRēēma kRēēstēē)

Emilia – Romagna

Food : cappelletti   (kapeletēē)   'little hats' of pasta with meat
                                     stuffing
       culatello   (kōōlatelo)   rump of pork
       mortadella   (moRtadela)   Bologna sausage
       parmigiano   Parmesan cheese
       (paRmēējano)
       salame and salted meats
       of many types
Wine : albana   (albana)   white
       lambrusco   red
       (lambRōōsko)
       monterosso   red
       (monteRoso)

Friuli – Venezia Giulia

Food : cacciaggione   game
       (kachajone)
       salsicce o luganeghe con   various types of sausage with
       polenta   (salsēēche o   maize pudding
       lōōganege kon polenta)

prosciutto di San Daniele (pRoshōōto dee san danyele)	San Daniele ham (raw and cured)
Wine: cabernet (kabeRne)	red
merlot (meRlo)	red
prosecco di Trieste (pRoseko dee tReeeeste)	white
tocai (tokay)	white

Lazio

Food: abbachio (abakyo)	roast suckling lamb
carciofi alla giudea (kaRchofee ala jōōdea)	large Roman artichokes
gnocchi alla romana (nyokee ala Romana)	semolina-flour dumplings (In other regions, but not in Lazio, 'gnocchi' are made with potato flour)
porchetta (poRketa)	roast suckling pig
spaghetti all'amatriciana (spagetee alamatReechana)	spaghetti with pork, onion and tomato sauce
Wine: colli Albani (kolee albanee)	white
est est est (est est est)	white
frascati (fRaskatee)	white

Liguria

Food: antipasto alla Genovese (anteeepasto ala jenovese)	hors d'oeuvres of béans, salame and cheese
foccaccia (fokachya)	pizza-tart
fritto misto di pesce (fReeto meesto dee peshe)	mixed fried fish
lumache (lōōmake)	snails
Wine: barbaresco	red
coronata di Genova (koRonata dee jenova)	white

219

Lombardia

Food: cotolette alla Milanese (kotolete ala mēēlanese)	Milanese veal cutlets
minestrone (mēēnestRone)	thick vegetable soup
panettone (panetone)	famous Italian cake, eaten particularly at Christmas
ossobuco (osobōōko)	shin of veal
zuppa Pavese (tsōōpa pavese)	broth with egg and fried bread sprinkled with cheese
Wine: barbacarlo (baRbakaRlo)	red
sassella (sasela)	red
grumello (gRōōmelo)	red

Marche

Food: cardi alla parmigiana (kaRdēē ala paRmēējana)	thistles cooked with parmesan cheese
minestra di passatelli (mēēnestRa dēē pasatelēē)	soup with egg, breadcrumbs, cheese and nutmeg
olive ripiene (olēēve Rēēpyene)	stuffed olives
tartufo nero (taRtōōfo neRo)	black truffle
trippe (tRēēpe)	tripe
Wine: bianchello di Metauro (byankelo dēē metaōōRo)	white
piceno (pēēcheno)	white and red
sangiovese (sanjovese)	red
verdicchio di Jesi (veRdēēchyo dēē yesēē)	white

Molise

Food: agnello e capretto al forno (anyelo e kapReto al foRno)	roast lamb and kid
pesce alla griglia (peshe ala gRēēlya)	grilled fish

220

spaghetti e maccheroni alla chitarra (spageTēē e makeRonēē ala kēētaRa)	finely-cut pasta
Wine: cerasuolo (cheRaswolo)	red
montepulciano (montepōōlchano)	red
trebbiano (tRebbyano)	white

Piemonte

Food:	bollito (bolēēto)	boiled meats
	cacciaggione (kachajone)	game
	fonduta con fontina (fondōōta kon fontēēna)	melted cheese dish
	gianduiotti (jandwēēotēē)	chocolates
	riso con tartufi (Rēēso kon taRtōōfēē)	rice with truffles
Wine:	astispumante (astēēspōōmante)	white sparkling
	barbera (baRbeRa)	red
	barolo (baRolo)	red
	nebbiolo (nebyolo)	red

Puglia

Food:	maccheroni alla ruta (makeRonēē ala Rōōta)	macaroni with rue-flavoured sauce
	minestra di fave (mēēnestRa dēē fave)	bean soup
	orecchiette col ragù d'agnello (oRekyete kol Ragōō danyelo)	pasta with lamb sauce
	salame piccante (salame pēēkante)	highly-spiced salame
Wine:	aleatico (aleatēēko)	red
	barletta (baRleta)	red
	bianco lacorotondo (byanko lakoRotondo)	white

221

Sardegna

Food: aragosta (aRagosta)   lobster
accarraxiau   suckling pig cooked in sheep's
   (akaRashaoo)   stomach
ciciones (cheechones)   dumplings served with sausage,
    sauce and cheese
culurrones (kuluRones)   ravioli
pecorino sardo   sheep's milk cheese
   (pekoReeno saRdo)
Wine: oliena (olyena)   red
malvasia (malvasya)   white
vernaccia (veRnacha)   white

Sicilia

Food: cassata (kasata)   type of ice cream
coniglio in agrodolce   rabbit in sweet-sour sauce
   (koneelyo een
   agrodolche)
pasta (pasta)   pasta
   p. con zucchine (pasta   p. with courgettes
   kon tsoocheene)
   p. con sarde (pasta   p. with sardines
   kon saRde)
   p. con ricotta (pasta   p. with cottage cheese
   kon Reekota)
provola (pRovola)   type of buffalo cheese often
    roasted
spiedini di fegatelli   chicken livers on the spit
   (spyedeene dee fegatelee)
Wine: corvo (koRvo)   white and red
marsala (maRsala)   red
Taormina (taoRmeena)   white and red
vini dell'Etna (veenee   white and red
   deletna)

Toscana

Food: costata Fiorentina   famous Florentine T-bone steak
   (kostata fyoRenteena)
panforte (panfoRte)   sort of gingerbread

risotto alla Fiorentina (Rēēsoto ala fyoRenfēēna)	risotto	
stracotto di bue (stRakoto dēē bōōe)	beef stew	
triglia alla livornese (tRēēlya ala lēēvoRnese)	red mullet	
Wine : chianti (kyantēē)	red	
candia rosé (kandya Rose)	rosé	
vernaccia di San Gimignano (veRnacha dēē san gēēmēēnyano)	white	
vinsanto (vinsanto)	white	

Trentino – Alto Adige

Food : farinata (faRinata)	meal porridge	
formaggi di montagna (foRmajēē dēē montanya)	mountain cheeses	
polenta (polenta)	cooked maize-flour	
selvaggina in salmì (selvajēēna ēēn salmēē)	game with ragout	
Wine : merlot (meRlo)	red	
val d'Adige (val dadēēje)	red	
val d'Isarco (val dēēsaRko)	red	

Umbria

Food : pizza di formaggio (pēētsa dēē foRmajo)	cheese pizza	
prosciutto di montagna (pRoshōōto dēē montanya)	mountain ham	
tartufi neri (taRtōōfēē neRēē)	black truffles	
Wine : Sangiovese (sanjovese)	red	
nebbiolo (nebyolo)	red	
Orvieto (oRvyeto)	white	

Valle d'Aosta

Food: cacciaggione   game
       (kacha**j**one)
       fonduta (fond$\overline{oo}$ta)   melted cheese dish
       gnocchi (**nyok**$\overline{ee}$)   potato-flour dumplings
Wine: bianco di Morgex   white
       (**byan**ko d$\overline{ee}$ mo**R**jeks)
       carema (ka**R**ema)   red
       malvasia de Nus   white, rare
       (mal**va**sya de n$\overline{oo}$s)
       torretta rosso (to**R**eta   red
       Roso)

Veneto

Food: anguilla fritta (ang**w**$\overline{ee}$la   fried eel
       f**R**$\overline{ee}$ta)
       baccalà alla Vicentina   salt cod
       (baka**la** ala
       v$\overline{ee}$chenf$\overline{ee}$na)
       fegato alla Veneziana   liver with onions
       (**fe**gato ala vene**ts**yana)
       polenta e osei (po**len**ta e   cooked maize-flour with small
       osey)   birds eg thrushes
       risi e bisi (**R**$\overline{ee}$s$\overline{ee}$ e   rice and peas
       b$\overline{ee}$s$\overline{ee}$)
Wine: Bardolino (ba**R**do**l**$\overline{ee}$no)   red
       prosecco (p**R**oseko)   white
       recioto (**R**e**cho**to)   red
       Soave (s**wa**ve)   white
       Valpolicella   red
       (valpo**l**$\overline{ee}$chela)

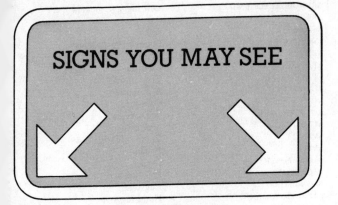

SIGNS YOU MAY SEE

ACCESSORI	Accessories
ACQUA POTABILE	Drinking water
AEREA	Airmail
AFFITTASI	To let
AGENZIA	Agency
AGENZIA DI VIAGGIO	Travel agency
ALBERGO	Hotel
ALBERGO DIURNO	Public washing facilities
ALLACCIARE LE CINTURE DI SICUREZZA	Fasten seat belts
ALLOGGIO	Accommodation
AL MARE	To the sea
ALT	Stop
ALTEZZA MASSIMA	Maximum height
AMBULANZA	Ambulance
AMBULATORIO	Surgery
ANDRÀ INCONTRO A SANZIONI PENALI CHI SARÀ TROVATO IN POSSESSO DI MERCE NON REGOLARMENTE PAGATA	Shoplifters will be prosecuted
ANFITEATRO	Amphitheatre
A NOLO	For hire
ANTICHITÀ	Antiques
APERTO	Open

ARMADIETTI PER BAGAGLI	Left luggage lockers
ARRIVI	Arrivals
ASCENSORE	Lift
ASSICURATE	Insured (Post Office)
ATTENTI AL CANE	Beware of the dog
ATTENZIONE	Caution
ATTRAVERSARE	Cross now
AUTOMATICO	Automatic
AUTO NOLEGGIO	Care hire
AUTO SERVIZIO	Self-service
AUTOSTRADA	Motorway
AVANTI	Come in/Cross now
AVVISO	Notice
BACINI PORTUALI	Docks
BAGAGLIAIO	Left luggage
BAGAGLIO	Luggage
BAGAGLIO A MANO	Hand luggage
BAMBINI	Children
BANCA	Bank
BARCHE A NOLEGGIO	Boats for hire
BENZINA	Petrol/petrol station
BIBITE FREDDE	Cold drinks
BIBLIOTECA	Library
BIGLIETTERIA	Box office/Booking office
BIGLIETTI	Tickets
BINARIO	Platform
CALDO (C)	Hot
CALZOLAIO	Heel bar/Shoe repairs
CAMBI NON SARANNO EFFETTUATI	Goods not exchanged
CAMBI NON SARANNO EFFETTUATI SE NON VERRÀ PRESENTATO LO SCONTRINO A COMPROVA DELL'AVVENUTO PAGAMENTO	Goods can only be exchanged on presentation of receipt
CAMBIO	Exchange
CAMPEGGIO	Camping
CAMPO DI GOLF	Golf course
CANCELLATO	Cancelled
CARABINIERI	Police
CARTE E GUIDE	Maps and guides
CASSA	Cash desk
CASSA CONTINUA	24 hour safe

226

CENTRO CITTÀ	City centre
CHIAMARE	Call (eg bell)
CHIESA	Church
CHIUDE ALLE ORE 14	Closes at 2 p.m.
CHIUSO	Closed
CHIUSO DALLE ORE 12.30 ALLE ORE 15.00	Closed from 12.30 to 3.00
CHIUSO PER INVENTARIO	Closed for stocktaking
CHIUSO PER RESTAURO	Closed for restoration
CHIUSO PER RINNOVO DEL LOCALE	Closed for refitting
CHIUSO PER SCIOPERO	Closed because of industrial action
CINTURE DI SALVATAGGIO	Lifebelts
CIRCO	Circus
COGNOME	Surname
COMPLETO	Full
CONTO CORRENTE	Current account
CORRIERA	Coach (sign at coach stops etc)
CORSIA	Ward
DEGUSTAZIONE CAFFÈ	Coffee tasting (not free!)
DEGUSTAZIONE VINI	Wine tasting (not free!)
DENTISTA	Dentist
DEPOSITO BAGAGLI	Baggage office
DESTINAZIONE	Destination
DEVIAZIONE	Diversion
DISCHI	Records
DISCOTECA	Disco
DIVIETO	Prohibited
DIVIETO DI AFFISSIONE	Stick no bills
DIVIETO DI BALNEAZIONE	No bathing
DIVIETO DI SCARICO	No rubbish
DIVIETO DI SOSTA	No parking
DIVIETO DI TRANSITO	No thoroughfare
DIVIETO DI TUFFARSI	No diving
DOGANA	Customs
DOMENICHE E FESTIVI CHIUSO	Closed on Sundays and holidays
DONNE	Women
DUE /PANETTONI/ AL PREZZO DI UNO	Two /panettoni/ (type of cake) for the price of one
ECCEZIONALI OCCASIONI	Special bargains
ENTRATA	Entrance

227

ENTRATA LIBERA	Admission free
ESAURITO	Sold out
ESTERO	Abroad (letter box)
FARMACIA	Chemist (look out for a square red cross)
FATTO IN ...	Made in ...
FERMARE	Shut
FERMATA	(Bus) stop
FERMO POSTA	Poste restante
FILA	Row
FINE	End
FIORISTA	Florist
FRANCOBOLLI	Stamps
FREDDO (F)	Cold
FUORI SERVIZIO	Out of order
GABINETTI	Toilets
GALLERIA	Tunnel
GELATI	Ice creams
GIOIELLERIA	Jewellery
GITE DI MEZZA GIORNATA	Half-day tours
GITE DI UN GIORNO	Day tours
GIÙ	Down
GRAN RISPARMIO	Big reductions
GRATIS	Free
GUARDAROBA	Cloakroom
GUIDA	Guide
H (OSPEDALE)	Hospital
IMMIGRAZIONE	Immigration
IMMUNIZZAZIONE	Immunisation
INDIRIZZO DI UFFICIO	Business address
INFORMAZIONI	Information/Enquiries
INGRESSO LIBERO	Admission free
IN RITARDO	Delayed
INTERNAZIONALE	International
INTERVALLO	Intermission
IN VENDITA QUI	On sale here
IVA	VAT
LA PERSONA CIVILE NON BESTEMMIA	Civilised people don't blaspheme
LAVAGGIO AUTO	Car wash
LAVANDERIA	Laundry

228

LAVANDERIA AUTOMATICA	Launderette
LETTERE	Letters
LETTERE RACCOMANDATE	Registered letters
LIBERO	Vacant
LIBRERIA	Bookshop
MESSAGGI	Messages
METÀ PREZZO	Half-price
M (METROPOLITANA)	Underground (Milan and Rome)
MONETA	Change
MULTA	Fine
NAZIONALE	National
NOLEGGIO	Rentals
NON CALPESTARE LE AIUOLE	Don't walk on the flowerbeds
NON CALPESTARE L'ERBA	Don't walk on the grass
NON DISTURBARE	Do not disturb
NON GETTARE BOTTIGLIE	Don't throw bottles
NON PARLARE CON L'AUTISTA	Do not speak to the driver
OCCASIONI	Bargains
OCCUPATO	Engaged
OFFERTA SPECIALE	Special offer
OLIO	Oil
ORARIO	Timetable/Office hours/Opening hours
ORARIO DI PARTENZA	Departure times
ORARIO D'UFFICIO DAL LUNEDÌ AL VENERDÌ 8.30 – 18.30	Office hours Monday to Friday 8.30 – 6.30
ORARIO SS MESSE FESTIVE 7 8.30 10 11.30 17	Mass times on Sundays and feast days 7, 8.30, 10, 11.30 and 5 o'clock
OSPEDALE	Hospital
OSTELLO DELLA GIOVENTÙ	Youth hostel
OTTICO	Optician
PACCHI RACCOMANDATI	Registered parcels
PARCHEGGIO (ESAURITO)	Parking/Car park (full)
PARRUCCHIERE	Hairdressing salon
PARTENZE	Departures
PASSAGGERI IN TRANSITO	Transit passengers
PASSAGGIO CARRABILE	Entrance in constant use
PASSAGGIO A LIVELLO	Level crossing
PASSAPORTI	Passports

229

PEDAGGIO	Toll
PENSIONE	Guest house
PERICOLO	Danger
PER LA CITTÀ	For the city (letter box)
PERMANENTE CONTINUA	No parking
PER TUTTE LE ALTRE DESTINAZIONE	All other destinations (letter box)
PISCINA	Swimming pool
PIZZERIA AL TAGLIO	Pizza sold by the slice
PORTATA MASSIMA	Maximum load (lift)
POSTA TELEGRAFO	Post and Telegraph Office
POSTE	Letter box
POSTO	Seat
PRENOTATO	Reserved
PRENOTAZIONI	Advance booking
PREZZI	Charges/prices
PREZZO MINIMO	Minimum charge
PRIMA CLASSE	First class
PRIVATO	Private
PROFUMERIA	Perfumery
PULITURA A SECCO	Dry cleaning
PULLMAN	Coach
REGALI	Gifts
REPARTO	Department (shop)
RESA VUOTI	Return empties
RIBASSATO	Reduction (price)
RICAMBI	Spare parts (car)
RICEVIMENTO	Reception
RIMBORSI NON SARANNO EFFETTUATI	No refunds given
RIMBORSI NON SARANNO EFFETTUATI SE NON VERRÀ PRESENTATO LO SCONTRINO A COMPROVA DELL'AVVENUTO PAGAMENTO	Refunds only given on presentation of receipt
RIPARAZIONE	Repairs
RISTORANTE	Restaurant
RIVISTE	Magazines
SALA DI ATTESA	Waiting room
SALA DI PARTENZA	Departure lounge
SALDI	Sale

230

SALDI DI FINE STAGIONE	End of season sale
SALOTTINI PROVA	Fitting rooms
SALOTTO	Lounge
SCALA MOBILE	Escalator
SCONTO 15%	15% discount
SCUOLA	School
SECONDA CLASSE	Second class
SENSO UNICO	One way
SERVIZIO (NON) COMPRESO	Service (not) included
SERVIZIO GRATIS	Free service
SERVIZIO IN CAMERA	Room service
SIGNORE	Ladies
SIGNORI	Gentlemen
SOLO RESIDENTI	Residents only
SOTTOPASSAGGIO	Subway
S. p. A. (SOCIETÀ PER AZIONI)	Limited company
SPESE	Charges/prices
SPETTACOLO	Performance
SPINGERE	Push
SPOGLIATOIO	Changing room
SPUNTINI	Snacks
STANZE DA AFFITTARE	Rooms to let
STAZIONE	Station
SU	Up
SULLE SCALE MOBILI TENETE BAMBINI IN BRACCIO, STACCATE GLI OMBRELLI DAI GRADINI, NON PORTARE CANI. GRAZIE.	On the escalators carry children, lift umbrellas clear, don't take dogs. Thank you.
SUPPLEMENTI	Extras/excess fares
T (TABACCAIO)	Tobacconist
TASSO DI CAMBIO	Rates of exchange
TASSA PER ECCESSO DI PESO	Excess baggage charge
TEATRO	Theatre
TELEGRAMMI	Telegrams
TELEVISIONE	Television
TERMINALE	Terminal
TIRARE	Pull
TOTOCALCIO	Football pools
TRAGHETTO	Ferry
UFFICIO CORRISPONDENZE E PACCHI	Post and parcels office

UFFICIO DI OGGETTI SMARRITI	Lost property office
ULTIMO TRENO	Last train
USCITA	Exit
USCITA DI SICUREZZA	Emergency exit
VELENO	Poison
VERIFICATE CHE L'IMPORTO DELLO SCONTRINO CORRISPONDA A QUANTO DA VOI PAGATO	Check your receipt
VIAGGI IN PULLMAN GUIDATI	Conducted coach tours
VIETATO	Prohibited
VIETATO AI MINORI DI 14 ANNI	No children under 14
VIETATO AI NON ADDETTI AL LAVORO	No entry to those not employed on the site
VIETATO ENTRARE	No entry
VIETATO FUMARE	No smoking
VIETATO INTRODURRE BICICLETTE E CANI	No bicycles or dogs
VOLO	Flight
VUOTO	Empty

Countries, currencies, nationalities and languages

Country, area or continent	Main unit of currency	Description & nationality (feminine form given in brackets)	Main language(s)
Africa	Africa	Africano (-na)	—
Albania	Albania	Albanese (m & f)	Albanese
Algeria	Algeria	Algerino (-na)	Arabo/Francese
Argentina	Argentina	Argentino (-na)	Spagnolo
Asia	Asia	Asiatico (-ca)	—
Australia	Dollar	Australiano (-na)	Inglese
Austria	Schilling	Austriaco (-ca)	Tedesco
Bahrain	Dinar	Bahrainese (m & f)	Arabo
Belgium	Franc	Belga (m & f)	Fiammingo/Francese
Bolivia	Peso	Boliviano (-na)	Spagnolo
Brazil	Cruzeiro	Brasiliano (-na)	Portoghese
Bulgaria	Lev	Bulgaro (-ra)	Bulgaro
Burma	Kyat	Birmano (-na)	Birmano
Canada	Dollar	Canadese (m & f)	Inglese/Francese
Chile	Peso	Cileno (-na)	Spagnolo
China	Yuan	Cinese (m & f)	Cinese
Colombia	Peso	Colombiano (-na)	Spagnolo
Costa Rica	Colon	Costaricano (-na)	Spagnolo
Cuba	Peso	Cubano (-na)	Spagnolo
Cyprus	Pound	Cipriota (m & f)	Greco/Turco
Czechoslovakia	Koruna	Cecoslovacco (-ca)	Ceco/Slovacco
Denmark	Krone	Danese (m & f)	Danese

Ecuador	Ecuador	Sucre	Ecuadoriano (-na)	Spagnolo
Egypt	Egitto	Pound	Egiziano (-na)	Arabo
Eire	Repubblica Irlandese	Punt	Irlandese (m & f)	Inglese/Irlandese
England	Inghilterra	Pound	Inglese (m & f)	Inglese
Ethiopia	Etiopia	Dollar	Etiopico (-ca)	Amarico
Europe	Europa	—	Europeo (-ea)	—
Finland	Finlandia	Markka	Finlandese (m & f)	Finlandese
France	Francia	Franc	Francese (m & f)	Francese
Germany	Germania			
West G.	G. Occidentale	Deutschmark	Tedesco (-ca)	Tedesco
East G.	G. Orientale	Mark	Tedesco (-ca)	Tedesco
Ghana	Gana	New Cedi	Ganese (m & f)	Inglese/Akan
Greece	Grecia	Drachma	Greco (-ca)	Greco
Guatemala	Guatemala	Quetzal	Guatemalteco (-ca)	Spagnolo
Guyana	Guiana	Dollar	Guianese (m & f)	Inglese
Holland	Olanda	Guilder	Olandese (m & f)	Olandese
Hong Kong	Hong Kong	Dollar	di Hong Kong (m & f)	Inglese/Cinese
Hungary	Ungheria	Forint	Ungherese (m & f)	Ungherese
Iceland	Islanda	Krona	Islandese (m & f)	Islandese
India	India	Rupee	Indiano (-na)	Hindi/Inglese
Indonesia	Indonesia	Rupiah	Indonesiano (-na)	Bahasa Indonesiano
Iran	Iran	Rial	Iranico (-ca)	Farsi
Iraq	Irak	Dinar	Iracheno (-na)	Arabo
Israel	Israele	Pound	Israeliano (-na)	Ebreo
Italy	Italia	Lire	Italiano (-na)	Italiano
Jamaica	Giamaica	Dollar	Giamaicano (-na)	Inglese
Japan	Giappone	Yen	Giapponese (m & f)	Giapponese
Jordan	Giordania	Dinar	Giordano (-na)	Arabo
Kenya	Kenia	Shilling	del Kenia (m & f)	Swahili
Kuwait	Kuwait	Dinar	del Kuwait (m & f)	Arabo

Country, area or continent	Main unit of currency	Description & nationality (feminine form given in brackets)	Main language(s)
Lebanon	Libano	Pound	Libanese (m & f)	Arabo
Libya	Libia	Dinar	Libico (-ca)	Arabo
Luxemburg	Lussemburgo	Franc	Lussemburghese (m & f)	Francese/Tedesco
Malaysia	Malesia	Dollar	Malese (m & f)	Malese/Cinese
Malta	Malta	Pound	Maltese (m & f)	Maltese/Inglese
Mexico	Messico	Peso	Messicano (-na)	Spagnolo
Morocco	Marocco	Dirham	Marocchino (-na)	Arabo/Francese
New Zealand	Nuova Zelanda	Dollar	Neozelandese (m & f)	Inglese
Nicaragua	Nicaragua	Cordoba	Nicaraguense (m & f)	Spagnolo
Nigeria	Nigeria	Naira	Nigeriano (-na)	Hausa/Ibo/Yorobua/Inglese
Northern Ireland	Irlanda del nord	Pound	Irlandese (m & f)	Inglese
Norway	Norvegia	Krona	Norvegese (m & f)	Norvegese
Pakistan	Pakistan	Rupee	Pakistano (-na)	Urdu
Paraguay	Paraguai	Guarani	Paraguaiano (-na)	Spagnolo
Peru	Peru	Sol	Peruviano (-na)	Spagnolo
Poland	Polonia	Zloty	Polacco (-ca)	Polacco
Portugal	Portogallo	Escudo	Portoghese (m & f)	Portoghese
Romania	Romania	Leu	Rumeno (-na)	Rumeno
Saudi Arabia	Arabia Saudita	Riyal	Arabo (-ba) Saudita (m & f)	Arabo
Scotland	Scozia	Pound	Scozzese (m & f)	Inglese/Gaelico
Singapore	Singapore	Dollar	di Singapore (m & f)	Malese/Cinese/Inglese/Tamil
South Africa	Sud Africa	Rand	Sudafricano (-na)	Afrikaans/Inglese

236

Spain	Spagna	Peseta	Spagnolo (-la)	Spagnolo
Sudan	Sudan	Pound	Sudanese (m & f)	Arabo
Sweden	Svezia	Krona	Svedese (m & f)	Svedese
Switzerland	Svizzera	Franc	Svizzero (-ra)	Francese/Tedesco/
				Italiano/Romancio
Syria	Siria	Pound	Siriano (-na)	Arabo
Tanzania	Tanzania	Shilling	Tanzaniano (-na)	Swahili
Thailand	Tailandia	Baht	Tailandese (m & f)	Tai
Tunisia	Tunisia	Dinar	Tunisino (-na)	Arabo/Francese
Turkey	Turchia	Lira	Turco (-ca)	Turco
Union of Soviet	Unione delle	Rouble	Russo (-sa)	Russo
Socialist Republics	Repubbliche			
(USSR)/Russia	Socialiste			
	Sovietiche			
	(URSS)/Russia			
United Kingdom	Regno Unito	Pound	Britannico (-ca)	Inglese
(UK) (England,	(Inghilterra,	sterling		
Northern Ireland,	Irlanda del nord,			
Scotland, Wales,	Scozia, Galles,			
Channel Islands)	Isole Normanne)			
United States of	Stati Uniti d'America	Dollar	Americano (-na)	Inglese
America (USA)	(USA)			
Uruguay	Uruguay	Peso	Uruguaino (-na)	Spagnolo
Venezuela	Venezuela	Bolivar	Venezuelano (-na)	Spagnolo
Vietnam	Vietnam	Dong	Vietnamita (m & f)	Vietnamita
Wales	Galles	Pound	Gallese (m & f)	Gallese/Inglese
Yugoslavia	Iugoslavia	Dinar	Iugoslavo (-va)	Serbo-croato
Zaire	Zaire	Zaire	dello Zaire (m & f)	Francese
Zimbabwe	Zimbabwe	Dollar	di Zimbabwe (m & f)	Inglese

The motorist abroad

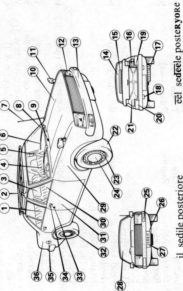

1 back seat — il sedile posteriore
2 roof rack — il portapacchi
3 head restraint — la poggiatesta
4 passenger's seat — il sedile anteriore destro
5 seat belt — la cintura di sicurezza
6 windscreen wiper blade — la spazzola tergicristallo
7 aerial — l'antenna
8 windscreen wiper arm — il braccio tergicristallo
9 windscreen washer — il lavacristallo

ēēl sedēēle posterȳore
ēēl portapakēē
la pojatesta
ēēl sedēēle anterȳore destro
la chēēntōōra dēē sēēkōōretsa
la spatsola terjēēkrēēstalo
lantena
ēēl brȧcho terjēēkrēēstalo
ēēl lavakrēēstalo

238

#	English	Italian	Pronunciation
10	bonnet	il cofano	eel kofano
11	exterior mirror	lo specchietto laterale	lo spekyeto lateRale
12	headlight	il proiettore	eel pRoyetoRe
13	bumper	il paraurti	eel paraŌŌRtee
14	rear window	il lunotto posteriore	eel lŌŌnoto posteRyoRe
15	rear window heater	il riscaldamento lunotto posteriore	eel RĒĒskaldamento lŌŌnoto posteRyoRe
16	spare wheel	la ruota di scorta	la Rwota dēē skoRta
17	fuel tank	il serbatoio	eel seRbatoyo
18	hazard warning light	il segnale luminoso di pericolo	eel senyale lŌŌmēēnoso dēē peRēēkolo
19	brake light	il fanalino dei freni	eel fanalēēno dey fRenēē
20	rear light	il fanalo posteriore	eel fanalo posteRyoRe
21	boot	il baule	eel baŌŌle
22	tyre	la gomma	la goma
23	front wheel	la ruota anteriore	la Rwota anteRyoRe
24	hubcap	la coppa	la kopa
25	sidelight	il fanalo laterale	eel fanalo lateRale
26	number plate	la targa	la taRga
27	registration number	il numero di targa	eel nŌŌmeRo dēē taRga
28	windscreen	il cristallo anteriore	eel kRēēstalo anteRyoRe
29	front wing	l'ala anteriore	lala anteRyoRe
30	driver's seat	il sedile di guida	eel sedēēle dēē gwēēda
31	door	la porta	la poRta
32	rear wheel	la ruota posteriore	la Rwota posteRyoRe
33	lock	la serratura	la seRatŌŌra
34	door handle	la maniglia	la manēēlya
35	petrol filler cap	il tappo della benzina	eel tapo dela bentsēēna
36	rear wing	l'ala posteriore	lala posteRyoRe

239

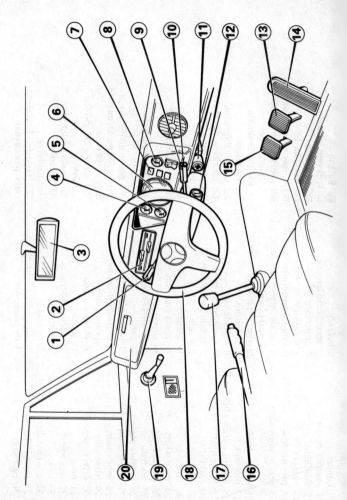

	English	Italian	Pronunciation
1	dipswitch	il commutatore luci	ēel komōōtatore lōōchēē
2	heater	l'impianto di riscaldamento (m)	lēempyanto dēē rēēskaldamento
3	interior mirror	lo specchio retrovisore	lo spekyo retrovēēzore
4	water temperature gauge	il termometro acqua	ēel termometro akwa
5	ammeter	il amperometro	ēel amperometro
6	speedometer	il contachilometri	ēel kontakēēlometrēē
7	oil pressure warning light	la spia pressione olio	la spēēa presyone olyo
8	fuel gauge	l'indicatore livello carburante (m)	lēendēēkatore lēēvelo karbōōrante
9	horn	la tromba	la tromba
10	direction indicator	l'indicatore di direzzione (m)	lēendēēkatore dēē dēēretsyone
11	choke	la valvola dell'aria	la valvola delarya
12	ignition switch	l'interruttore accensione (m)	lēenterōōtore achensyone
13	brake pedal	il pedale freni	ēel pedale frenēē
14	accelerator	il pedale acceleratore	ēel pedale acheleratore
15	clutch pedal	il pedale frizione	ēel pedale frēētsyone
16	handbrake	il freno a mano	ēel freno a mano
17	gear lever (selector)	la leva cambio	la leva kambyo
18	steering wheel	il volante	ēel volante
19	window winder	la maniglia alzacristallo	la manēēlya altsakrēēstalo
20	glove compartment	il cassetto ripostiglio	ēel kaseto rēēpostēēlyo

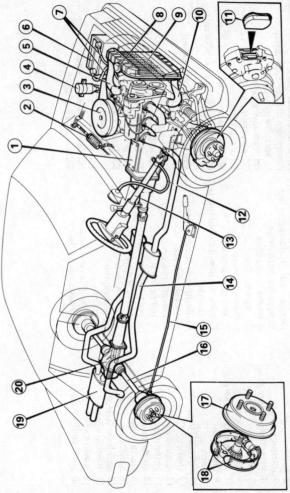

242

#	English	Italian	Pronunciation
1	gearbox	la scatola cambio	la **skatola kambyo**
2	fuse box	la scatola porta fusibili	la **skatola pOrta** fōozēebēelēe
3	air filter	il filtro dell'aria	ēel **fēeltro** delaRYa
4	ignition coil	l'accensione (m)	lachensyone
5	radiator hose (top)	il tubo radiatore superiore	ēel **tōōbo** RadyatoRe sōōpeRYORe
6	battery	la bateria	la bateRĒea
7	leads (battery) (pl)	i conduttori	ēe kondōōtoRĒe
8	filler cap (radiator)	il tappo	ēel **tapo**
9	radiator	il radiatore	ēel RadyatoRe
10	radiator hose (bottom)	il tubo radiatore inferiore	ēel **tōōbo** RadyatoRe ēenfeRYORe
11	disk brake pad	la pastiglia (del freno)	la pastēelya (del **fR**eno)
12	speedometer cable	il caveto per contachilometri	ēel kaveto per kontakēelometrēe
13	steering column	l'albero volante	lalbeRo volante
14	exhaust pipe	il tubo scarico	ēel **tōōbo** skaRēeko
15	handbrake cable	il caveto freno a mano	ēel kaveto **fR**eno a **mano**
16	rear axle	l'asse posteriore (m)	lase posteRYORe
17	brake drum	il tamburo di freno	ēel tam**bōō**Ro dēe **fR**eno
18	brake shoe	il ceppo del freno	ēel **chepo** del **fR**eno
19	silencer	il silenziatore	ēel sēelentsyatoRe
20	differential	il differenziale	ēel dēefeRentsyale

243

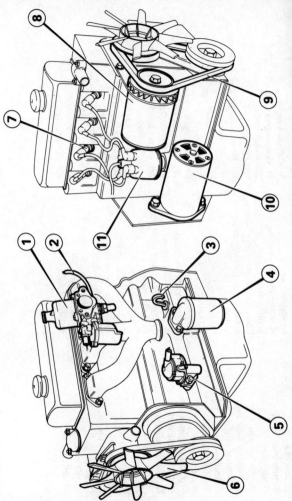

244

1 carburettor	il carburatore	ēēl karbōōratore
2 cable	il cavo per traino	ēēl kavo per trayno
3 oil dip stick	l'asticella per controllo livello olio	lastēēchela per kontRolo lēēvelo olyo
4 oil filter	il filtro olio	ēēl fēēltRo olyo
5 fuel pump	la pompa carburante	la pompa karbōōRante
6 fan	il ventilatore	ēēl ventēēlatore
7 sparking plug	la candela	la kandela
8 alternator	il dinamo	ēēl dēēnamo
9 fan belt	la cinghia per ventilatore	la chēēngya per ventēēlatore
10 starter motor	il motorino di avviamento	ēēl motorēēno dēē avyamento
11 distributor	il distributore	ēēl dēēstrēēbōōtore

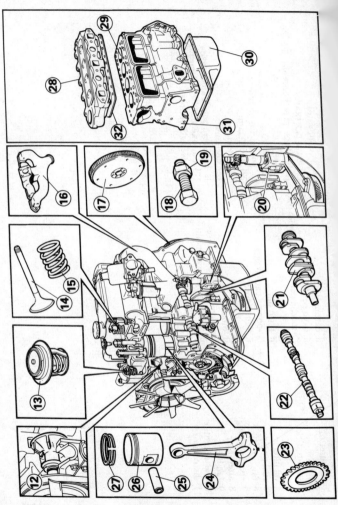

English	Italian	
12 water pump	la pompa acqua	la **pomp**a akwa
13 thermostat	il termostato	ēēl teRmostato
14 valve	la valvola	la valvola
15 spring (n)	la molla	la **mo**la
16 manifold, inlet and exhaust	il collettore d'ammissione e scarico	ēēl koletoRe damēēsyone e skaRēēko
17 fly wheel	il volano	ēēl volano
18 bolt	il bullone	ēēl bōōlone
19 nut	il dado	ēēl dado
20 oil pump	la pompa olio	la **pomp**a olyo
21 crankshaft	l'albero motore	lalbeRo motoRe
22 camshaft	l'albero a camme	lalbeRo a kame
23 sprocket	la ruota dentata	la **Rwo**ta dentata
24 connecting rod	la biella	la byela
25 gudgeon pin	lo spinotto	lo spēēnoto
26 piston	il pistone	ēēl pēēstone
27 piston rings (pl)	gli anelli del pistone	ly anelli del pēēstone
28 cylinder head	la testa del cilindro	la **te**sta del chēēlēēndRo
29 cylinder	il cilindro	ēēl chēēlēēndRo
30 oil sump	la coppa olio	la **ko**pa olyo
31 cylinder block	il monoblocco	ēēl monobloko
32 gasket	la guarnizione	la gwaRnēētsyone

247

The motorist abroad

Useful words and expressions

Remember: It's /the battery/	È /la bateria/	e /la bateREEa/
accident	l'incidente (m)	leencheEEdente
air pressure	la pressione delle gomme	la presyone dele gome
could you check /the tyre pressure/ please?	mi può controllare /la p. delle g./ per favore?	mee pwo kontROLare /la pREsyone dele gome/ peR favoRE

lb/sq. in.	=	kg/cm²	lb/sq. in.	=	kg/cm²	lb/sq. in.	=	kg/cm²
20	=	1.40	24	=	1.68	30	=	2.10
21	=	1.47	26	=	1.82	34	=	2.39
22	=	1.54	28	=	1.96	40	=	2.81

antifreeze	l'anti-gelo	lanteEjelo
a can of a.	un barattolo di a.	oon baRatolo dee anteEjelo
automatic (adj)	automatico	aOOtomateEko
a. transmission	la trasmissione automatica	la tRasmeEsyone aOOtomateEka
axle	l'asse (m)	lase
rear a.	l'a. posteriore	lase posteRYoRE
battery	la batteria	la bateREEa
I'd like the b. charged	vorrei far caricare la b.	voRey faR kaREEkaRe la bateREEa
I've got a flat b.	ho la b. scarica	o la bateREEa skaREEka
braking system/brakes	i freni (mpl)	ee fReNEE
brake fluid	il liquido dei freni	eel leEkweEdo dey fReNEE
brake pads/linings for disc brakes	le pastiglie (fpl) (del freno)	le pasfeElye (del fReno)
for drum brakes	i guarmazioni (mpl) (del freno)	ee gwaRmatsyoNEE (del fReno)

248

breakdown (n)	il guasto	ēēl gwasto
b. service	il soccorso stradale	ēēl sokoRso stRadale
b. vehicle	il veicolo di soccorso	ēēl veēēkolo dēē sokoRso
I have broken down	ho un g. alla macchina	o ōōn gwasto ala makēēna
cable	il cavo (per traino)	ēēl cavo
car	la macchina	la makēēna
by c.	in m.	ēēn makēēna
c. wash	lavaggio della m.	lavajo dela makēēna
car sickness	il mal di macchina	ēēl mal dēē makēēna
I get c. s.	soffro il m. di m.	sofRo ēēl mal dēē makēēna
change (vb)	cambiare	kambyaRe
I'd like /the tyre/ changed	vorrei far c. /la gomma/	voRey faR kambyaRe /la goma/
change gear	cambiare la marcia	kambyaRe la maRcha
charge (vb)	caricare	kaRēēkaRe
I'd like the battery charged	vorrei far c. /la batteria/	voRey faR kaRēēkaRe /la bateRēēa/
chassis	il telaio	ēēl telayo
check	controllare	kontRolaRe
could you c. /the oil and water/ please?	mi può c. /l'olio e l'acqua/ per favore?	mēē pwo kontRolaRe /lolyo e lakwa/ peR favoRe
could you c. /the tyre pressure/ please?	mi può c. /la pressione delle gomme/ per favore?	mēē pwo kontRolaRe /la pRèsyone dele gome/ peR favoRe
clutch	la frizione	la fRēētsyone
crash	il scontro	ēēl skontRo
crash (into)	scontrarmi (con)	skontRaRmēē (kon)
cross-ply tyres (pl)	le gomme diagonali	le gome dēēagonalēē
deicer	lo spray antighiaccio	lo spRey antēēgyacho
derv	la nafta per motori diesel	la nafta peR motoRēē dyesel

diesel oil	la nafta	la **naf**ta
dip (vb)	abbassare i fari	abasaʀe ee faʀee
dipstick	l'asticella per controllo livello olio	l'asteechela peʀ kontʀolo leevelo olyo
disc brakes (pl)	i freni a disco	ee fʀenee a deesko
distributor	il distributore	eel deestʀeeboootoʀe
drive (vb)	guidare	gweedaʀe
driver	l'autista	laooteesta
drive shaft	l'albero principale	lalbeʀo pʀeencheepale
electrical system	il sistema elettrico	eel seestema eletʀeeko
exhaust system	il sistema scarico	eel seestema skaʀeeko
fit (eg exhaust)	montare	montaʀe
fly wheel	il volano	eel volano
footpump	la pompa a piedi	la pompa a pyedee
garage	il garage	eel gaʀaje
gears	le marcie	le maʀche
first gear	la prima marcia	la pʀeema maʀcha
second gear	la seconda marcia	la sekonda maʀcha
third gear	la terza marcia	la teʀtsa maʀcha
fourth gear	la quarta marcia	la kwaʀta maʀcha
fifth gear	la quinta marcia	la kweenta maʀcha
reverse	la retromarcia	la ʀetʀomaʀcha
grease (n)	il grasso	eel gʀaso
grease (vb)	ingrassare	eengʀasaʀe
headlamp bulb	la lampadina per faro	la lampadeena peʀ faʀo
hire (vb)	noleggiare	nolejaʀe
hood (sports car)	il capote	eel kapote
hose	il tubo di gomma	eel toobo dee goma
hub	il mozzo	eel modzo
hydraulic brakes (pl)	i freni idraulici (mpl)	ee fʀenee eedʀaooleechee
ignition system	il sistema accensione	eel seestema achensyone
inner tube (tyre)	la camera d'aria	la kameʀa daʀya
insurance certificate	il certificato di assicurazione	eel cheʀteefeekato dee aseekooʀatsyone

250

English	Italian	Pronunciation
international driving licence	la patente internazionale	la patente eenternatsyonale
jack	il cricco	eel kreeko
jeep	il jeep	eel jeep
key	la chiave	la kyave
layby	piazzuola di sosta	pyadswola dee sosta
leak (n)	la perdita	la perdeeta
leak (vb)	spandere	spandere
/the radiator/ is leaking	/il radiatore/ spande	eel radyatore/ spande
licence (driving licence)	la patente	la patente
log book	il libretto	eel leebreto
lorry	l'autocarro	laootokaro
make (n) (car)	la marca	la marka
mechanic	il meccanico	eel mekaneeko
mend	riparare	reeparare
I'd like /the tyre/ mended please	vorrei far r. /la gomma/ per favore	vorey far reeparare /la goma/ per favore
oil (engine oil)	l'olio	lolyo
could you check /the o. and water/ please?	mi può controllare /l'o. e l'acqua/ per favore?	mee pwo kontrolare / lolyo e lakwa/ per favore
can of o.	il bidone di o.	eel beedone dee olyo
o. filter	il filtro olio	eel feeltro olyo
o. pump	la pompa olio	la pompa olyo
overdrive	quinta marcia	kweenta marcha
overheat	surriscaldare	sooreeskaldare
overheated	surriscaldato	sooreeskaldato
part (car)	il pezzo	eel petso
petrol	la benzina	la bendseena
** (91/92 oct) *** (94/95 oct)	normale	normale
**** (97/98 oct)	super	sooper
/18/ litres of /3 star/ please	/diciotto/ litri de /normale/, per favore	/deechoto/ leetree de /normale/ per favore

251

/19,000 lire's/ worth of /4 star/ please	/diciannovemila lire/ di /super/ per favore	/deechanovemeela leeRe/ dee /soopeR/ peR favoRe
fill it up please	il pieno per favore	eel pyeno peR favoRe
petrol can	il bidone per benzina	eel beedone peR bendseena
petrol coupon	il buono per benzina	eel bwono peR bendseena
petrol station	la stazione di servizio	la statsyone dee seRveetsyo
puncture	la foratura	la foratoora
I've got a p.	ho forato una gomma	o foRato oona goma
radial tyres (pl)	i radiali (mpl)	ee Radyalee
radio (car)	la radio	la Radyo
repair (vb)	riparare	ReepaRaRe
reverse (n)	retromarcia	RetRomaRcha
reverse (vb)	fare retromarcia	faRe RetRomaRcha
run over	investire	eenvesfeeRe
seat	il sedile	eel sedeele
service (n)	il servizio	eel seRveetsyo
service (vb)	controllare	kontRolaRe
it needs servicing	deve essere controllata	deve eseRe kontRolata
shammy leather	la pelle di camoscio	la pele dee kamoshyo
shock absorber	l'ammortizzatore (m)	lamoRteetzatoRe
rear s.a.	l'a. posteriore	lamoRteetzatoRe posteRyoRe
spare parts (pl)	i pezzi (mpl) di ricambio	ee petsee dee Reekambyo
sparking plug	la candela	la kandela
sports car	la macchina sportiva	la makeena spoRfeeva
spring (n)	la molla	la mola
start (vb)	avviare	avyaRe
it won't s.	non si avvia	non see avya
starter motor	il motorino di avviamento	eel motoReeno dee avyamento
steer (car)	guidare	gweedaRe
steering	la guida	la gweeda

252

suspension	la sospensione	la sospensyone
front s.	la s. anteriore	la sospensyone anteRyoRe
rear s.	la s. posteriore	la sospensyone posteRyoRe
switch (n)	l'interruttore (m)	leenteROOtore
switch off (vb)	spegnere	spenyeRe
switch on (vb)	accendere	achendeRe
tow rope	il cavo per traino	eel kavo peR tRayno
I need a tow	mi occorre del traino	mee okoRe del tRayno
trailer	il rimorchio	eel Reemorkyo
transmission	la trasmissione	la tRasmeesyone
automatic t.	la trasmissione automatica	la tRasmeesyone aootomateeka
t. shaft	l'albero di trasmissione	lalbero dee tRasmeesyone
tubeless (tyre)	il tubeless	eel toobleš
twin carburettor	i carburatori doppi (mpl)	ee karboORatoRee dopee
tyre	la gomma	la goma
could you check /the tyres/ please?	mi può controllare /le gomme/ per favore?	mee pwo kontRolaRe /le gome/ peR favoRe
I've got a flat t.	ho una g. sgonfia	o oona goma sgonfya
tyre pressure	la pressione delle gomme	la pResyone dele gome
van	il furgone	eel fooRgone
water	l'acqua	lakwa
could you check /the oil and w./ please?	mi può controllare /l'olio e l'a./ per favore?	mee pwo kontRolaRe /lolyo e lakwa/ peR favoRe
wheel	la ruota	la Rwota
window	il cristallo	eel kReestalo
wing	l'ala	lala
work (vb)	funzionare	foontsyonaRe
it doesn't w.	non funziona	non foontsyona

Mini Grammar

This section is for reference only and is not intended to be a complete grammar of Italian. It contains a summary of the more important grammatical forms which occur in the Study Section.

NOUNS

Gender
All nouns are feminine or masculine, whether they indicate persons, occupations, animals or things:

Masculine		Feminine	
uomo	man	donna	woman
ragazzo	boy	ragazza	girl
cameriere	waiter	cameriera	waitress
cavallo	horse	cavalla	mare
biglietto	ticket	stanza	room
passaporto	passport	busta	envelope
giornale	newspaper	chiave	key

Most masculine nouns end in 'o'.
Most feminine nouns end in 'a'.
But some nouns, both masculine and feminine, end in 'e' and other letters.

Plural
To form the plural of most nouns, change the final vowel.

The regular plural of masculine nouns ending in 'o' is 'i'.
The regular plural of feminine nouns ending in 'a' is 'e'.
(All irregular plurals are given in the Mini Dictionary)

Masculine		Feminine	
ragazzo	ragazzi	ragazza	ragazze
biglietto	biglietti	stanza	stanze
passaporto	passaporti	busta	buste

The regular plural of nouns ending in 'e' (mostly masculine) is 'i':

Masculine		Feminine	
cameriere	camerieri	chiave	chiavi
giornale	giornali		

With all nouns ending in 'ca' or 'ga', the hard 'c' or 'g' (as in 'cat' or 'gun') is preserved in the plural by adding 'h' after 'c' or 'g'. 'h' is also added to some – but not all – nouns ending in 'co' and 'go'.

biblioteca	biblioteche	(f)	library (-ies)
collega	colleghi	(m)	colleague (-s)
albergo	alberghi	(m)	hotel (-s)

ARTICLES

The article changes according to whether the noun which follows it is masculine or feminine.

In the singular
Before masculine nouns 'the' is 'il':

| il conto | the bill |
| il treno | the train |

Before feminine nouns 'the' is 'la':

| la busta | the envelope |
| la chiave | the key |

Before nouns beginning with a vowel 'il/la' is shortened to 'l':

| l'appartamento (m) | the flat |
| l'ambulanza (f) | the ambulance |

Note: Before masculine nouns beginning with 'z', or with 's' followed by another consonant, 'the' is 'lo':

| lo zio | the uncle |
| lo studente | the student |

In the plural
Before masculine nouns 'the' is 'i':

| i conti | the bills |
| i treni | the trains |

255

Before feminine words 'the' is 'le':

le buste	the envelopes
le chiavi	the keys
le ambulanze	the ambulances

Note: Before masculine words beginning with a vowel, or with 'z', or with 's' followed by another consonant, 'the' is 'gli':

gli appartamenti	the flats
gli studenti	the students

Joined prepositions

In some expressions, eg 'to the', 'from the', 'of the', 'in the', 'on the' etc, the preposition ('to', 'from', 'of', etc) is joined to the different Italian forms of 'the' to make a single word.

	Singular				Plural		
	+il(m)	+la(f)	+l'(m/f)	+lo(m)	+i(m)	+le(f)	+gli(m)
a (to, at)	al	alla	all'	allo	ai	alle	agli
da (from, by)	dal	dalla	dall'	dallo	dai	dalle	dagli
di (of)	del	della	dell'	dello	dei	delle	degli
in (in, at)	nel	nella	nell'	nello	nei	nelle	negli
su (on, about)	sul	sulla	sull'	sullo	sui	sulle	sugli

Here are some examples

alla stazione (f)	to the station/at the station
al centro (m)	to the centre
all'aeroporto (m)	to the airport/at the airport
dagli Stati Uniti (mpl)	from the United States
della ragazza (f)	of the girl
nel frigorifero (m)	in the fridge
informazioni sugli alberghi (mpl)	information about hotels

Note that Italian prepositions can be used in different ways from their English equivalents:

al braccio	in the arm
alla romana	cooked in the Roman style

The most important use of di + 'the' is to mean 'some':

della birra	some beer
del tè	some tea
delle cartoline	some postcards
dei posti	some seats

Sometimes a preposition + 'il/la/i/le' is used in Italian where it would not be in English (and vice versa):

dall'Inghilterra	from England – literally 'from the England'
in centro	in the centre – literally 'in centre'

The preposition 'con' (with) can only be combined with the masculine articles 'il' and 'i':

col ('con' + 'il') treno	by train – literally 'with the train'

A/an

In the singular
Before masculine nouns 'a/an' is 'un':

un albergo	a hotel
un telefono	a telephone

But note 'uno' before a noun beginning with 'z' or 's' followed by another consonant:

uno studente	a student

Before feminine nouns 'a/an' is 'una':

una macchina	a car
una pizza	a pizza

But note 'un'' before a vowel:

un'insalata	a salad

for 'some' and 'any' use 'di' + 'il/la/i/le' (see previous section):

della birra	some beer
del caffè	some coffee, etc

257

ADJECTIVES

Adjectives 'agree' with the noun they describe and thus have masculine, feminine and plural forms.

Adjectives ending in 'o'
Most adjectives end in 'o' in their masculine form:

il barattolo piccol<u>o</u>	the little can (m)
sono italian<u>o</u>	I'm Italian (m)

The ending changes to 'a' in their feminine form:

la borsa piccol<u>a</u>	the little bag (f)
sono italian<u>a</u>	I'm Italian (f)

To form the plural of adjectives ending in 'o', change 'o' to 'i'.

i barattoli piccol<u>i</u>	the little cans (mpl)
siamo italian<u>i</u>	we're Italian (mpl)

To form the plural of adjectives ending in 'a', change 'a', to 'e':

le borse piccol<u>e</u>	the little bags (fpl)
siamo italian<u>e</u>	we're Italian (fpl)

Adjectives ending in 'e'
Adjectives ending in 'e' can be both masculine and feminine forms:

il barattolo verd<u>e</u>	the green can (m)
la borsa verd<u>e</u>	the green bag (f)
sono ingles<u>e</u>	I'm English (m & f)

To form the plural of adjectives ending in 'e', change 'e' to 'i':

i barattoli verd<u>i</u>	the green cans (mpl)
le borse verd<u>i</u>	the green bags (fpl)
siamo ingles<u>i</u>	we're English (mpl & fpl)

Position of adjectives
In Italian most adjectives follow the noun they describe:

la borsa verde	the green bag
un libro inglese	an English book

But some very common adjectives precede the noun:

una bella stanza	a beautiful room
una brutta stazione	an ugly station
uno corto circuito	a short circuit
la giovane donna	the young lady
un vecchio albergo	an old hotel

258

But be careful! By putting some adjectives after the noun you may change their meaning:

un grand'uomo	a great man
un uomo grande	a tall man
Povera donna!	Poor (ie unfortunate) woman!
una donna povera	a poor ie not rich woman

Irregular adjectives

Certain very common adjectives – 'bello' (beautiful), 'buono' (good), 'grande' (big) and 'santo' (saint) are irregular when they precede a noun.

'Bello' changes in the same way as 'di' + 'il/la/l'/lo' etc eg 'del/della/dell'/dello' etc (see 'Jointed' prepositions p00):

una bella città	a beautiful city
un bel duomo	a beautiful cathedral
Bell'idea	Good idea! (f)
un bello studio	a beautiful studio
belle scarpe	beautiful shoes
due bei bambini	two beautiful children
begli alberi	beautiful trees

'Buono' is regular in the plural but when it is in the singular changes in the same way as 'un/una' (see A/an p257):

un buon vino	a good wine
un buono studente	a good student
una buon'educazione	a good education

'Grande' becomes 'gran' and 'santo' becomes 'san' in the masculine singular before a noun beginning with a consonant (except 's' or 'z' when they do not change). 'Grande' becomes 'grand'' and 'santo' becomes 'sant'' before a noun beginning with a vowel:

un gran fracasso	a great crash
un grande scrittore	a great writer
un grand'uomo	a great man
San Pietro	Saint Peter
il Santo Spirito	the Holy Spirit

Remember that all these adjectives are regular when they come after the noun they describe or are separated from it.

Comparisons

To compare people or things, use 'più' (more) or 'meno' (less):

più grande	bigger
meno costoso	less expensive

259

To compare two things, use 'più . . . di'/'meno . . . di' (more . . . than/less . . . than):

La sua macchina è <u>più</u> grande <u>della</u> (di + la) mia	His car is bigger than mine
Questo ristorante è <u>meno</u> costoso <u>di</u> quello	This restaurant is less expensive than that one

To express the superlative, put 'il/la/i/le' (the) before 'più'.
Remember that both 'il/la/i/le' and the adjective must agree with the noun:

Questo ristorante è il più costoso della città	This restaurant is the most expensive in the town
Questa stanza è la più grande della casa	This room is the biggest in the house

But note that 'la stanza più grande' means both 'the biggest room' and 'the bigger room' (there is no difference in Italian).

Note that some adjectives have alternative forms for comparative adjectives:

'buono' (good)	'più buono' or	'migliore' (better)
'grande' (big)	'più grande' or	'maggiore' (bigger)
'piccolo' (little)	'più piccolo' or	'minore' (smaller)

Superlative adjectives are often used for emphasis:

Questa città è bellissima	This city is really beautiful (literally, most beautiful)
Il caffè è buonissimo	The coffee is excellent (literally, most good)

Note that 'ottimo' is an alternative form of 'buonissimo' (excellent).

This /that, this one/that one

Questo (this) and Quello (that) are used both as adjectives:

questo mese	this month (m)
questa mattina	this morning (f)
quello formaggio	that cheese (m)
quella mela	that apple (f)

and as pronouns:

Questo per favore	This one please (m)
Quello per favore	That one please (m)
Vorrei quella grande	I'd like that big one (f)

They must agree with the noun to which they refer.

PRONOUNS

Subject		After a preposition		Direct object		Indirect object	
I	**io**	me	**me**	me	**mi**	to me	**mi (me)**
you (informal)	**tu**	you	**te**	you	**ti**	to you	**ti (te)**
he/it	**lui**	him	**lui**	him/it	**lo**	to him	**gli (glie)**
she/it	**lei**	her	**lei**	her/it	**la**	to her	**le (glie)**
you (polite)	**lei**	you	**lei**	you	**la**	to you	**le (glie)**
we	**noi**	us	**noi**	us	**ci**	to us	**ci (ce)**
you (plural informal)	**voi**	you	**voi**	you	**vi**	to you	**vi (ve)**
they	**loro**	them	**loro**	them	**li (m) le (f)**	to them	**loro**
you (plural polite)	**loro**	you	**loro**	you	**le**	to you	**loro**

For explanation of words in brackets see the note on indirect object pronouns (p263).

Subject pronouns

Subject pronouns are not usually necessary in Italian:

(Io) sono italiano   I'm Italian
(Lui) parla italiano   He speaks Italian

Use the pronoun for emphasis or to make the meaning absolutely clear:

<u>Lui</u> parla italiano, <u>lei</u> parla francese (He speaks Italian, she speaks French).

Use 'tu', 'te', 'ti' (you, to you) with someone you know well or with a child. Wait for other people to use 'tu' to you first! The plural of 'tu' is 'voi'.
Use 'lei' (you) with someone you don't know well. The plural of 'lei' is 'loro'. 'Lei' (you) and 'lei' (she) sound exactly the same, as do 'loro' (you) and 'loro' (they). They are sometimes written differently, with the capital letter 'L' when lei/loro mean 'you', although this is becoming less common nowadays.

Pronouns after prepositions

These pronouns are usually used after a preposition which follows a verb:

Questa lettera è per <u>me</u>	This letter is for me
Vieni con <u>me</u>	Come with me

Direct object pronouns

Direct object pronouns precede the verb. They agree in number and gender with the thing they refer to:

<u>Lo</u> prendo	I'll take it (m)
<u>Lo</u> scriva per favore	Write it please (m)
<u>Lo</u> vorrei cotto bene	I'd like it well done (m)
<u>L'</u>abbiamo veduto	We have seen her

But note that the pronoun comes after a verb in its infinitive form:

Non riesco a far<u>lo</u> (<u>fare</u> + <u>lo</u>)	literally 'I don't succeed to do it' ie 'I can't do it').

Indirect object pronouns

Indirect object pronouns, except 'loro' usually precede the verb:

Il signor Fermi <u>le</u> parla	Mr Fermi is talking to her
Cosa <u>mi</u> consiglia?	Literally, What to me do you recommend? ie What do you recommend?
Maria parla <u>loro</u>	Maria is talking to them

The indirect object pronoun usually carries the sense of 'to someone' or 'for someone'. It is often used in Italian where you might not expect it in English:

<u>Mi</u> dispiace molto	I'm very sorry (literally 'to me it displeases much')
<u>Mi</u> tiene il posto	Could you keep my seat? (literally 'to me keep the seat?')
<u>Mi</u> fa male la gamba	My leg hurts (literally 'to me makes bad the leg')
<u>Le</u> presento la signora Fermi	This is Mrs Fermi (literally 'to you I present Mrs Fermi')
<u>Le</u> piace questo?	Do you like this? (literally 'to you pleases this?')
Cosa <u>mi</u> occorre?	What do I need? (literally 'what to me is wanting?')

Note that when indirect and direct object pronouns are used together, the form of the indirect object pronoun changes: 'mi' becomes 'me' etc ('loro' is not affected as it comes after the verb): See words in brackets on p261.

Paolo le da un libro   Paul gives her a book
but
Paolo glie lo da   Paul gives it to her

The indirect pronoun comes before the direct pronoun.

Reflexive pronouns/Possessive pronouns and adjectives

Reflexive pronouns		Possessive pronouns/adjectives			
		m	**f**	**mpl**	**fpl**
myself	**mi**	my/mine	il mio	la mia	i miei	le mie
yourself (informal)	**ti**	your/yours	il tuo	la tua	i tuoi	le tue
himself, herself	**si**	his/his her/hers	il suo	la sua	i suoi	le sue
yourself (polite)	**si**	your/yours	il suo	la sua	i suoi	le sue
ourselves	**ci**	our/ours	il nostro	la nostra	i nostri	le nostre
yourselves (informal)	**vi**	your/yours	il vostro	la vostra	i vostri	le vostre
themselves	**si**	their/theirs	il loro	la loro	i loro	le loro
yourselves (polite)	**si**		il loro	la loro	i loro	le loro

Reflexive pronouns

Some very common verbs are combined with 'myself', 'yourself' etc. The reflexive pronoun usually precedes the verb:

Come si chiama?   What's your name? – literally, 'How do you call yourself?'

Come si scrive?   How do you spell it? – literally, 'How does it write itself?'

The reflexive pronoun is also used in expressions when 'you do something' really means 'one does something':

Come si va?   How do you/does one get there?
Quando si chiude?   When do you close?

The reflexive pronoun comes immediately after the verb when it is in the infinitive:

Vorrei lavar<u>mi</u>   I'd like to have a wash

In the Mini Dictionary, verbs which take the reflexive pronoun are shown with the 'mi' form:

have a wash   lavar<u>mi</u> (lavare+mi)
I'm having a wash   <u>mi</u> lavo

Possessive pronouns and adjectives

The word for 'my/mine', 'your/yours' etc in Italian is the same:

<u>il mio</u> passaporto   my passport
questo passaporto è <u>il mio</u>   this passport is mine

Note that, in Italian, 'il/la/i/le' precedes the possessive pronoun:

<u>il</u> mio/<u>la</u> tua etc   literally, <u>the</u> mine, <u>the</u> yours etc.

However, in some short expressions, 'il/la/i/le' is dropped:

È mio   It's mine
È suo questo?   Is this yours?

Possessive pronouns and adjectives agree with the noun they precede:

<u>la tua</u> valigia   your suitcase (f)
<u>i miei</u> biglietti   my tickets (mpl)
queste scarpe sono <u>le tue</u>   these are your shoes (fpl)

The word for 'his' 'her' and 'your' (polite) is the same – 'il suo' – but it is usually clear from the context to whom one is referring:

Maria è nella <u>sua</u> stanza   Maria is in <u>her</u> room
Paolo è nella <u>sua</u> stanza   Paul is in <u>his</u> room

When talking about one of your close relatives (father, mother, brother, sister) omit il/la:

<u>mio</u> padre   my father
<u>mia</u> madre   my mother
<u>mio</u> fratello   my brother
<u>mia</u> sorella   my sister

But note:

<u>i miei</u> fratelli   my brothers

In Italian you don't use the possessive adjective when talking about parts of the body. Instead you use 'the':

Mi fa male <u>la</u> gamba   My leg hurts
Ho male <u>al</u> braccio   I've got a pain in my arm

264

VERBS

The present tense
Most verbs used in Survive in Italian are in the present tense:

Sono inglese	I'm English
Sono all'albergo Jolly	I'm staying at the Hotel Jolly
Abito a Londra	I live in London
Cos'è?	What is it?
Quando parte il treno?	When does the train leave?

Regular verbs
There are three groups of regular verbs in Italian; those ending in:
'are' eg abitare (to live), parlare (to speak), mangiare (to eat)
'ere' eg vendere (to sell), perdere (to lose), prendere (to take)
'ire' eg partire (to leave), dormire (to sleep) finire (to finish)

To form the present tense of verbs ending in 'are', take off 'are' and add the following endings:

	Abitare (to live)	Mangiare (to eat)
I	abito	mangio
you (informal)	abiti	mangi
he/she/you (polite)	abita	mangia
we	abitiamo	mangiamo
you (plural informal)	abitate	mangiate
they/you (polite plural)	abitano	mangiano

Note that if the verb ends in 'iare' the 'you' (informal) form drops the 'i'.

To form the present tense of verbs ending in 'ere', take off 'ere' and add the following endings:

	Vendere (to sell)	Prendere (to take)
I	vendo	prendo
you	vendi	prendi
he/she/you (polite)	vende	prende
we	vendiamo	prendiamo
you (plural informal)	vendete	prendete
they/you (polite plural)	vendono	prendono

To form the present tense of verbs ending in 'ire', take off 'ire' and add the following endings. Verbs which follow the 'finire' pattern are marked with an asterisk in the Mini Dictionary.

	Partire (to leave)	***Finire** (to finish)
I	part**o**	fin**isco**
you	part**i**	fin**isci**
he/she/you (polite)	part**e**	fin**isce**
we	part**iamo**	fin**iamo**
you (plural informal)	part**ite**	fin**ite**
they/you (polite plural)	part**ono**	fin**iscono**

Irregular verbs

Many common verbs are irregular in Italian. You will hear them often, and if you use them often, you will soon learn their peculiarities!

	Essere (be)	**Avere** (have)	**Andare** (go)	**Dare** (give)	**Fare** (do)	**Venire** (come)	**Dire** (say)
I	sono	ho	vado	do	faccio	vengo	dico
you	sei	hai	vai	dai	fai	vieni	dici
he/she/you (polite)	è	ha	va	da	fa	viene	dice
we	siamo	abbiamo	andiamo	diamo	facciamo	veniamo	diciam
you (plural informal)	siete	avete	andate	date	fate	venite	dite
they/you (polite plural)	sono	hanno	vanno	danno	fanno	vengono	dicono

'Avere'

There is no literal equivalent in Italian for 'I've got . . .' You simply use 'ho' (I have . . .):

Ho un posto prenotato	I've got a reserved seat
Ha il biglietto?	Have you got the ticket?
Ho la tosse	I've got a cough

In some expressions 'avere' is used instead of 'essere' (to be):

Ho caldo	I'm cold
Che nazionalità ha?	What nationality are you?

266

Here are some more irregular verbs which express desire, ability and obligation:

	Volere (want, wish)	Potere (can, be able)	Sapere (know)	Dovere (must, have to)
I	voglio	posso	so	debbo/devo
you	vuoi	puoi	sai	devi
he/she/you (polite)	vuole	può	sa	deve
we	vogliamo	possiamo	sappiamo	dobbiamo
you (plural informal)	volete	potete	sapete	dovete
they/you (polite plural)	vogliono	possono	sanno	debbono

'Volere'
Although the present tense of 'volere' is quite common in Italian:

Vuole noleggiare una   Do you want to hire a car?
macchina?

Non voglio andare in autobus   I don't want to go by bus

the conditional tense is more polite and often used:

Vorrei andare al cinema   I would like to go to the cinema
Cosa vorrebbe fare?   What would you like to do?

'Potere'
The present tense of 'potere' can be used to express 'can', 'may' or 'could':

Posso entrare?   Can I come in?
Posso prendere in prestito la   May I/Could I borrow your
sua penna?   pen?

However, when asking someone to do something for you in Italian, it is more usual to use the imperative with 'please':

Mi tieni il posto per favore   Could you keep my seat for me
please

Per favore ripeta   Could you repeat that please

See The imperative p269.

'Sapere'

'Sapere' means 'to know (a fact)' or 'to know how to (do something)'

Cos'è? Non lo so	What's this? I don't know
So nuotare	I know how to swim

When referring to a place or a person, use 'conoscere':

Non lo conosco	I don't know him

'Dovere'

Note the alternative forms of 'I must':

Devo pagare ora?	Must I pay now?
Debbo partire	I must leave

Be careful with 'non debbo' – it doesn't mean 'I must not' but 'I don't have to' or 'I need not':

Non debbo prendere il prossimo treno	I needn't catch the next train

The future tense

To form the future tense, take the final vowel (usually e) off the infinitive form of the verb and add the following endings:

	Abitare (to live)	Vendere (to sell)	Finire (to finish)
I	abiterò	venderò	finirò
you	abiterai	venderai	finirai
he/she/you (polite)	abiterà	venderà	finirà
we	abiteremo	venderemo	finiremo
you (plural informal)			
they/you (polite plural)	abiterete	venderete	finirete
	abiteranno	venderanno	finiranno

Note that with verbs which end in 'are' in the infinitive form, the 'a' is changed to 'e':

abitare (to live) – abiterò (I will live)

In Italian, it is often possible to use the present tense instead of the future tense:

Torno fra dieci minuti	I'll be back – literally 'I am back' – in ten minutes

And if you are unsure about the future tense, you can often survive by using the present tense:

Quando parte il treno?   When does the train leave?
Quando partirà il treno?   When will the train leave?

A few common verbs have irregular future forms, though their endings are the same as in the chart above:

avere (to have)	avrò, avrai etc (I will have, you will have etc)
essere (to be)	sarò, sarai etc (I will be, you will be etc)
andare (to go)	andrò, andrai etc (I will go, you will go etc)
potere (to be able)	potrò, potrai etc (I will be able, you will be able etc)
sapere (to know)	saprò, saprai etc (I will know, you will know etc)
vedere (to see)	vedrò, vedrai etc (I will see, you will see etc)
venire (to come)	verrò, verrai etc (I will come, you will come etc)
fare (to do, make)	farò, farai etc (I will make, you will make etc)
dare (to give)	darò, darai etc (I will give, you will give etc)

The imperative

Use the imperative when you want to ask someone to do something, or to make a suggestion. Here are a few common expressions:

Guardi!	Look!
Scusi!	Excuse me!
Andiamo	Let's go
Mi lasci in pace	Leave me alone
Si fermi qui	Stop here
Vediamoci alle nove	Let's meet at nine

To make your request more polite, add 'please':

Per favore mi chiami alle sette   Please call me at seven o'clock

The imperative endings of regular verbs are:

		Parlare (to speak)	Vendere (to sell)	Partire (to leave)
you (informal)	**tu**	parla	vendi	parti
you (polite)	**lei**	parli	venda	parta
you (plural informal)	**voi**	parlate	vendete	partite
you (polite plural)	**loro**	parlino	vendano	partano

Here are some irregular imperatives:

	Essere (be)	Avere (have)	Andare (go)	Dare (give)	Fare (do)	Dire (say)
you (informal)	sii	abbi	va	da	fa	di
you (polite)	sia	abbia	vada	dia	faccia	dica
you (plural informal)	siate	abbiate	andate	date	fate	dite
you (polite plural)	siano	abbiano	vadano	diano	facciano	dicano

The negative

It's easy to make a negative statement in Italian; simply put 'non' before the verb:

Ho una stanza singola	I've got a single room
<u>Non</u> ho una stanza singola	I haven't got a single room
Ci sono posti	There are some seats
<u>Non</u> ci sono posti	There aren't any seats

Asking a question

This is easy in Italian; you don't have to change the word order, simply change your tone of voice:

| Vieni con me | You're coming with me |
| Vieni con me? | Are you coming with me? |

Another way of forming a question is to change the order of the subject and verb:

| L'aereo è in orario | The plane's on time |
| È in orario l'aereo? | Is the plane on time? |

If you want to check something you can add 'non è vero?' (literally 'is it not true?') at the end of a statement:

| Fa caldo, non è vero? | It's cold, isn't it? |

The past

The most common way of expressing the past in Italian is by means of 'avere' (to have) + the past participle of the verb you want to use. To form the past participle of verbs ending in:

'are' change 'are' to 'ato' eg parlare → parlato (to speak)
'ere' change 'ere' to 'uto' eg vedere → veduto (to see)
'ire' change 'ire' to 'ito' eg finire → finito (to finish)

		Parlare	Vedere	Finire
I	ho	parlato	veduto	finito
you	hai	parlato	veduto	finito
he/she/you (polite)	ha	parlato	veduto	finito
we	abbiamo	parlato	veduto	finito
you (plural informal)	avete	parlato	veduto	finito
they/you (polite plural)	hanno	parlato	veduto	finito

All irregular past participles are given in the Mini Dictionary
eg nascere – nato (to be born, born), venire – venuto (to come, come)

Note that some verbs are combined with 'essere' (to be) rather than 'avere' (to have) to form the past tense. Here are the most common verbs:

andare	andato	(to go, gone)
arrivare	arrivato	(to arrive, arrived)
entrare	entrato	(to enter, entered)
nascere	nato	(to be born, born)
partire	partito	(to go, gone)
restare	restato	(to stay, stayed)
ruiscire	ruiscito	(to succeed, succeeded)
venire	venuto	(to come, come)

With these verbs, the ending must agree in number and gender with the subject:

'ato' (masculine singular)   'ati' (masculine plural)
'ata' (feminine singular)   'ate' (feminine plural)

		Andare
I	sono	andato (-ata)
you	sei	andato (-ata)
he/she/you (polite)	è	andato (-ata)
we	siamo	andati (-ate)
you (plural informal)	siete	andati (-ate)
they/you (polite plural)	sono	andati (-ate)

271

Letters you may need to write

Letter of thanks

                        Your address
                        /September 4th 19—/

Dear Mr/Mrs/Mr and Mrs/...

(I've/We've just returned) home after (a wonderful holiday/stay) in (Italy) and (I am/we are writing) to thank you again for being so kind to (me/us).
(I/We spent) (a marvellous/day/afternoon/ evening) with you and it gave (me/us) a real glimpse of life in (Italy). (I/We do hope) you will be able to come and (see me/us) (if/when) you come to England.
Warmest regards to (your family/mother/children/ father/parents).

      Yours (sincerely),

NB In Italian, days and months do not begin with a capital letter.

/4 settembre 19–/

Pregmo. Signor /Gentma. Signora /Gentma. Famiglia,

(Sono appena tornato /Siamo appena tornati) a casa dopo (una meravigliosa vacanza /un meraviglioso soggiorno) in (Italia) e (desidero /desideriamo) [ringraziarla /ringraziarvi] di nuovo per [la sua/la vostra] gentilezza verso di (me/noi).

(Ho passato/Abbiamo passato) (una meravigliosa giornata/una meravigliosa serata/un meraviglioso pomeriggio) con [lei/voi] che (mi/ci) ha permesso di avere una viva impressione della vita in (Italia). (Spero/Speriamo) che [lei possa/voi possiate] venire a (trovarmi/trovarci) (se/quando) [verrà/verrete] in Inghilterra.

Cordialissimi saluti([alla sua/alla vostra] famiglia/ mamma/ [ai suoi /ai vostri] figli [al suo/al vostro] papa/ [ai suoi/ai vostri] genitori).

Distinti saluti,

Your address

NB If you are writing to one person, use the words in square brackets which are *not* underlined. If you are writing to more than one person, use the underlined words. Note that in Italian your address always comes at the bottom of the letter.

273

Booking accommodation

Your address
/February 2nd 19—/

The Manager
Address of hotel

Dear Sir,

   I would like to book (a room/(two) rooms) with
you for the nights of (July 27th) to (July 31st)
inclusive. I would like (a single room/a double room/a
twin-bedded room/(two) single rooms/(two) double
rooms/(two) twin-bedded rooms) (with/without)
(bath/shower).
   I would be grateful if you could let me know if you
have (a room/rooms available) for this period and
what your terms are for (bed and breakfast/half board/
full board).
   I look forward to hearing from you in the near
future.

        Yours faithfully,

Date/2 febbraio 19—/

Spett. Direzione
Address of hotel

Egregio Signore,

Vorrei riservare (una stanza/ (due) stanze) dal (27
luglio) al (31 luglio) incluso. Desidererei (una stanza
singola/una stanza matrimoniale/una stanza a due
letti/ (due) stanze singole/ (due) stanze matrimoniali/
(due) stanze a due letti) (con/senza) (bagno/doccia).

Vi sarei grato se poteste farmi sapere se avete (una
stanza libera/stanze libere) per questo periodo e i
vostri prezzi per (stanza e prima colazione/mezza
pensione/pensione completa).

In attesa di una vostra sollecita risposta saluto
distintamente.

Distinti saluti,

Your address

Informal letter

Your address
/3rd May 19–/

Dear /Carlo/,
Dear /Giovanna/,

Just a short note to thank you for putting me up.
I spent (four) really fantastic days with you and your
friends. I hope to see you all very soon in (York). My
flat is very small but if you bring your sleeping bags
there won't be any problem fitting you all in.
Thanks again! I'll write soon!

Love,

PS Lots of love to /Riccardo/

/3 maio 19--/

Caro /Carlo/,
Cara/Giovanna/,

   Due righe soltanto per ringraziarti della tua
ospitalità. Ho passato (quattro) giornate meravigliose
con te e con i tuoi amici. Spero di rivedervi tutti molto
presto a (York). Mio appartamento è molto piccolo ma
se portate i vostri sacchi a pelo non sarà difficile
trovare posto per tutti.

   Grazie di nuovo -- e ti scriverò presto.

        Saluti affettuosi,

P.S. Cari saluti a /Riccardo/

Your address

Equivalents in

Italian money

Lira = L

Coins (Monete)
L5   cinque lire
L10 dieci lire
L20 venti lire
L50 cinquanta lire
L100 cento lire
L200 duecento lire

Notes (Banconote)
L500   cinquecento lire
L1000 mille lire
L2000 duemila lire
L5000 cinquemila lire
L10,000 diecimila lire
L20,000 ventimila lire
L50,000 cinquantamila lire
L100,000 centomila lire

In a bank you can specify how you would like the money:

in ten thousands
in twenty thousands
in fifty thousands
in hundred thousands

in biglietti da diecimila
in biglietti da ventimila
in biglietti da cinquantamila
in biglietti da centomila

Distances

1 mile = 1.6 kilometres   1.6 chilometri = 1 mile

Miles	10	20	30	40	50	60	70	80	90	100	Miles
Kilometres	16	32	48	64	80	97	113	128	145	160	Chilometri

Lengths and sizes

Some approximate equivalents:

British			*Metric*
1 inch		=	2.5 centimetri
6 inches		=	15 centimetri
1 foot	= 12 inches	=	30 centimetri
2 feet	= 24 inches	=	60 centimetri
1 yard	= 36 inches or 3 feet =		91 centimetri
1 yard 3 inches		=	1 metro

278

General clothes sizes (including chest/hip measurements)

GB	USA	Europe	ins	cms
8	6	36	30/32	76/81
10	8	38	32/34	81/86
12	10	40	34/36	86/91
14	12	42	36/38	91/97
16	14	44	38/40	97/102
18	16	46	40/42	102/107
20	18	48	42/44	107/112
22	20	50	44/46	112/117
24	22	52	46/48	117/122
26	24	54	48/50	122/127

Waist measurements

(ins) GB/USA 22 24 26 28 30 32 34 36 38 40 42 44 46 48 50
(cms) Europe 56 61 66 71 76 81 86 91 97 102 107 112 117 122 127

Collar measurements

(ins) GB/USA 14 $14\frac{1}{2}$ 15 $15\frac{1}{2}$ 16 $16\frac{1}{2}$ 17 $17\frac{1}{2}$
(cms) Europe 36 37 38 39 40 41 42 43

Shoes

GB 3 $3\frac{1}{2}$ 4 $4\frac{1}{2}$ 5 $5\frac{1}{2}$ 6 $6\frac{1}{2}$ 7 $7\frac{1}{2}$ 8 $8\frac{1}{2}$ 9 10 11 12
USA $4\frac{1}{2}$ 5 $5\frac{1}{2}$ 6 $6\frac{1}{2}$ 7 $7\frac{1}{2}$ 8 $8\frac{1}{2}$ 9 $9\frac{1}{2}$ 10 $10\frac{1}{2}$ $11\frac{1}{2}$ $12\frac{1}{2}$ $13\frac{1}{2}$
Europe 36 37 38 39 40 41 42 43 44 45

Hats

GB $6\frac{5}{8}$ $6\frac{3}{4}$ $6\frac{7}{8}$ 7 $7\frac{1}{8}$ $7\frac{1}{4}$ $7\frac{3}{8}$ $7\frac{1}{2}$ $7\frac{5}{8}$
USA $6\frac{3}{4}$ $6\frac{7}{8}$ 7 $7\frac{1}{8}$ $7\frac{1}{4}$ $7\frac{3}{8}$ $7\frac{1}{2}$ $7\frac{5}{8}$ $7\frac{3}{4}$
Europe 54 55 56 57 58 59 60 61 62

Glove sizes are the same in every country.

Weights

Some approximate equivalents:
Grammi (g) (Grams) and chilogrammi (kg) (kilograms)
1000 grammi (1000 g) = 1 chilogrammo (kilo/kg)

1 oz.	=	25 grammi
4 ozs.	=	100/125 grammi
8 ozs.	=	225 grammi
1 pound (16 ozs.)	=	450 grammi
1 pound 2 ozs.	=	500 grammi ($\frac{1}{2}$ chilogrammo)
2 pounds 4 ozs.	=	1 chilogrammo (1 chilo/kg)
1 stone	=	6 chilogrammi

Body weight
Body weight in Italy is measured in kilograms (chilogrammi)
Some approximate equivalents:

POUNDS	STONES	KILOGRAMS
28	2	12$\frac{1}{2}$
42	3	19
56	4	25
70	5	32
84	6	38
98	7	45
112	8	51
126	9	57$\frac{1}{2}$
140	10	63
154	11	70
168	12	76
182	13	83
196	14	90

Liquid measure

In Italy all liquids are measured in litres.
Some approximate equivalents:
1 pint = 0.57 litri (litres)   1 gallon = 4.55 litres

GB Measures		Litres
1 pint	=	0.5
(20 fluid ounces)		
(fl. ozs.)		
1.7 pints	=	1
1.1 gallons	=	5
2.2 gallons	=	10

3.3 gallons	=	15
4.4 gallons	=	20
5.5 gallons	=	25
6.6 gallons	=	30
7.7 gallons	=	35
8.8 gallons	=	40
9.9 gallons	=	45

Temperature

	Fahrenheit (F)	Centigrade (C)
Boiling point	212°	100°
	104°	40°
Body temperature	98.4°	36.9°
	86°	30°
	68°	20°
	59°	15°
	50°	10°
Freezing point	32°	0°
	23°	−5°
	0°	−18°

(Convert Fahrenheit to Centigrade by subtracting 32 and multiplying by 5/9. Convert Centigrade to Fahrenheit by multiplying by 9/5 and adding 32.)

Useful information for travellers

Useful addresses

Every town has its own 'Ente Turismo' (tourist) office which will supply free leaflets, maps and information. At most stations there is an 'Ufficio Informazioni' (information office) which offers a similar service. Usual opening hours: 9.00 to 12.30, 3.0 p.m. to 7.0 p.m. (Usually closed on Sunday.)

Social behaviour

Shaking hands is common in Italy, both on meeting and parting. When being introduced, say 'Piacere' and your *surname* as you shake hands. A woman is usually addressed as 'Signora' (when married) and 'Signorina' (when not). 'Signore', for a man, is less common.

To attract attention say 'Scusi.'

Queues are rare in Italy. It's every man for himself, but without being aggressive about it.

Bargaining is getting rarer. Only try it if you feel the atmosphere is right.

Lunch or dinner guests usually take flowers or chocolates for their host.

Accommodation

Contact any 'Ente Turismo' office. All big stations have a hotel information service. Hotel categories: luxury, I, II, III and IV. 'Pensioni' are roughly British B & B standard, can be excellent and cheap. They are also divided into categories – I, II and III. Student hostels (ostelli della gioventù) can be found in some places.

Getting around

Allow for big city rush hours which can cause serious hold-ups, particularly in Milan and Rome. Maps can be bought from all stationers and booksellers, and the 'Ente Turismo' office will always give you one of its own city.

By taxi You don't usually stop taxis in the street. The normal system is to go to a rank (common in all big cities) or telephone. Most public telephones have taxi numbers prominently displayed. The colour of Italian taxis varies from place to place, but they are always very distinctive. Payment is shown on the meter. Add 10 per cent for the tip.

By bus Again things vary from city to city. If there is a conductor you pay him. if not tickets are sold in tobacconists and many newspaper kiosks. Sometimes there are ticket machines in the bus itself. Bus doors open automatically, and you get on at the back and off in the middle or at the front.

By underground Underground networks can only be found in Rome and Milan, and they cover very little ground by comparison with London or Paris. There is usually one first class compartment, but for all the difference it makes, you might as well go second. Tickets on sale at the station newspaper kiosk.

By train Remember that Italian trains are usually crowded, and it's rarely worth travelling first in the hope of getting a seat because of the shortage of first class accommodation. The exception to this rule is provided by the 'rapidi' (express trains) which are excellent and extremely comfortable, but for which you always have to pay a supplement and sometimes are obliged to travel first class as well. 'Rapidi' are perfect for inter-city travel.

NB There are special rates for rail travel on Sundays and public holidays.

By coach It's simpler to travel by train, but coaches are the only means of transport to many villages. Coach

283

Useful information for travellers

services are not all that frequent, and the price corresponds with a second-class rail fare. Ask for information at any travel agency.

Changing money

Banks are open from 8.30–1.30 Mon-Fri except on public holidays. Hotels and bigger shops will usually accept travellers' cheques.

Note that exchange, and most other banking operations, are carried out in two distinct phases. First you do the necessary form filling etc with the clerk who will then say 'Alla cassa', sending you to the cash counter where you are handed the money.

Shopping

Shops Opening hours vary, but can be approximately summed up as 8.30–1.0 and 4.30–7.30. If you're relying on food shops, it's as well to ask about the early closing day which differs from town to town. In the mid to late seventies, there was an acute change shortage in Italy. This has improved greatly, but you are still liable to be offered stamps, sweets or, particularly, telephone tokens as change. Telephone tokens have the status of money.

Post Offices Life can be complicated in Italian post offices, but fortunately stamps are obtainable from tobacconists where you can also buy express letters – which is advisable if you don't want your mail to take a couple of weeks.

Food and drink

Restaurant meals are expensive, and only the bigger cities offer snack bar or café alternatives. Most young people, and a lot of their elders as well, opt for the 'rosticceria' or the 'pizzeria', where other dishes besides 'pizza' are served. Most cafés do snacks and a toast (pronounced 'tost' and signifying a toasted ham and cheese sandwich). This makes a very good light meal. You can usually get food and drink up to midnight in cities and, at the height of the summer, way into the small hours. In cafés and motorway self-service bars you are usually expected to go to the cash-desk and pay before you are served.

Tipping

Ten per cent is a good rule, but needn't be followed slavishy. When you get over the ten thousand lire mark you can start to scale it down slightly according to your own judgement. If the person who serves you is obviously the proprietor you don't tip. Railway porters – a dying race anyway – have fixed rates per piece of baggage, but don't object to a small tip over and above this.

Entertainments

To find out what's going on look at entertainments column of daily or evening paper. Remember that Italian entertainments start late (never before nine and often after the advertised time of starting), and include at least one long interval. You book at the 'biglietteria' (theatre box office). Much sought-after shows like the opera at 'La Scala' in Milan are often sold out for months in advance. The seating in Italian theatres is divided up as follows (with slight variations from theatre to theatre): 'platea' (stalls) consisting of 'poltronissime' (front stalls) and 'poltrone' (back stalls), 'balconate' (dress circle), 'prima galleria numerata' (numbered seats in the upper circle), 'seconda galleria non numerata' or 'loggione' (gallery) and 'palchi' (boxes). In many theatres the boxes are 'rented' by families for an entire season.

Matinées (spettacolo pomeridiano) are extremely rare in Italy. The evening show ('spettacolo' or 'spettacolo serale') usually starts at 9.0 or 9.30.

Museums and galleries Closing days vary, but are usually on a Monday. A student card will get you in free or at a reduced rate to many national museums and galleries. Sunday mornings are free.

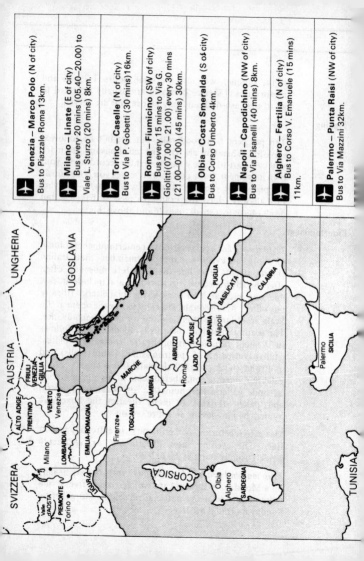

✈ **Venezia – Marco Polo** (N of city)
Bus to Piazzale Roma 13km.

✈ **Milano – Linate** (E of city)
Bus every 20 mins (05.40–20.00) to
Viale L. Sturzo (20 mins) 8km.

✈ **Torino – Caselle** (N of city)
Bus to Via P. Gobetti (30 mins) 16km.

✈ **Roma – Fiumicino** (SW of city)
Bus every 15 mins to Via G.
Giolitti (07.00 – 21.00) every 30 mins
(21.00–07.00) (45 mins) 30km.

✈ **Olbia – Costa Smeralda** (S of city)
Bus to Corso Umberto 4km.

✈ **Napoli – Capodichino** (NW of city)
Bus to Via Pisanelli (40 mins) 8km.

✈ **Alghero – Fertilia** (N of city)
Bus to Corso V. Emanuele (15 mins)
11km.

✈ **Palermo – Punta Raisi** (NW of city)
Bus to Via Mazzini 32km.

NOTES

NOTES

NOTES